# HERE'S WHAT PEOPLE
# ARE SAYING ABOUT THIS BOOK!

*"Gene Getz is the opposite of a cloistered monk. He's persistently engaged with all sorts of busy people and, at the same time, deeply occupied with the ancient wisdom of Scripture and its applications to the tensions of every day. For me, having Gene along is like driving with St. Paul through the traffic jams of life and asking him how the Bible would make sense of it."*

> BOB BUFORD—Founder, Leadership Network;
> Author, *Halftime—Changing Your Game Plan from Success to Significance*

*"We are indebted to Dr. Gene Getz for this book. Nothing quite as comprehensive or challenging has appeared in recent times. I warmly commend it for three reasons: It is biblical. The book is rooted in the Old Testament but covers the entire New Testament. It is practical. It pinpoints 102 supracultural principles for personal and general application. It is critical. It searches 'the thoughts and intents of the heart' on many matters, and it speaks to the materialism and 'me-ism' of our present day."*

> STEPHEN F. OLFORD—Founder and Senior Lecturer, Olford Ministries International

*"What I like about this book is the clear connection of the principles with the time-proven truth of God's Word. Of course we are not surprised that Gene Getz would give us clarity of truth in the context of up-to-date, practical application!"*

> DR. JOSEPH M. STOWELL—President, Moody Bible Institute

"Dr. Gene Getz's biblical research is thoughtful, insightful, and provocative. He deals with Scripture itself, which has a power no man's words can equal. A veteran pastor and teacher with integrity and a vision for churches and leaders, Dr. Getz unearths from the Bible challenging perspectives vitally needed by today's church."

RANDY ALCORN—Author, *The Treasure Principle*

"This updated, revised classic is more than timely for our present generation. For those who are serious about understanding steward leadership in this day and age, I recommend buying a case for your church and a copy for every Christian leader you are in contact with! This classic book will undoubtedly set the stage for stewardship education for this new century."

SCOTT PREISSLER, PHD—President and CEO, Christian Stewardship Association

# ABOUT THE AUTHOR

Dr. Gene Getz has been involved in a variety of ministry experiences, including church planting, pastoring, Christian education, radio, music, conference speaking, and college and seminary teaching. He has authored more than sixty books that have been translated into thirty-five foreign languages. He is the founder of the Fellowship Bible Church movement, with more than 350 churches tying their roots back to the original Fellowship Bible Church in the Dallas area. He is currently serving as executive director of the Center for Church Renewal, host and teacher of Renewal Radio, and pastor emeritus of Fellowship Bible Church North in Plano, Texas.

# RICH

## IN EVERY WAY

# RICH
## IN EVERY WAY

*everything God says about*

*money and possessions*

# DR. GENE GETZ

HOWARD
PUBLISHING CO.

**Our purpose at Howard Publishing is to:**

- *Increase faith* in the hearts of growing Christians
- *Inspire holiness* in the lives of believers
- *Instill hope* in the hearts of struggling people everywhere

**Because He's coming again!**

*Rich in Every Way* © 2004 by Dr. Gene A. Getz
All rights reserved. Printed in the United States of America
Published by Howard Publishing Co., Inc.
3117 North 7th Street, West Monroe, Louisiana 71291-2227
www.howardpublishing.com

04 05 06 07 08 09 10 11 12 13     10 9 8 7 6 5 4 3 2 1

Edited by Between the Lines
Cover design by Terry Dugan Design
Interior design by Gabe Cardinale

Library of Congress Cataloging-in-Publication Data

Getz, Gene A.
    Rich in every way : everything God says about money and possesions : 101 supracultural principles for handling material possessions / Gene Getz ; foreword by Howard Dayton.
      p. cm.
    ISBN 1-58229-390-2
    1. Wealth—Biblical teaching. 2. Stewardship, Christian—Biblical teaching. I. Title.

BS2545.W37G492 2004
241'.68—dc22
                                                             2004047594

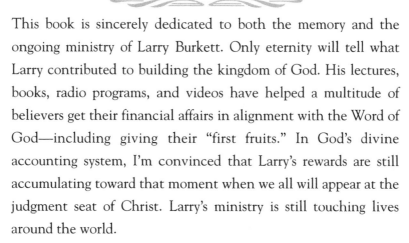

This book is sincerely dedicated to both the memory and the ongoing ministry of Larry Burkett. Only eternity will tell what Larry contributed to building the kingdom of God. His lectures, books, radio programs, and videos have helped a multitude of believers get their financial affairs in alignment with the Word of God—including giving their "first fruits." In God's divine accounting system, I'm convinced that Larry's rewards are still accumulating toward that moment when we all will appear at the judgment seat of Christ. Larry's ministry is still touching lives around the world.

# Contents

## Part 7: Principles from the Prison Epistles

## Part 8: Principles from the Pastoral Letters

## Part 9: The Final Letters

## Conclusion: The Principles Compiled

## Appendix:

## Graphics:

## Maps:

# Foreword

All of us tend to be influenced by the culture in which we live. And for those living in our affluent country, that means the pervasive impact of consumerism.

We are constantly bombarded with the message that the "fulfilling, beautiful, wrinkle-free life" can be ours if only we are willing to buy it. Costly, manipulative advertising encourages us to adopt an image-conscious lifestyle that claims to satisfy the human heart's deepest needs.

None of us are immune to this message. As someone once said, "People buy things they do not need with money they do not have to impress people they do not even like."

The practical consequences of this culture of spending can be devastating. Personal consumer debt has increased dramatically, while the habit of saving has all but disappeared. A tidal wave of government-sponsored gambling has swept our nation. There are now an estimated 5.5 million pathologically addicted gamblers, 1.1 million of whom are teenagers. These and other factors have contributed to millions of people each year filing for bankruptcy. Approximately 56 percent of all divorces are the result of financial tension in the home.

Unfortunately, there's almost no difference between the spending habits of those who know Christ and those who don't. Giving among Christians, as measured by percentage of income, has declined almost every year for the past three decades. We're not investing our resources in that which is eternally significant. For example, the average American gambles $1,174 a year, while the average church member gives $20 annually for foreign missions.

Many people are enjoying financial stability or prosperity, but materialism has robbed them of their spiritual vitality. They fit the description of the church in Laodicea: "You say, 'I am rich, and have become wealthy, and have need of nothing,' and you do not know that you are wretched and miserable and poor and blind and naked" (Revelation 3:17 NASB).

Against this discouraging backdrop, the Lord has given his people a wonderful gift in Dr. Gene Getz and this book, *Rich in Every Way*. Gene has established one of the most effective church models in the world. He has pastored churches that have no direct denominational affiliation, yet approximately three hundred Fellowship Bible Churches have been spawned out of his original vision in Dallas thirty years ago.

*Rich in Every Way* is powerful because it is rooted in the Bible. Romans 12:2 reads, "Do not be conformed to this world, but be transformed by the renewing of your mind, that you may prove what the will of God is, that which is good and acceptable and perfect" (NASB). The Amplified Bible reads this way: "Do not be conformed to this world (this age), [fashioned after and adapted to its external, superficial customs]." Too often God's people have become conformed to our culture of consumerism and are ineffective in influencing others for the cause of Christ. We have lost our salt.

When our cofounder Larry Burkett first became acquainted with Gene's research and writings, he made the following comment: "Dr. Getz is a rare breed of man devoted to the ministry of Christ who can write a theological work and make it both fascinating and interesting reading."

I agree. And what makes this book even more significant is that it has resulted from a study group composed of businessmen who, with Gene's guidance, studied every passage in the Scriptures on the subject of material possessions. Furthermore, Gene has been applying the principles you'll learn in this book in his own life and in the life of his church. *Rich in Every Way* is desperately needed at this time in history and is destined to become a classic. I recommend it without reservation.

Howard Dayton
Cofounder, Crown Financial Ministries

Preface
# Pressure or Providence

The title for this book emerged out of a dynamic experience. I sat with the management team at Howard Publishing for several hours one afternoon brainstorming. Jokingly, they threatened that they weren't going to let me fly back to Dallas until we had all agreed on a title that captured the essence of this study on material possessions. We threw idea after idea on the table, and in each case the consensus was thumbs down.

Then it happened! Call it pressure or providence—or both—but the phrase *rich in every way* popped into my head and out onto the "table." It immediately brought a thumbs-up response. We all agreed that this phrase not only captured Paul's original intent but the essence of the message in the book you now hold in your hands.

Note Paul's statement in 2 Corinthians 9:11: "You will be made *rich in every way* so that you can be generous on every occasion, and through us your generosity will result in thanksgiving to God."

In the immediate context, Paul unquestionably had material possessions in mind when he penned these words. However, when we

understand all of the circumstances as well as the context of Scripture, it's also clear that Paul was addressing a much larger issue.

The Greek word *ploutizo*, which Paul used here and which is translated "rich" in the NIV, can indeed mean "to make wealthy" in a material sense. But note how Paul used a similar word in his first letter to the Corinthians: "Already you have all you want! Already you have become rich [*plouteo*]! You have become kings!" (1 Corinthians 4:8).

Even more importantly, note how Paul used this word in his second letter, just a few paragraphs prior to his "rich in every way" comment: "You know the grace of our Lord Jesus Christ, that though he was rich [*plousios*], yet for your sakes he became poor, so that you through his poverty might become rich [*plouteo*]" (2 Corinthians 8:9).

Clearly Paul was not speaking here of material wealth but rather of the incomparable riches [*ploutos*] of God's grace (see Ephesians 1:7; 2:7). Even more specifically, Paul identified our calling in Christ as a result of "the unsearchable riches of Christ" (Ephesians 3:8).

We'll look more carefully at the larger context of eternal wealth in the main body of this book, but suffice it to say, Paul was not promising the Corinthians material wealth and abundance as we use these terms today. He *was* promising them God's grace—not only to meet their material needs but also to enable them to be generous regardless of their material resources. Let's not forget how Paul began this section in his letter:

We want you to know about the *grace* that God has given the Macedonian churches. Out of the most severe

trial, their overflowing joy and their extreme *poverty* welled up in *rich generosity*. For I testify that they gave as much as they they were able, and even beyond their ability. Entirely on their own, they urgently pleaded with us for the privilege of sharing in this service to the saints. (2 Corinthians 8:1–4)

Perhaps this scripture explains and illustrates more fully than any other what Paul had in mind with the phrase *rich in every way*. Indeed, we feel this title captures the essence of what the Bible teaches about Christians and material possessions.

# Acknowledgments

This book is a result of a community project. Once a week for six months, I originally met with eleven dedicated Christian men to study everything the Bible has to say about material possessions. Together, we evaluated scriptural stories and texts and then outlined what we believe are supracultural principles that can be applied anywhere in the world and at any moment in history. To these following men, I owe a debt of gratitude:

Ed Burford

Jack Cole

Mike Cornwall

Bill Fackler

Jim Harris (now deceased)

Earl Lindgren

Don Logue

Steve Meyer

Richard Pascuzzi

Stan Potocki

Jim Wilson

I must add that all of these men are godly models of how

Christians should view and use their material possessions.

I also want to thank two very special assistants in the Center for Church Renewal, Iva Morelli and Sue Mitchell, who have gone beyond the call of duty in helping me prepare this edition for publication.

And finally, I'm deeply grateful to my wife, Elaine, who has always encouraged me in my writing projects. In this case, she deserves a special word of thanks for allowing a group of men to invade her home once a week for a three-hour meeting—and to even provide us with refreshments.

## Introduction
# A Quest for God's Agenda

### Tried by Fire

One Monday morning—about 2:00 a.m.—I was suddenly jolted out of a sound sleep. The phone was ringing! The voice on the other end of the line was somber. "Gene, an arsonist has just torched our church offices."

My wife and I rushed to the scene, where fire engines had already arrived from four major areas in the Dallas Metroplex. Helicopters were hovering overhead, and a crowd was gathering. By dawn the four major television networks in Dallas had crews on the scene. I vividly remember one pointed question: "Pastor, how do you feel at a time like this?" In shock, I could only quote Romans 8:28.

My office on the second floor was obviously the center of the blaze. Through the smoke, we could see my personal library engulfed in flames. By the time firefighters had brought the flames under control, fifty of our offices had been destroyed, and fifteen of our pastors at Fellowship Bible Church North had lost their personal libraries.

With the help of inspectors, we were able to reconstruct what happened. The arsonist struck my office first, pouring gasoline on the sofa where I had counseled a couple a few days before. The husband, bitter with rage, decided to attack not only me but our entire pastoral staff—and in essence, the whole church. He had hit four other strategic locations with accelerants, deliberately destroying our whole complex.

A few days later, my wife and I entered the building. We donned our hard hats and made our way through the charred debris to the second floor and the space where my office had been. Nothing remained but piles of ash and metal beams sagging from the ceiling.

On what once was a credenza below my bookshelves, I had placed a lot of personal items. One was a gift from a man in Brazil to whom I had ministered. Sculpted out of metal, it was a replica of Moses holding the Ten Commandments. It was a beautiful piece of art created by one of the most brilliant metal sculptors in all of Brazil.

Could it be that this marvelous statue had survived? Taking a large shovel, I dug into the heap on the floor. When I turned over the first scoop of ashes, embedded in the debris was—no, not the sculpture of Moses—but a book I had written, titled *A Biblical Theology of Material Possessions*. Though singed, it was intact. My wife and I couldn't believe our eyes. It was as though God were asking me directly and personally, "Gene, do you *really* believe what you've written in that book?" To be frank, at that moment my wife and I burst into laughter. Though there was comic relief for the moment, deep down, this experience sent me a powerful message.

To this day, I have that book—just as I found it—on display in my office. It's a constant reminder that the material possessions we have are of no eternal value unless we use them to build the kingdom of God. In the end, everything will be destroyed by fire. All that will endure is the way we've used these temporal gifts to achieve God's purposes in the world.

*A Biblical Theology of Material Possessions*

What you're about to read is a new publication of this book—refined, updated, and more fully illustrated. In many respects, what I first shared about material possessions from God's perspective is more relevant today than it was when it was first published.

## Our Quest

This book is also the result of the exciting and challenging process of doing "theology in community." This may sound complicated, but it's really simple. In essence, this kind of Bible exploration involves a group of Christians—few enough to study together in an interactive environment—looking carefully at aspects of the biblical story as the Holy Spirit unfolded this dynamic saga over a period of time.

The group involved in this study—including myself as facilitator—was made up of twelve men. Most of them are Peter, James, and John types—all active in their own business communities. No, we weren't trying to imitate Jesus's strategy in choosing the apostles, though I must admit that twelve seems an ideal number for this kind of scriptural study.

Meeting almost every Wednesday evening for a number of months, we traced through the Bible what God has said regarding material possessions—and how Christians in every culture of the world should view and use these gifts from God. We began our study where the church began in Jerusalem. Analyzing Luke's descriptive narrative in the book of Acts, we followed this unfolding story through the rest of the New Testament.

## A Divine Framework

Very quickly in this report, Luke recorded a basic outline for understanding Christ's answer to the apostles' nervous inquiry on the Mount of Olives just before he left this earth: "Lord, are you at this time going to restore the kingdom to Israel?"

Responding calmly but with intensity, Jesus answered their question: "It is not for you to know the time or dates the Father has set by his own authority. But you will receive power when the Holy Spirit comes on you; and you will be my witnesses in

*Jerusalem,* and in *all Judea and Samaria,* and to *the ends of the earth*" (Acts 1:7–8).

Jesus's response served as a divine framework for Luke's personal report to Theophilus. The book of Acts fills in many of the details as the apostles and their representatives began to carry out the Great Commission—to "go and make disciples of all nations" (Matthew 28:19). But as these men traveled beyond Judea and Samaria, preaching and teaching the Good News, they introduced us to another means for communicating God's plan of salvation and spiritual growth. The Holy Spirit inspired some of them to write reports (the Gospels) and to compose letters (the Epistles) that were sent to the churches that had been planted throughout the Roman world, or to individuals—like Timothy and Titus—who had helped to establish these churches. Today we call these marvelous documents the New Testament, which is composed of twenty-seven books. The apostle Peter carefully described this divine and human process: "Above all, you must understand that no prophecy of Scripture came about by the prophet's own interpretation. For prophecy never had its origin in the will of man, but men spoke from God as they were carried along by the Holy Spirit" (2 Peter 1:20–21).

If the New Testament is the Word of God—and we believe it is—then it's only when we carefully read these written documents and letters as they were inscribed chronologically and allow the Holy Spirit to enlighten the eyes of our hearts that we will be able to know and understand more fully God's will for us today.

Furthermore, there is safety in numbers when it comes to Bible interpretation. The Holy Spirit is able to work uniquely in a community—part of God's divine plan. It's "as each part does its work" that the body of Christ "builds itself up in love" (Ephesians 4:16)—which certainly includes the process described by Paul: "Let the word of Christ dwell in you richly as you teach and admonish one another with all wisdom" (Colossians 3:16).

This was our challenge—and our goal was to zero in on what the Holy Spirit has revealed in Scripture regarding God's gift of material possessions and his specific will as to how we are to view and use them today. (The paradigm for our study is presented graphically on page 7.)

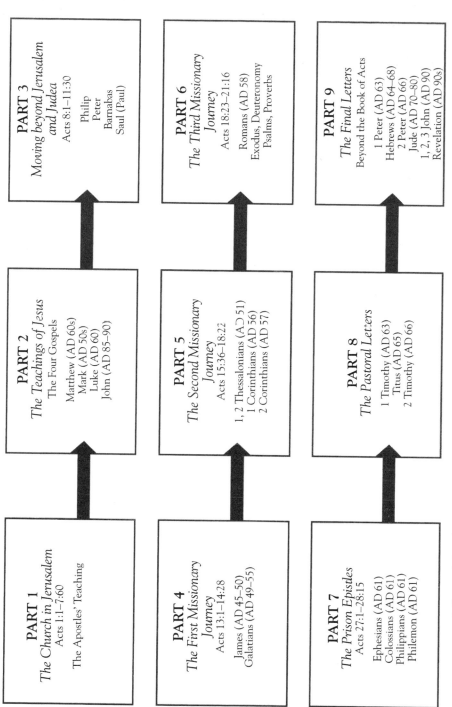

**PART 1**
*The Church in Jerusalem*
Acts 1:1–7:60

The Apostles' Teaching

**PART 2**
*The Teachings of Jesus*
The Four Gospels

Matthew (AD 60s)
Mark (AD 50s)
Luke (AD 60)
John (AD 85–90)

**PART 3**
*Moving beyond Jerusalem
and Judea*
Acts 8:1–11:30

Philip
Peter
Barnabas
Saul (Paul)

**PART 4**
*The First Missionary
Journey*
Acts 13:1–14:28

James (AD 45–50)
Galatians (AD 49–55)

**PART 5**
*The Second Missionary
Journey*
Acts 15:36–18:22

1, 2 Thessalonians (AD 51)
1 Corinthians (AD 56)
2 Corinthians (AD 57)

**PART 6**
*The Third Missionary
Journey*
Acts 18:23–21:16

Romans (AD 58)
Exodus, Deuteronomy
Psalms, Proverbs

**PART 7**
*The Prison Epistles*
Acts 27:1–28:15

Ephesians (AD 61)
Colossians (AD 61)
Philippians (AD 61)
Philemon (AD 61)

**PART 8**
*The Pastoral Letters*

1 Timothy (AD 63)
Titus (AD 65)
2 Timothy (AD 66)

**PART 9**
*The Final Letters*
Beyond the Book of Acts

1 Peter (AD 63)
Hebrews (AD 64–68)
2 Peter (AD 66)
Jude (AD 70–80)
1, 2, 3 John (AD 90)
Revelation (AD 90s)

A Research Paradigm (For studying the subject of material possessions as described in the biblical story.)

## Biblical Continuity

We soon discovered, however, that this subject could not be adequately understood without carefully reading the Old Testament. As in most areas of biblical truth, we cannot understand God's will adequately unless we observe the continuity that is built into the entire biblical story—from Genesis to Revelation. For example, we cannot comprehend God's will regarding the Second Coming of Jesus Christ without consulting both Old and New Testament prophets. Just so, we cannot understand God's will regarding our material possessions unless we study both the history of God's people (the church) in the New Testament and the history of God's people (Israel) in the Old Testament.

## Our Point of Reference

For nearly two thousand years, we have been a new covenant people living under grace as members of the body of Christ. Our position in Christ, both individually and corporately, is a very important biblical and theological grid for understanding how Old Testament teachings regarding material possessions relate to what we are taught in the New Testament.

Our primary purpose in this study was to look for timeless truths that are applicable at any moment in history and in every people group that has and will ever inhabit planet Earth. We've identified these truths as *supracultural principles*. In fact, to our surprise, we discovered that the Bible says more about our material possessions than about any other subject other than God himself.[1]

## God's Agenda

Once we completed this basic study, I had the privilege of both writing this book and teaching these principles to the people I've served as senior pastor of Fellowship Bible Church North in Plano, Texas. Following one of these teaching sessions, I was greatly encouraged by the comment of one of our lay leaders. "Gene," he said with excitement in his eyes, "what makes this material so powerful is that it's God's agenda, not yours!" He went on to explain that most presentations he had heard before—and he had heard many—described someone's personal agenda using a variety of proof texts to support that agenda.

Needless to say, this was an encouraging comment, since that's exactly what we had hoped to accomplish with this study—to discover what God's will actually is in this very important arena that permeates all of our lives. By God's design, we live in a material world. How can we live as citizens on earth when our true citizenship is in heaven? God answers this question by unveiling *his agenda*! It's not surprising that many believers in our church began rethinking their priorities regarding their personal possessions.

## Moving from Principles to Practice

The Holy Spirit inspired the authors of Scripture to record God's eternal Truth. If stated correctly, biblical principles are specific statements of that Truth. However, it's only as we as Christians internalize this Truth that changes will take place in our lives. These changes must start with a clear knowledge and understanding of biblical revelation. As Paul reminded Timothy, "All

Scripture is God-breathed and is useful for teaching, rebuking, correcting and training in righteousness, so that the man of God may be thoroughly equipped for every good work" (2 Timothy 3:16–17).

To internalize biblical truth, we must allow the author of Scripture—the Holy Spirit—not only to open the eyes of our hearts to know and understand Scripture but also to change our lives. Here the second part of Paul's prayer for the Ephesian Christians is our secret, as well, in applying biblical truth:

> I pray that out of his glorious riches he may strengthen you with power through his Spirit in your inner being, so that Christ may dwell in your hearts through faith. And I pray that you, being rooted and established in love, may have power, together with all the saints, to grasp how wide and long and high and deep is the love of Christ, and to know this love that surpasses knowledge—that you may be filled to the measure of all the fullness of God. (Ephesians 3:16–19)

I'm indeed grateful to Howard Publishing for encouraging me to present this material in a new and fresh way. The truth that lies between the covers of this book certainly was not destroyed by the fire I described earlier. The principles we've outlined are as old as Scripture, since what you read reflects what God has inscribed about material possessions in both the Old and New Testaments—the Word of God that will abide forever.

But what God has revealed to us in the Bible is also as current as today. And the society we're living in—particularly in

America—is perhaps more materialistic than at any time in the history of Western culture. To be in God's will, we must listen and respond to the Savior who, on the mount overlooking the Sea of Galilee, told his eager audience, "Seek first his kingdom and his righteousness, and all these things will be given to you as well" (Matthew 6:33).

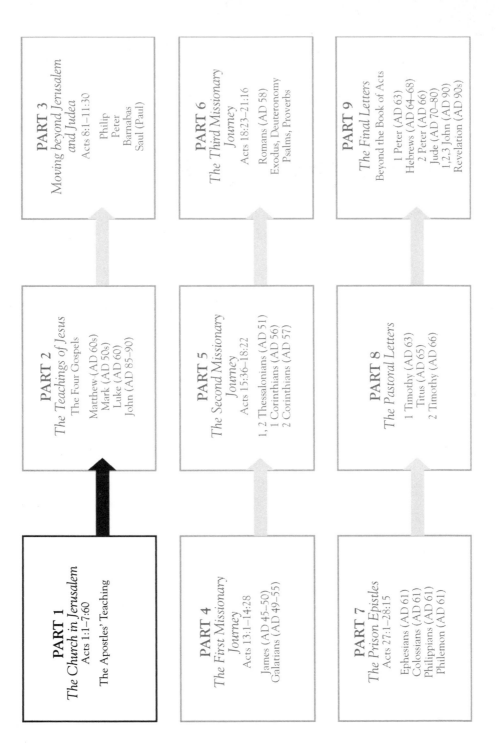

**PART 1**
*The Church in Jerusalem*
Acts 1:1–7:60

The Apostles' Teaching

**PART 2**
*The Teachings of Jesus*
The Four Gospels

Matthew (AD 60s)
Mark (AD 50s)
Luke (AD 60)
John (AD 85–90)

**PART 3**
*Moving beyond Jerusalem and Judea*
Acts 8:1–11:30

Philip
Peter
Barnabas
Saul (Paul)

**PART 4**
*The First Missionary Journey*
Acts 13:1–14:28

James (AD 45–50)
Galatians (AD 49–55)

**PART 5**
*The Second Missionary Journey*
Acts 15:36–18:22

1, 2 Thessalonians (AD 51)
1 Corinthians (AD 56)
2 Corinthians (AD 57)

**PART 6**
*The Third Missionary Journey*
Acts 18:23–21:16

Romans (AD 58)
Exodus, Deuteronomy
Psalms, Proverbs

**PART 7**
*The Prison Epistles*
Acts 27:1–28:15

Ephesians (AD 61)
Colossians (AD 61)
Philippians (AD 61)
Philemon (AD 61)

**PART 8**
*The Pastoral Letters*

1 Timothy (AD 63)
Titus (AD 65)
2 Timothy (AD 66)

**PART 9**
*The Final Letters*
Beyond the Book of Acts

1 Peter (AD 63)
Hebrews (AD 64–68)
2 Peter (AD 66)
Jude (AD 70–80)
1,2,3 John (AD 90)
Revelation (AD 90s)

A Research Paradigm (For studying the subject of material possessions as described in the biblical story.)

# PART 1

## PRINCIPLES FROM
## THE CHURCH IN JERUSALEM

What happened in the holy city in AD 33, after Jesus Christ ascended and the Holy Spirit descended, launched a dynamic movement that has spanned the globe. To this day all people, regardless of economic status, ethnic background, color, or language, are a part of that movement if they have sincerely put their faith in the Lord Jesus Christ for salvation.

Though these early believers initially had a very limited view of God's ultimate plan for the church, how they viewed and used their material possessions has probably never been equaled. During the first five years as a corporate community, they exemplified a generosity that challenges believers for all time. In fact, approximately half of the events recorded in the early chapters of the book of Acts focus on the way these first-century Christians used their material possessions to further the work of God's kingdom.

Chapter 1
# The Mystery Revealed

Thousands of faithful pilgrims from all over the Roman Empire were present in Jerusalem when the Holy Spirit descended on the Day of Pentecost. Luke identified them as *"God-fearing Jews* from every nation under heaven" (Acts 2:5).[1] Many of these visitors would have arrived earlier to participate in the Passover celebration and so would have been in Jerusalem at the time of Christ's crucifixion (the day after Passover).[2] Jeremias estimated that the permanent inhabitants of Jerusalem totaled about 55,000 and that during the Feast of Pentecost there were approximately 125,000 visitors.[3]

Imagine the setting! Jerusalem teemed with worshipers from all over the Roman Empire—and beyond. They came to offer sacrifices at the temple, to pay their temple tax, and to use their "second tithe"[4] to participate in this great festival. Together with the residents of Jerusalem and the outlying districts, they were expressing their Jewish faith.

## If You Were a Jew (Acts 2)
What would you have done if you had been a God-fearing, Grecian Jew—a father of a large family, let us say from Rome?

Your family had spent days traveling by land and sea in order to worship God in the temple in Jerusalem.

While there, you witnessed Jesus's crucifixion. In fact, you got caught up in the mob psychology that permeated the atmosphere. Though you didn't fully understand why you participated, you joined the crowd and shouted, "Crucify him! Crucify him!" You were convinced that this man was guilty of blasphemy. After all, one of your best friends, a member of the Sanhedrin, told you he had heard Jesus claim to have existed before Abraham was born (John 8:58). Such arrogance, you concluded, deserves death.

## Your Enlightenment

You now realize that Jesus actually *was* the Messiah. The rumors you had heard about a supposed resurrection were true! You heard the sound like a mighty rushing wind that swept through Jerusalem. Again you followed the crowd, this time to a location where you heard twelve men from Galilee speaking in various languages—languages they had never learned. You recognized most of them as uneducated men, yet one of them spoke in your Latin dialect, "declaring the wonders of God" (Acts 2:11).

Then you heard Peter speak. You learned that he was a former fisherman who had left his boats and nets nearly three and a half years ago to follow Christ. You were utterly amazed when he stood and quoted a lengthy section from the prophet Joel, explaining that the disciples were speaking by the influence and power of the Holy Spirit (Acts 2:17–18).

*Your Conversion*

At that moment, you were overwhelmed with conviction—"cut to the heart." With a number of other listeners, you cried out, "Brothers, what shall we do?" (Acts 2:37).

"Repent and be baptized . . . in the name of Jesus Christ for the forgiveness of your sins," Peter responded, "and you will receive the gift of the Holy Spirit" just as they had (Acts 2:38).

You rushed back to the inn where you were staying and where your family was eagerly awaiting a report of this unusual disturbance. You shared what you had seen and heard, and because your wife and your sons and daughters (and their spouses) respected you as their spiritual leader, your entire family—including your servants—eagerly responded to the Good News. All of you put your faith in Jesus Christ.

Together, you and your extended family elbowed your way back through the crowds where the apostles were baptizing thousands of people. All of you joyfully volunteered to be baptized to demonstrate to your fellow Jews that you acknowledged Christ as the true Messiah. With this act of public confession, you let everyone know that you had joined the ranks of those who were disciples of Christ.

*Your Critical Decision*

The fifty-day celebration of Pentecost had come to a close. The money and food (your second tithe) you had saved for the trip were nearly depleted, with just enough resources left to travel back to your home in Rome.

You soon found out that thousands of other Grecian Jews,

including numerous widows, were facing the same critical decision: should you return home or stay in Jerusalem?

You were aware, of course, that the Old Testament prophets predicted that the Messiah would occupy the throne of David and reign as king in Jerusalem. It would be a perfect kingdom. As you retired that night, you reminded your family of the words of Isaiah: "I will create new heavens and a new earth. The former things will not be remembered, nor will they come to mind. But be glad and rejoice forever in what I will create, for I will create *Jerusalem* to be a delight and its people a joy. I will rejoice over *Jerusalem* and take delight in my people; the sound of weeping and of crying will be heard in it no more" (Isaiah 65:17–19).

## *Your Reflections*

You could hardly sleep that night, thinking about Isaiah's words. You thought about the Roman emperor, Tiberius, whose throne was just a few miles from your home. He was a godless man. Though he had made some good decisions and had established some helpful policies in the Roman Empire, he was an arrogant leader. The experience just two years ago (AD 31) when Aelius Sejanus, the captain of the Praetorian Guard, had tried to seize his throne had left Tiberius extremely paranoid and even more cruel than before.

Then there was Herod Antipas, the tetrarch of Galilee and Perea. Though a Jew by religion, he was an insensitive and immoral leader. To placate his wife, Herodias, who was intensely angry with John the Baptist for accusing the couple of having an adulterous relationship, Herod had had John beheaded (Matthew 14:1–12).

Two months ago, when this ruthless leader arrived in

Jerusalem for the Passover celebration, it was with his usual pomp and circumstance—actually pride and arrogance. You had heard about the way he treated Jesus when Pilate sent him to Herod for a hearing—how he and his soldiers had ridiculed and mocked him, dressing him in an elegant robe (Luke 23:11).

And how could you forget Pontius Pilate, appointed by the Roman emperor as procurator of Judea. You'd seen him in action the day Christ was sentenced to death. In some respects, you felt sorry for him because he had wrestled with the decision, knowing full well that Jesus was innocent of the charges brought against him.

These events churned and then congealed in your thoughts. You finally began drifting toward sleep, reflecting on Peter's sermon, when he had quoted the prophet Joel. Your mind jumped ahead to the next section of the prophecy:

> In those days and at that time, when I restore the fortunes of Judah and Jerusalem, I will gather all nations and bring them down to the Valley of Jehoshaphat. There I will enter into judgment against them concerning my inheritance, my people Israel, for they scattered my people among the nations and divided up my land. . . . Then you will know that I, the Lord your God, dwell in Zion, my holy hill. Jerusalem will be holy; never again will foreigners invade her. (Joel 3:1–2, 17)

Hadn't Zechariah prophesied the same future for Jerusalem? "On that day," he wrote, "living water will flow out from Jerusalem. . . . The LORD will be king over the whole earth. On that day there will be one LORD, and his name the only name" (Zechariah 14:8–9).

By then your mind was half awake, half in slumber. In your semiconscious dreams, you saw Herod and Pilate—even the Roman Emperor Tiberius—all bowing low and kneeling before Jesus Christ, who was sitting on the throne in Jerusalem. And beyond, you saw people coming from all parts of the world to pay homage to the King of kings, the one and final great King of the Jews.

## The Scene in Perspective

Though this is an imaginary scenario, it fits what was happening in Jerusalem. It reconstructs what may have been the thinking of many God-fearing Jews who came from all over the New Testament world to worship. Those who were relatively wealthy had been in Jerusalem for at least two months. They had witnessed the crucifixion and now had been confronted with their sin of rejecting the Messiah.

Others had come for a shorter period of time. Though their knowledge of everything that had transpired was more limited, others in Jerusalem would have quickly filled them in on the details. Many had actually heard Jesus teach and had seen him work miracles. They would have felt the impact of their sin more forcefully, since they had witnessed and participated in his life as well as in his death.

Most of the Grecian Jews who responded to Peter's message evidently decided to stay in Jerusalem so as not to miss the next chapter in this exciting story. After all, the last words the apostles received directly from the Lord came via the two men dressed in white. As Christ was disappearing from sight, these heavenly messengers had appeared to the apostles as they were looking up into the sky. Speaking to these men, who must have been utterly over-whelmed, they informed them that Jesus would come back the same way they had seen him go into heaven (Acts 1:11).

You can be sure the apostles shared this message immediately with all those who responded to the gospel—and this information would have spread like wildfire.

## Their View of the Future

We have no historical evidence that the Holy Spirit gave the apostles, at this moment, a time line for these events. In fact, some of the specific details regarding the return of Christ to earth have never been revealed, even to this day.

The apostles, then, did not understand clearly what was to transpire in the days to come, even though Jesus had given them some specific information about their responsibility. When they asked him if he was "going to restore the kingdom to Israel" at that time, Jesus responded by saying, "It is not for you to know the times or dates the Father has set by his own authority. But you will receive power when the Holy Spirit comes on you; and you will be my witnesses in Jerusalem, and in all Judea and Samaria, and to the ends of the earth" (Acts 1:6–8).

With this explanation and directive, Jesus made clear that he would not return to restore the kingdom to Israel until these men had at least *begun* the process of proclaiming his death and resurrec-tion "to the ends of the earth." The apostles didn't fully understand what this meant, nor did they give much attention to it initially. But in God's sovereign plan, the Holy Spirit began to unfold the future in broad brush strokes, enabling Peter to interpret the prophecies of Joel and David even without a specific understanding of that great era of which he was now a part—the age of the church. Peter didn't even understand at that point that Gentiles would be a part of the kingdom. This insight did not come until at least five years later, when he was confronted with the task of witnessing to a Gentile named Cornelius. At that time he confessed, "I now realize how true it is that God does not show favoritism but accepts men from every nation who fear him and do what is right" (Acts 10:34–35).

The apostle Paul was the first to explain clearly what had happened in Jerusalem when the Holy Spirit came on the Day of Pentecost. When he wrote to the Ephesians, he identified this phenomenon as the "mystery of Christ":

> In reading this, then, you will be able to understand my insight into the mystery of Christ, which was not made known to men in other generations as it has now been revealed by the Spirit to God's holy apostles and prophets. This mystery is that through the gospel the Gentiles are heirs together with Israel, members together of one body, and sharers together in the promise in Christ Jesus. (Ephesians 3:4–6)

## Chapter 2
# An Unparalleled Work of Faith

When the church was born in Jerusalem, the majority of those Jews who had come from distant places and who had responded to the gospel settled in to wait for Christ to return and to restore the earthly kingdom to Israel. In view of what they knew from the Old Testament and of the final message the apostles had received from the two angels as Jesus ascended, we cannot blame them. They simply responded to the information they had. They had been told that this same Jesus would return as they had seen him ascend. In the meantime, they demonstrated mutual concern for one another that is still unparalleled in the history of Christianity.

It was no doubt from his experience during those years that James, the half brother of Christ and the person who eventually became the head elder and pastor in the Jerusalem church, later penned a powerful letter explaining that "faith without deeds is dead" (James 2:26). He declared, "Show me your faith without deeds, and I will show you my faith by what I do" (James 2:18). This personal witness reflects the testimony of the community of believers in Jerusalem in the early days of the church.[1]

In this chapter, we will examine six situations in the early church in Jerusalem from which we will abstract our first nine supracultural principles.

# BIBLICAL BASIS

*A Dynamic Community Witness*—Acts 2:42–47

As we've already noted, thousands of families decided to stay in Jerusalem, even though many of them had already used up their surplus of money and food. Those who were staying in public inns would need to pay rent, and everyone needed food daily. To solve this problem, the believers—those who lived in Jerusalem and those who lived in other parts of the Roman Empire—decided to have "everything in common." But it was the believers in Jerusalem who had to take the first steps.

This they did willingly and unselfishly: "Selling their possessions and goods, they gave to anyone as he had need" (Acts 2:45). Jerusalem residents opened their doors to those from other places in the world: "They broke bread in their homes and ate together with glad and sincere hearts" (Acts 2:46). Through this demonstration of love and unselfishness, new believers were "enjoying the favor of all the people." More and more Jews recognized that Jesus Christ was the true Messiah, and "the Lord added to their number daily those who were being saved" (Acts 2:47).

As we look at these dynamic events in the book of Acts, we'll see powerful principles that apply in any culture of the world and at any moment in history. And when we look at the rest of the biblical story as it unfolds, we'll see how additional first-century events and biblical directives reinforce and expand these initial supracultural principles.

## *Supra*cultural Principle 1

### THE POWER OF LOVE AND UNITY

*Using our material possessions in harmony with the will of God will create love and unity among believers, which in turn will motivate and encourage non-Christians to believe in Jesus Christ.*

When Jesus spent his final days with the apostles in the Upper Room, he gave them a new commandment: "Love one another." He demonstrated and illustrated his love in the middle of the Passover meal when he washed the disciples' feet. Christ said, "As I have loved you, so you must love one another" (John 13:34). Then he declared what would result from this kind of love: "All men will know that you are my disciples, if you love one another" (John 13:35).

Later Jesus prayed for these men—and for all of us who would believe in Jesus Christ through their message (John 17:20). Jesus was very specific in saying that as Christians love one another, the unity this creates will convince unbelievers that Jesus Christ was one with the Father and was sent into the world by the Father to be the Savior (John 17:20–22).

This is what was happening in Jerusalem. As these believers shared their material possessions with anyone who had needs, unbelievers could see clearly that they "were one in heart and mind" (Acts 4:32). Consequently, the believers were "enjoying the favor of all the people," which in turn caused many more to believe that Jesus Christ was actually who he said he was—the Messiah and Savior. Luke reported that "the Lord added to their number daily those who were being saved" (Acts 2:47).

This principle—the power of love and unity—is just as true and applicable today as it was in first-century Jerusalem. Unbelievers are attracted to unselfish, generous Christians—and as a result, they will be open to the message of salvation. Conversely, selfish Christians who are not demonstrating Christ's love often destroy unity in the church. It goes without saying that this is not a positive witness to unbelievers. It drives them away from the gospel. Unfortunately, in today's world, Satan has a wide-open door in our materialistic culture. It shouldn't surprise us that he'll use every opportunity to try to destroy our witness in the world, and there's no debate: One of the chinks in our armor is selfishness! The giving patterns of American Christians, sadly, illustrates our vulnerability to Satan's "flaming arrows" (Ephesians 6:16).

# BIBLICAL BASIS

*A Startling Contrast*—Acts 3:1–10

The first miracle recorded by Luke involved Peter and John as they were going to the temple to pray. As they were approaching the temple gate called Beautiful, they encountered a man who had been crippled from birth. Some of his friends were carrying him to a place inside the temple courts where he was allowed to beg. It's doubtful he knew who Peter and John were, so he went about his daily routine and asked them for money. But note Peter's response: "Silver or gold I do not have, but what I have I give you. In the name of Jesus Christ of Nazareth, walk" (Acts 3:6).

Here was a man begging for money, but Peter and John were unable to respond. They had no "silver or gold." Rather, they used the grace God had bestowed upon them to heal. They then shared the message of eternal life in Christ that could be received as a free gift—apart from money.

There is a dynamic message in this interchange. The other religious leaders in Jerusalem were among the wealthy. Unfortunately, many of the poor people felt that this wealth was a result of God's blessing on their leaders, who had concocted their own brand of prosperity theology by distorting Old Testament promises. But here were two former fishermen who had left their boats and nets and who had very little of this world's goods. Yet they had the power to heal and the message of salvation that could give eternal life.

The contrast must have been startling. These men were willing to give up the accumulation of material possessions in order to serve Jesus Christ and his kingdom—an act of love and concern that put the spotlight on the hypocrisy of the religious leaders in Jerusalem.

## *Supra*cultural Principle 2
### MODELING GENEROSITY

*Spiritual leaders should model the way all Christians are to use material possessions.*

Modeling giving is not just a New Testament principle. David announced to the whole assembly what he had decided to give to the temple (see 1 Chronicles 28 and 29), from both his corporate resources as king of Israel (1 Chronicles 29:2) to his personal resources (1 Chronicles 29:3–5). Consequently, those listening were so encouraged that they, in turn, gave willingly toward the work of the temple of God (1 Chronicles 29:7). This leadership model impacted all Israel: "The people rejoiced at the *willing response of their leaders*, for they had given freely and wholeheartedly to the LORD" (1 Chronicles 29:9).

Paul often modeled this principle, actually giving up his material rights in order to offer the gospel free of charge (1 Corinthians 9:18). Though he taught that spiritual leaders should be cared for financially (1 Timothy 5:17–18), he also modeled integrity, unselfishness, and pure motives—particularly among unbelievers and new Christians (1 Thessalonians 2:9).

God's people need visible leadership models in terms of what God expects regarding the use of material possessions. How this fleshes out methodologically will vary greatly in different cultural circumstances. What must be consistent in every situation, however, is the model itself.

# BIBLICAL BASIS

*A Voluntary Liquidation System*—Acts 4:32–35

When Luke recorded that people "shared everything they had," he did not mean that *everyone* sold *everything* and put the total proceeds in a common fund. Rather, he clarified this statement when he said, "There were no *needy* persons among them. For *from time to time* those who owned lands or houses sold them" (Acts 4:34). In other words, as the needs of people became obvious, those who could, and desired to do so, responded by liquidating their properties in order to provide money to meet these needs. This was a voluntary system, which must have greatly impacted the God-fearing but non-Christian Jews who were used to a rather rigid, legalistic approach to giving. The believers shared their material possessions out of love—because of their commitment to the Lord Jesus Christ and their compassion for humans in need.

## *Supra*cultural Principle 3

### SPECIAL NEEDS AND SPECIAL SACRIFICES

*Be willing to make sacrifices to meet special material needs within the body of Christ.*

There are always special circumstances that create special needs among God's people. In New Testament days, sometimes it was a famine, such as the one Jerusalem Christians would face later. In that case, the church in Antioch came to the rescue (Acts 11:25–30; see discussion in Part 3). Later Paul faced special needs because of his imprisonment in Rome, and the Philippian church rose to the occasion and met his needs (Philippians 4:10–20).

And so it is today. Special needs emerge, and when they do, God's people should respond to meet those needs. Not to respond when it is possible to do so is to violate the will of God (Proverbs 3:27).

Don't misunderstand. These special opportunities to give don't alleviate our responsibility to follow God's will by being regular and consistent givers. Both principles emerge from the study of the New Testament. But the fact remains that throughout Scripture, human needs were a primary motivating factor for giving among God's people. Frequently, we see directives to meet the physical needs of the poor. We see exhortations to care for the needs of those who minister to us through the Word of God. And we're commanded to show hospitality to friends and strangers alike.

# BIBLICAL BASIS

*A Son of Encouragement*—Acts 4:36–37

The Holy Spirit inspired Luke to record one exemplary event to illustrate what was happening in Jerusalem. Joseph was a Levite from Cyprus who evidently had been in Jerusalem for some time. Perhaps he had moved to Jerusalem and invested in properties, or he operated his business from his home in Cyprus. In any case, he owned property in Jerusalem, and when the need arose, he "sold a field he owned and brought the money and put it at the apostles' feet" (Acts 4:37).

The apostles dubbed him Barnabas, which means Son of Encouragement. His actions tell us a great deal about his generous spirit. Luke's account also demonstrates the open and public way the Jerusalem believers shared their material possessions with others. In fact, this succinct but power-packed paragraph regarding Barnabas introduces us to at least three dynamic supracultural principles.

## *Supracultural* Principle 4

### BECOMING ENCOURAGERS

*Share your material possessions to encourage
others in the body of Christ.*

The keyword in this principle is *encourage*. Barnabas, the Son of Encouragement, is a marvelous example of this principle at work in the Jerusalem church (Acts 4:36). Anyone who has been in Christian leadership and responsible for meeting the needs of others can identify with the reason the apostles changed Joseph's name to Barnabas. People who are generous are special encouragers.

## *Supra*cultural Principle 5

### SHOWING APPRECIATION

*Show appreciation to Christians who are*
*faithful in sharing their material possessions.*

This principle is demonstrated throughout the New Testament in appreciation shown to individuals as well as to groups of Christians. Paul wrote to Philemon, "Your love has given me great joy and encouragement, because you, brother, have refreshed the hearts of the saints" (Philemon 7). Paul was no doubt referring to the way Philemon used his material possessions, particularly his home, to show Christian hospitality (see chapter 22).

On another occasion, Paul showed appreciation to a group of Christians when he wrote to the Corinthians. Referring to the Macedonian churches, he said, "We want you to know about the grace that God has given the Macedonian churches. Out of the most severe trial, their overflowing joy and their extreme poverty welled up in rich generosity. For I testify that they gave as much as they were able, and even beyond their ability" (2 Corinthians 8:1–3; see chapter 16).

Today Christian leaders need to develop sensitive but specific ways to show appreciation to fellow believers, in both a personal and a corporate way, for their generosity. It's true that people need to be taught their responsibility to be good stewards, but they also need to be commended when they're faithful—even more so when they've gone beyond what God expects.

## *Supra*cultural Principle 6

### PERSONAL AND CORPORATE MODELS

*Christians need to be able to observe other believers who*
*are faithful in sharing their material possessions.*

This principle runs counter to the strong emphasis on confidentiality that often accompanies Christian giving today. No one can deny that what Barnabas did was visible not only to the apostles but also to other Christians and even to non-Christians in Jerusalem. Otherwise, Ananias and Sapphira wouldn't have attempted to do the same thing but with wrong motives. We must not miss the point that the Holy Spirit wanted Barnabas specifically and the Jerusalem church corporately to be a visible model to believers throughout the centuries. That's why he inspired Luke to record these events.

On another occasion, Paul used the generosity of Christians in Achaia to motivate Macedonian believers to be liberal as well. Later, in 2 Corinthians 9:1–2, he wrote that the Achaians' enthusiastic desire to give had motivated most of the Macedonian Christians to do the same thing (see chapter 17).

Just like Christians in the New Testament era, believers today need personal and corporate models to inspire them to use their material possessions to further the kingdom of God. Verbal teaching alone will not motivate this action.

# BIBLICAL BASIS

*An Act of Pride—Acts 5:1–11*

The next major recorded event also involved the liquidating of property and giving to meet the needs of the church. And again, specific individuals were identified by name. But here the similarities end.

The two people mentioned are a husband and wife named Ananias and Sapphira. Like Barnabas, they were probably well-to-do businesspeople who "also sold a piece of property." However, this couple had agreed to keep part of the money from the sale and to bring the remainder to the apostles. That was their right, but they wanted to give the impression that they were giving the total sum from the sale of the property.

The results were devastating. When Ananias brought the money, Peter knew (through the power of the Holy Spirit) that he was lying about the gift. "Didn't it belong to you before it was sold?" Peter asked. "And after it was sold, wasn't the money at your disposal? What made you think of doing such a thing?"

Both Ananias and Sapphira were severely judged for their wrongdoing. At once, Ananias "fell down and died" (Acts 5:5). Sapphira arrived on the scene about three hours later, also lied, and paid the same price. Predictably, "great fear seized the whole church and all who heard about these events" (Acts 5:11).

Luke didn't record this scene to demonstrate that Ananias and

Sapphira were outside of God's will when they gave this money publicly. Many others throughout Jerusalem were doing the same thing. Neither was it wrong to keep part of the money. They were under no obligation either to sell the land or to give the money. The odious aspect of this sin to God was their lying to the Holy Spirit (Acts 5:4).

This account is meant to be read and interpreted as a back-to-back contrast to the Barnabas story. The two events together demonstrate dramatically how the use of our material possessions reflects our relationship with God and with Jesus Christ. They are inseparable concepts, particularly as they relate to honesty and integrity.

Furthermore, these stories reflect the importance of the way we view and use our material possessions in maintaining a proper witness for Jesus Christ, both to our fellow Christians and to the unbelieving world. The way these believers used their money was highly visible, and God didn't want false impressions given to those who were looking on.

## *Supra*cultural Principle 7

### PURE MOTIVES

*Our material gifts should always be given
to honor God, not ourselves.*

In contrast with Barnabas's generous act of love, Ananias and Sapphira's motives were wrong. They wanted self-glory, so much so that they gave a false impression and actually lied to the Holy Spirit.

Thankfully, serious punishment is not God's normal way of dealing with this kind of sin in the lives of his children. But on this rare occasion, God was reminding believers in a very dramatic way how serious it is to ignore his instructions and to purposely act outside of his will.

# BIBLICAL BASIS

*Helping People in Need*—Acts 6:1–7

As the church grew in numbers, the predictable happened. Certain individuals were neglected in this semicommunal system: "The Grecian Jews among them complained against the Hebraic Jews because their widows were being overlooked in the daily distribution of food" (Acts 6:1).

Because of their conversions to Jesus Christ, the widows who would ordinarily be taken care of through the Jewish social system were cut off from that support. Those who suffered first were the Grecian widows who had come as visitors to Jerusalem. Naturally they would run out of resources before those Hebrew widows who were part of community and who would be cared for by their own relatives nearby.

The apostles responded to this organizational challenge. They gathered all the disciples together and proposed a solution. From an administrative and organizational point of view, it would seem likely that this included only "all" of those Grecian Jews who had brought the complaint. It would have been virtually impossible to hold a public meeting in Jerusalem involving hundreds and perhaps thousands of people. Christians were, by this time, deeply resented by the religious leaders and not permitted to meet in the temple courts.

The first part of the apostles' solution involved their own priorities. They made clear that the work was getting too complex for them to take time to meet the need personally. They in no way negated the importance of this ministry to widows, but it would not be appropriate for them to "neglect the ministry of the Word of God," which was their primary calling. Neither were they unwilling to be involved in resolving the problem.

The apostles proposed that the Grecian brothers select seven men who were highly qualified—men known to be full of the Holy Spirit and wisdom (Acts 6:3)—to oversee the ministry to widows. Once these men were selected, the apostles turned this responsibility over to them and gave their own attention to prayer and the ministry of the Word (Acts 6:3–4).

Positive results were immediate! The apostles were free to spend their time preaching the gospel, and God continued to bless as the gospel spread and the number of disciples in Jerusalem increased rapidly. Even more significantly, a large number of priests, the elite among the Jews, became obedient to the faith (Acts 6:7).

This story may seem far removed from our own experiences in the twenty-first century—particularly in Western culture. However, at least two important principles emerge that should guide the church no matter what the cultural dynamics.

## *Supra*cultural Principle 8

### ADEQUATE FORMS

*Every church should have an efficient system for
helping to meet the true material needs of
others in the body of Christ.*

Though the church in Jerusalem was unique in its structure, what they did in meeting the needs of widows illustrates this principle.

When there is a true need among Christians that cannot be met in other ways, that need should be met by members of the body of Christ. Consequently, any given church in any given cultural situation should develop a system to determine what the needs are and how to meet them in an equitable fashion.

## *Supra*cultural Principle 9

### DELEGATING TASKS

*Spiritual leaders must at times delegate administrative responsibilities to other mature believers who can help them in meeting material needs.*

It's clear in Scripture that spiritual leaders in every local church are to manage and shepherd the people just as a father is to manage his family well (1 Timothy 3:4–5). This certainly includes overseeing the financial aspects of the church. But it is not the will of God that pastors and elders be burdened with the detailed responsibility of meeting the material needs of people.

This principle was clearly illustrated in the Jerusalem church. Though the apostles were responsible for making sure that the widows' needs were met by setting up a proper system, they were not responsible for the actual distribution of food. The reason is simple: God does not want those designated primarily as elders and pastors to become sidetracked from fulfilling their primary ministry.[2]

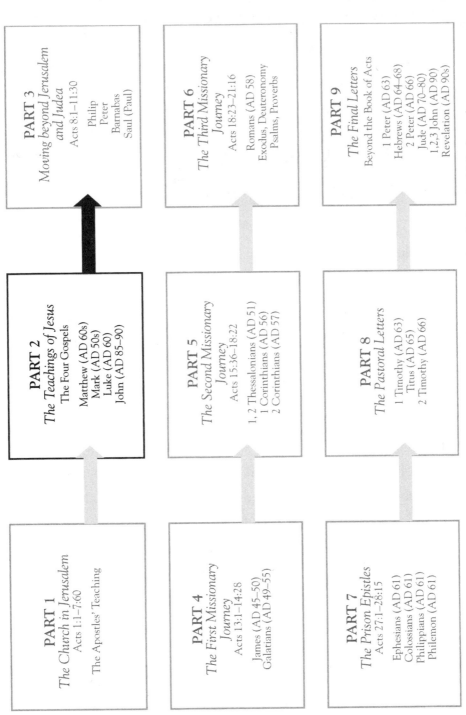

**PART 1**
*The Church in Jerusalem*
Acts 1:1–7:60

The Apostles' Teaching

**PART 2**
*The Teachings of Jesus*
The Four Gospels

Matthew (AD 60s)
Mark (AD 50s)
Luke (AD 60)
John (AD 85–90)

**PART 3**
*Moving beyond Jerusalem and Judea*
Acts 8:1–11:30

Philip
Peter
Barnabas
Saul (Paul)

**PART 4**
*The First Missionary Journey*
Acts 13:1–14:28

James (AD 45–50)
Galatians (AD 49–55)

**PART 5**
*The Second Missionary Journey*
Acts 15:36–18:22

1, 2 Thessalonians (AD 51)
1 Corinthians (AD 56)
2 Corinthians (AD 57)

**PART 6**
*The Third Missionary Journey*
Acts 18:23–21:16

Romans (AD 58)
Exodus, Deuteronomy
Psalms, Proverbs

**PART 7**
*The Prison Epistles*
Acts 27:1–28:15

Ephesians (AD 61)
Colossians (AD 61)
Philippians (AD 61)
Philemon (AD 61)

**PART 8**
*The Pastoral Letters*

1 Timothy (AD 63)
Titus (AD 65)
2 Timothy (AD 66)

**PART 9**
*The Final Letters*
Beyond the Book of Acts

1 Peter (AD 63)
Hebrews (AD 64–68)
2 Peter (AD 66)
Jude (AD 70–80)
1,2,3 John (AD 90)
Revelation (AD 90s)

A Research Paradigm (For studying the subject of material possessions as described in the biblical story.)

# PART 2
## PRINCIPLES FROM
## THE TEACHINGS OF JESUS

As a result of Peter's teaching on the Day of Pentecost, three thousand people responded in faith and were baptized in order to demonstrate that they had received Jesus as the promised Messiah and Savior. They immediately "devoted themselves to the *apostles' teaching*" (Acts 2:42). Much of what these people heard from the lips of the Twelve were no doubt the very teachings of Christ himself. Jesus had assured them that when the Counselor (the Holy Spirit) came, he would remind them of everything he had taught them (John 14:26). Ultimately, the Spirit of truth would guide them into all truth (John 16:13).

Included in these truths would be what Jesus taught regarding material possessions, some of which was later recorded in the four Gospels. And it's surely no coincidence that the Holy Spirit chose Matthew, a former tax collector and a first-century materialist, to record most of what we have in Scripture of Jesus's words.

So Jesus's teachings regarding material possessions became the apostles' teaching—which, as we'll see, was being dramatically worked out in the lives of the New Testament believers in Jerusalem.

In part 2, we will look at the teachings of Jesus and how they were implemented into the early church.

## Chapter 3
# The Sermon on the Mount
### (Matthew 5)

When Jesus began his public ministry in Galilee, both teaching and healing, his popularity expanded rapidly. Soon "large crowds from Galilee, the Decapolis, Jerusalem, Judea and the region across the Jordan followed him" (Matthew 4:25). In order to teach more in-depth, he took his disciples—a much smaller group that he invited to follow him—to a secluded spot on a hillside overlooking the Sea of Galilee. There he sat down and began to teach (Matthew 5:2). We often designate what Jesus taught that day as the Sermon on the Mount, and it's significant that much of it focuses on material possessions.

## BIBLICAL BASIS

*Blessed are the poor in spirit, for theirs is the kingdom of heaven.*
—Matthew 5:3

Luke's record is more specific: "Blessed are you who are poor, for yours is the kingdom of God" (Luke 6:20). Jesus was addressing many people who had very little of this world's goods. If these people responded to Christ's message of eternal life, Jesus assured them, they would have a special place in God's kingdom.

In fact, their lack of wealth helped them to recognize their "impoverished spirits," motivating them to respond to Christ's call to be his followers.

This is one of the points Jesus was making to his disciples following his encounter with the rich young ruler who came asking what he must do to inherit eternal life (Matthew 19:16). To his surprise, Jesus told him to sell what he had and give the proceeds to the poor. Then he would have treasure in heaven (Matthew 19:21). But "when the young man heard this, he went away sad, because he had great wealth" (Matthew 19:22).

When the disciples watched this man turn and walk away, Jesus told them, "It is hard for a rich man to enter the kingdom of heaven." They "were greatly astonished and asked, 'Who then can be saved?'" (Matthew 19:25). Jesus responded, "With man this is impossible, but with God all things are possible" (Matthew 19:26).

Jesus wasn't telling this young man or the disciples that they must sell everything and give away the proceeds in order to be saved. That would contradict the whole of Scripture, for no one can be saved by doing good works (Romans 4:1–3; 5:1; Ephesians 2:8–9). Furthermore, Jesus did not require this kind of sacrifice from other rich people who followed him. Rather, he was dealing with a man who was in love with his material possessions. He had "great wealth," and it was his stumbling block. Though the man did many good things with his life, his love of money kept him from experiencing God's saving love and grace. Evidently, he was not even willing to discuss the matter further with Jesus. He simply walked away with a heavy heart.

So as Jesus taught that day on the hillside, he urged those who were poor, both materially and spiritually, to be encouraged. Their lack of this world's goods could serve as a means to open their hearts to God. The fact that they were poor in a material sense enabled them to be "poor in spirit." To be rich materially may have given them a sense of being "rich in spirit," which can interfere with a person's response to God's invitation to be saved. Unfortunately, some people feel no need for God when they're rich and self-satisfied.

### The Church in Jerusalem

Did the Holy Spirit remind Matthew of Jesus's teachings about being "poor in spirit" during those early days of the church? If so, many poor people would have been encouraged. Yes, there were many well-to-do people present—like Barnabas—but I believe the poor widow Jesus referred to in the temple was probably among those who first responded to the gospel. In a real sense, those who were poor in spirit were already experiencing what Jesus meant when he said, "Theirs is the kingdom of heaven" (Matthew 5:3). They had come to know the Lord Jesus Christ as personal Savior. The kingdom of God was already within them (Luke 17:21).

## Supracultural Principle 10

### BLINDING SELF-SUFFICIENCY

*Having a lot of material possessions may make it difficult to recognize and acknowledge our need for God's grace in salvation.*

This principle does not mean that wealthy people cannot or will not respond to the gospel. Zacchaeus certainly illustrates that they can and do, and so do others who came to Christ when the church was born in Jerusalem. As we continue our study, we will encounter more well-to-do people like the Ethiopian eunuch, Cornelius, Lydia, Priscilla and Aquila, and Philemon—all of whom responded to the gospel once the church expanded beyond Jerusalem.

The facts are, however, that an abundance of things and a desire to accumulate more and more can cause any of us to be self-satisfied, self-indulgent, and even cruel.

# BIBLICAL BASIS

*First go and be reconciled to your brother; then come and offer your gift.*
—Matthew 5:24

When Jesus was teaching that day, he also demonstrated the interrelatedness of the two great commandments, which are foundational for *all* the commandments. The first and greatest commandment (Matthew 22:37–38) is that we should fervently love the Lord our God. The second is that we should love our neighbors as ourselves (Matthew 22:39).

Applied to giving, Jesus taught his followers that before they offered their material possessions to God, they must seek forgiveness from those they had wronged. To be out of harmony with their fellow believers was to be out of harmony with God. Under these conditions, their gifts were not acceptable to God—no matter what the size or how perfect. In other words, their love for God was marred because of their lack of love for their neighbor.

Does this mean that the gifts these people offered at the altar were not acceptable to God unless they had righted every wrong they had ever committed toward others? That would have put them—and us—in an impossible situation. Jesus said, "If you are offering your gift at the altar and there *remember* that your brother has something against you. . . . First go and be reconciled to your brother; then come and offer your gift" (Matthew 5:23–24). In other words, they were not to make offerings to God until they had made the things right that they were purposely refusing to "remember"—that is, to seek forgiveness and make restitution. Jesus probably also had in mind contemplated actions toward others that were vindictive (Matthew 5:21–22). In such a case, the thought and intent of the heart had become just as sinful as the action itself.

## The Church in Jerusalem

Imagine the scene. Believers were meeting regularly in various homes to worship God. The apostles joined them, going from house to house teaching and preaching (Acts 5:42). On many occasions, Matthew may have actually shared Jesus's teaching on reconciliation—which he would later record in his Gospel under the inspiration of the Holy Spirit.

We must remember that not all those in Jerusalem at the time the church was born were residents. Many came from all over the New Testament world to offer gifts on the altar in the temple. Among these people were those guilty of serious sins against their fellow Jews. Some had cheated in business—such as Matthew and Zacchaeus when they were still tax collectors. Others were guilty of coveting or lying. Or they had committed private sins involving intense hatred or even adultery.

As new believers, these people would have felt convicted by the Holy Spirit, causing them to seek forgiveness not only from God but from others as well. To be reconciled with their brothers and sisters in Christ before offering gifts to God must have contributed to the love and unity that first existed in the church in Jerusalem. Not only were these new Christians reconciled with one another, but they also stopped cheating and mistreating one another. In fact, they were doing just the opposite— sharing what they had in order to meet one another's needs. In the midst of this community of love, those who were being added to the church daily would also seek reconciliation. What Jesus had taught was probably being carried out all over Jerusalem.

## *Supracultural* Principle 11

### MAKING RESTITUTION

*Material gifts are acceptable and pleasing to God only when we've done our part to be in harmony with brothers and sisters in Christ.*

Christians who are harboring conscious memories of sinning against others and have not asked forgiveness are to do all they can to be at peace with those persons before continuing to offer their possessions to the Lord. Just as the apostle Paul exhorted the Corinthians to examine themselves before they participated in eating and drinking at the Lord's Supper (1 Corinthians 11:27–29), so Christians should examine themselves when they worship God with their material gifts. If we discover sin in our lives, we should seek forgiveness as soon as possible.

Paul affirmed this principle in his letter to the Romans. When exhorting all Christians to pay whatever they owe people—taxes, revenue, respect, honor—Paul concluded with this specific, and yet general, admonition: "Let no debt remain outstanding, except the continuing debt to love one another" (Romans 13:8).

# BIBLICAL BASIS

*Give to the one who asks you, and do not turn away from the one who wants to borrow from you.* —Matthew 5:42

On several occasions in the Sermon on the Mount, Jesus used exaggerated and paradoxical statements to get the attention of his listeners and to make his points. Such is the case when he seemingly instructed his disciples to both give and loan money with indiscretion to people who asked for it. It may appear that Jesus was teaching his followers to be vulnerable to every individual who asked them for money—including thieves, robbers, cheats, selfish manipulators, and false teachers. But note that in the same immediate context, Jesus also commanded:

- If someone strikes you on the right cheek, turn to him the other also (Matthew 5:39).
- If someone wants to sue you and take your tunic, let him have your cloak as well (Matthew 5:40).
- If someone forces you to go one mile, go with him two miles (Matthew 5:41).

Jesus also used hyperbole earlier in the Sermon on the Mount in dealing with other areas of sin. For example, when teaching against adultery, he said:

- If your right eye causes you to sin, gouge it out and throw it away (Matthew 5:29).
- If your right hand causes you to sin, cut it off and throw it away (Matthew 5:30).

Obviously, Jesus didn't mean for his disciples to take these statements regarding physical mutilation literally. Neither did he mean for his followers to take all of his exhortations regarding material possessions literally. In the case of the rich young ruler, Jesus was attempting to deal with the major area of weakness in that man's life—his love of material possessions more than of God or anything else in this world—not commanding that we all must sell everything we own in order to follow Christ.

What, then, was Jesus teaching? The context demonstrates that Christ was dealing with basic attitudes toward those who are our enemies—those who hate us. We are not to demand an "eye for eye" and a "tooth for tooth" (Matthew 5:38). William Hendriksen summarized this passage with the following conclusion: "We have no right to hate the person who tries to deprive us of our possessions. Love even towards him should fill our hearts and reveal itself in our actions."[1]

## The Church in Jerusalem

Though we don't have specific evidence of the apostles or of any of the Christians in the Jerusalem church actually giving money, food, clothing, or shelter to those who hated them, we do have a dynamic illustration of loving one's enemies as Christ loved his enemies. When Stephen was being stoned because of his witness for Christ, "he fell on his knees and cried out, 'Lord, do not hold this sin against them'" (Acts 7:60). In essence, this is what Christ did when he died on the cross. Looking down on his enemies, he cried, "Father, forgive them, for they do not know what they are doing" (Luke 23:34).

We can conclude that a Christian like Stephen, who loved those who were stoning him, would never hesitate to help meet his enemies' economic needs (Matthew 5:42). This is also a remarkable demonstration of "turning the other cheek" (Matthew 5:39), "giving your cloak as well as your tunic" (Matthew 5:40), and going two miles when your enemy "forces you to go one mile" (Matthew 5:41). Jerusalem was filled with believers who were willing to practice these attitudes and actions toward their enemies—a marvelous demonstration of God's grace enabling these believers to follow the teachings of Jesus Christ.

## *Supra*cultural Principle 12
### LOVING OUR ENEMIES

*We should minister not only to those who love us but also to those who resent or even try to harm us.*

Jesus wasn't saying we should allow people to manipulate and take advantage of us. If we do, we're contributing to their irresponsibility. Paul made this clear when he said that a person who is lazy and will not work should not be provided with food (2 Thessalonians 3:10). But it is possible to express, at least in a token way, the same love Christ demonstrated toward his enemies. When he miraculously fed the five thousand people, he knew that the majority of them were not true disciples and would eventually turn their backs on him. But he fed them anyway. When he explained to them the next day that he was the bread of life and that to inherit eternal life they would need to partake of him, "many of his disciples turned back and no longer followed him" (John 6:66).

Who knows how many of those who turned away that day had since become part of the great multitude of true disciples in Jerusalem. They would surely never forget that incredible experience when Jesus fed them in spite of their shortcomings. We must remember this dynamic principle because there are times when we can follow Christ's example and help even our enemies. God may use our generosity and concern to eventually bring these people to saving faith in Jesus Christ.

Chapter 4
# The Sermon on the Mount
(Matthew 6)

In this chapter, we'll continue our look at Jesus's teaching in the Sermon on the Mount, beginning in Matthew 6:3–4.

## BIBLICAL BASIS

*When you give to the needy, do not let your left hand know what your right hand is doing, so that your giving may be in secret.* —Matthew 6:3–4

To understand what Jesus meant by this rather unusual exhortation, we must consider several important factors. First, the Lord was again using hyperbole to make a point. Taken literally, not allowing the left hand to be aware of what the right hand is doing would mean individuals wouldn't know what they themselves were giving. But Jesus wasn't speaking literally in this case any more than when he said, "If your right hand causes you to sin, cut it off and throw it away" (Matthew 5:30).

Second, we must interpret Jesus's exhortation to give in secret in light of a similar teaching in the very next paragraph: "When you pray, go into your room, close the door, and pray to your Father, who is unseen" (Matthew 6:6). If Jesus was teaching that all giving was to be private, we must also conclude that all praying must be private. Not only would we have to avoid being heard as we pray, but we would also have to avoid being seen. This would contradict the extensive emphasis on public and corporate prayer in the rest of the New Testament.

Third, we must look at what Jesus actually practiced and promoted. Generally speaking, he didn't condemn people who gave publicly. In fact, as the poor widow put her gift in the temple treasury, he used her public offering to illustrate sacrificial giving to those who were watching (Luke 21:1–4). Jesus also prayed in public (e.g., Luke 23:34; John 11:41–42; 17:1–26) and in a public setting taught his disciples to pray (Matthew 6:9–13).

Fourth, we must look at what actually happened in the early church. Public giving, as well as public prayer and praise, was a vital part of the way Christians in Jerusalem demonstrated their love for one another and for God. The Holy Spirit used both their personal and corporate witness in these areas to draw others into the kingdom of God (Acts 2:42–47).

Finally, and perhaps most importantly, we must understand the historical and cultural setting. Many of the religious leaders and wealthy people within Judaism at the time of Christ paraded their good works before others. When they gave to the needy, they would "announce it with trumpets" (Matthew 6:2). Their motivation was to be honored by men.

By teaching that giving should be a private matter, Jesus was putting his finger on their prideful motivation. If they couldn't be seen, they would have felt no compulsion to give—or to pray. Their motivation to help the poor was selfish. It didn't spring from their love for God or concern for those who were needy. Motive, then, was the deeper issue. Giving gifts to God or to others to glorify ourselves is a serious violation of the will of God.

### The Church in Jerusalem

Ananias and Sapphira were guilty of violating this teaching. Their motivation for giving was self-glorification—so much so that they lied directly to the Holy Spirit. Consequently, they suffered extreme judgment (Acts 5:1–11). But the vast majority of Christians in Jerusalem had the right perspective on what Jesus was teaching when he said, "Do not let your left hand know what your right hand is doing." Their personal giving was public, but their hearts and motives were pure. They wanted to minister to one another and, in the process, glorify God—not themselves.

## *Supracultural* Principle 13

### GLORIFYING GOD

*Evaluate your motives to see whether you're giving to glorify God or to glorify yourself.*

Paul affirmed this principle when he exhorted the Corinthians to maintain pure motives in everything they did: "Whether you eat or drink or whatever you do, do it all for the glory of God" (1 Corinthians 10:31). "Whatever you do" includes our giving.

To check our motives as Christians, we can stop and ask ourselves several questions: What if no one knew what we were giving? Would we give as much? On the other hand, what if others did know what we were giving? Would we be embarrassed and ashamed?

If we look at the context of what Jesus taught, particularly in the light of the whole of Scripture, we will see that a doctrine of public giving taken to an extreme (which is often promoted by religious groups that teach a works-oriented salvation) can lead to self-glorification and self-righteousness. Conversely, a doctrine of private giving can lead to another form of sin—selfishness and deceit. We are particularly tempted to engage in this kind of sin when we are not held accountable to be good stewards of what God has given us. In short, we may be using this false doctrine of privacy to cover up our disobedience.

It's possible to blend and balance these extremes. Our motive for public giving should always be God's glory. Once we understand his perspective on this issue and are giving as God intended us to, we won't be concerned that our gifts be kept confidential. We'll feel good (not proud) that we're obeying God and modeling his will for others. In fact, once we have a biblical perspective on the way God wants us to use our material possessions, we won't want to keep this aspect of our Christian lives private any more than we want to keep private our commitment to moral and ethical behavior.

## BIBLICAL BASIS

*Give us today our daily bread.* —Matthew 6:11

The people of Israel often became independent and ungrateful. Moses warned them against this tendency before they even came into the Promised Land: "When you eat and are satisfied, be careful that you do not forget the LORD, who brought you out of Egypt, out of the land of slavery" (Deuteronomy 6:11–12). Moses warned further that when they received cities, houses, wells, and many other good things they had not worked for, they must be on guard against the temptation to say to themselves, "My power and the strength of my hands have produced this wealth for me" (Deuteronomy 8:17).

Unfortunately, Israel's history is a story of disobedience. And even though they were not dwelling in the land in freedom, as God had promised they would someday, they still were a self-reliant people when Jesus walked among them. Seeking God's daily guidance for provisions was not a part of their mentality. Though they had their regular ritualistic prayer times in the temple and in the synagogues, personal, intimate prayer with the heavenly Father was a foreign concept. This is why one of his disciples (no doubt one of the twelve apostles), who was watching Jesus pray, asked him to teach them to pray as John had taught his disciples (Luke 11:1). Among other things, Jesus taught them to pray for their daily bread.

*The Church in Jerusalem*

Was the Lord's prayer for daily bread part of the message the apostles shared with the believers in Jerusalem? I would think so. These new Christians also learned that they didn't have to go to the temple or a synagogue to pray. They could pray at any time and in any place. Jesus was their high priest, the only mediator between themselves and God (1 Timothy 2:5). This was a new experience.

Many of the visitors in Jerusalem were at that time without daily bread. Their resources were depleted. But when they devoted themselves to prayer as Jesus had taught the apostles to pray, God moved especially on the hearts of those who lived in Jerusalem to be a part of the answer to their request for daily bread (Acts 2:42–45).

## *Supra*cultural Principle 14

### PRAYER AND PETITION

*Pray and thank God for daily sustenance.*

The apostle Paul both affirmed and broadened Jesus's specific exhortation to pray for daily bread: "Do not be anxious about anything, but in everything, by prayer and petition, with thanksgiving, present your requests to God" (Philippians 4:6). In Jesus's model prayer, he gave specificity to the "everything" Paul would mention in his exhortation to the Philippians.

In terms of our material needs, we should also remember that God in his sovereignty sometimes allows difficult economic situations in order to refocus our thinking from dependency on ourselves to dependency on him. How easy it is during times of plenty to revert to Israel's behavior and take credit for our material accomplishments.

It's our privilege, then, to ask God for daily bread. God wants to bless us and provide us with the necessities of life. Though there are times when Christians suffer—along with all humanity—because of natural disasters and human frailty, God wants to encourage us whether we have little or much. We should never hesitate to ask him to meet our needs. Not to do so is to violate his will for our lives.

## BIBLICAL BASIS

*Do not store up for yourselves treasures on earth. . . . But store up for yourselves treasures in heaven.* —Matthew 6:19–20

Jesus told the story of a wealthy farmer whose land was so productive that he decided to tear down his granaries and build larger ones. He was satisfied with his material accumulations and eventually concluded that he had enough resources to retire. Unfortunately, he didn't realize he was going to die suddenly. He had made preparation for this life, but not for eternity. Jesus then made an application that is directly related to his teaching in the Sermon on the Mount: "This is how it will be with anyone who stores up things for himself but is not rich toward God" (Luke 12:21).

### The Church in Jerusalem

As the apostles met with the new believers in Jerusalem, it would not be surprising if they shared this perspective on material possessions. If so, many of those who had their focus on material things evidently felt convicted of this particular sin. The property they had purchased and the houses they had built no longer held the same meaning. With love in their hearts produced by the Holy Spirit, they were able to relinquish some of these possessions in order to store up "treasures in heaven, where moth and rust do not destroy, and where thieves do not break in and steal" (Matthew 6:20).

## *Supra*cultural Principle 15

### CREATIVE GIVING

*Whatever excess material possessions God enables
us to accumulate should be used in creative
ways to further his kingdom.*

Applying this principle in modern culture doesn't mean it's wrong to plan ahead. Neither does it mean that it's wrong to accumulate material possessions or to have a plan to care for ourselves and our families in the future. Many teachings in the book of Proverbs affirm that we should be responsible Christians. Proverbs 6:6–8, for example, says, "Go to the ant, you sluggard; consider its ways and be wise! It has no commander, no overseer or ruler, yet it stores its provisions in summer and gathers its food at harvest." (See also Proverbs 10:5; 13:22; 21:5; 24:27; 27:23.)

When Jesus warned us not to store up treasures on earth but rather to store up treasures in heaven, he never intended to give the impression that it's wrong to accumulate material possessions. Rather, he was teaching us that our focus should always be on eternal values and accomplishing the will of God by the way we *use* our material possessions. Those who have much should give much—as Paul taught—in proportion to what they have. In this way, we're using our excess to accomplish God's will in the world.

It's difficult, of course, to define *excess*. What is excessive in terms of the kinds of houses we live in, the cars we drive, or the clothes we wear? What is ample in terms of planning for future needs, including retirement? How much insurance should we carry? How much should we plan to leave for our children or even for our grandchildren? In some cultures, these questions are answered by default. People live and die with barely enough to meet their basic needs. But in more affluent areas of the world, sincere Christians face these decisions every day.

There are no simple answers. What counts as excess must be addressed at a personal level by each Christian. But the principles that emerge from this study will enable all of us, in all cultural situations, to answer these questions satisfactorily—assuming we take them seriously and providing we're honest with God and with ourselves. Each of us should be able to develop an approach for using, in creative ways, whatever excess material possessions God has given in order to further the kingdom of God without neglecting human responsibility. Best of all, we'll find joy in this process because we're storing up for ourselves treasures in heaven.

# BIBLICAL BASIS

*Where your treasure is, there your heart will be also.* —Matthew 6:21

Though the Greek word for heart (*kardia*) literally refers to the chief organ that gives life to the human body, in Scripture it refers to "man's entire mental and moral activity, both the rational and emotional elements." In other words, the heart is used figuratively for "the hidden springs of the personal life."[1] "Treasure" refers to our dearest possessions—those things that occupy our minds and hearts. Our treasure is what we think about and what affects our emotions.

Jesus was teaching that we can gauge our priorities regarding material possessions by what occupies our thoughts and actions. If we're constantly concerned about our possessions on earth— thinking about them, worrying about them, demonstrating jealousy and greed, mistreating others to gain more or to keep what we have—our treasures are on earth. That's where our heart is. Conversely, if we're consistently thinking in terms of how we can use our material possessions to glorify God—how we can meet others' needs, how we can further God's work, how we can invest in eternal things—our treasure is in heaven because that's where our hearts are.

*The Church in Jerusalem*

From the evidence we have in Scripture, there's little question as to where the hearts of most Jerusalem Christians were in the early days of the church. With the exception of a few like Ananias and Sapphira, these believers' focus was on eternal values. Rather than thinking about how much they could accumulate for themselves and how they could use their material possessions for self-gratification and self-glorification, they thought in terms of how to honor Jesus Christ and serve one another. What an incredible example this is for Christians of all time—no matter what our economic and social structures.

## *Supra*cultural Principle 16

### TRUE PERSPECTIVE

*We can detect our true perspective on material possessions by evaluating the consistent thoughts and attitudes of our hearts.*

Consider the following questions:

- What do I think about most?
- What occupies most of my emotional and physical energy?
- How do I respond emotionally when I see human needs?
- How do I respond emotionally when I hear biblical messages on what God says my attitudes and actions should be regarding material possessions?
- How do I respond when I feel I may need to part with some material possessions so they can be better used to meet someone else's needs or to help carry out the Great Commission?

- What priorities do I have other than making money (such as worshiping God, learning God's Word, spending quality time with my family, serving others in my church, or bettering the community)?
- What is my attitude when I do give?

These questions will help all of us determine whether our treasures are on earth or in heaven. For where our treasure is, there our hearts will be also.

We all react negatively at times to the way some Christian leaders attempt to raise money—when they use manipulation, guilt, or pressure. But this shouldn't cause us to respond negatively to what God says about the way we should use our material possessions. Though some people use God's Word in inappropriate ways, this does not give us an excuse to ignore God's will for our lives.

# BIBLICAL BASIS

*You cannot serve both God and Money.* —Matthew 6:24

This is an extension of what Christ had just taught regarding the heart (Matthew 6:21). Money can become our master. Elaborating, Jesus stated that we "will hate the one and love the other," or we "will be devoted to the one and despise the other" (Matthew 6:24).

This was the rich young ruler's dilemma. Money was his master. Jesus knew this to be true because he could penetrate the man's thoughts and the intents of his heart. Unfortunately, the young man walked sadly away, not aware that he could master his money for the glory of God and experience great joy in doing so.

*The Church in Jerusalem*

It's conceivable that this subject came up for discussion on numerous occasions as the new church grew and flourished in Jerusalem. All around these new believers were fellow Jews— including the religious leaders of their day—who were serving money. They claimed to know God, but by their actions they denied him. In contrast, coming to know Christ had set many people free from their slavery to material possessions. They began to experience the joy of open hearts and open hands.

## *Supra*cultural Principle 17

### MATERIAL BONDAGE

*It is possible for a Christian to be in bondage to material possessions.*

Not only was the rich young ruler in bondage to money, but it also kept him from becoming a true disciple of Jesus. In that sense, he had to make a choice between his material possessions and salvation in the Lord Jesus Christ. Paul agreed with the Savior when he stated that people who consistently engage in various acts of the sinful nature "will not inherit the kingdom of God" (Galatians 5:21). That's why it's important for people who claim to be Christians but who are in love with "things" to search their hearts to see if their relationship with Christ is personal and real.

Still, many true Christians have allowed themselves to become slaves to material possessions. In this sense, they are serving money—even as believers. Just as some Christians may be serving other carnal and sinful desires, as outlined by Paul in his letter to the Galatians (sexual immorality, impurity, jealousy, etc.;

Galatians 5:19–21), some are guilty of being in bondage to material things. If this is true of us, we must not abuse God's grace and patience by continuing to sin. If we do, at some point in time, he will discipline us as a loving father (Hebrews 12:8).

Though God chooses various ways to discipline his children when they persistently sin, perhaps the most common is allowing us to reap what we sow (Galatians 6:7). It may take years to harvest this painful crop. Some materialistic parents experience it when their own children grow up and become even more materialistic than they are. They may even become materialistic in the ultimate sense and, like the rich young ruler, reject Jesus Christ.

Having been a pastor for many years, I know of Christian parents who grieve that their adult children have rejected their faith. These children spend weekends indulging themselves with grown-up toys. In some cases these children are simply living the way their parents did, focusing on material possessions, earthly pleasures, and getting ahead in life. Though the parents were believers and attended church, they never modeled and taught generosity—only materialism. Unfortunately, their children have concluded that they really don't need God in their lives. How tragic!

## BIBLICAL BASIS

*Seek first his kingdom and his righteousness, and all these things will be given to you as well.* —Matthew 6:33

Spiritual realities and material things are not irreconcilable entities. It's a matter of *priorities*. Jesus recognized that we live in the midst of a material world. We cannot live without food, clothing, and shelter. We need these things to survive.

### The Church in Jerusalem

When the widows' needs in Jerusalem were uncared for, the Grecian widows became discontented, as did others who knew them. Consequently, the apostles made sure those needs were met. But these new Christians were not placing a *priority* on material things. Rather than focusing on their own physical needs, they concentrated on seeking God's will. In the process, the things they needed were given to them as well—just as Jesus said they would be (Matthew 6:33).

## *Supra*cultural Principle 18

### PUTTING GOD FIRST

*If we put God first in all things, he will meet our needs.*

When Jesus taught this principle, he wasn't referring to some ethereal eternity but to the physical world in which these people lived. Paul affirmed this promise to the Philippians when they had been faithful in sharing their material possessions to meet his needs: "God will meet all your needs according to his glorious riches in Christ Jesus" (Philippians 4:19).

Paul wrote similarly to the Corinthians when he was encouraging them to be generous in their giving. In order to reassure them, Paul followed his exhortation with this promise: "God is able to make all grace abound to you, so that in all things at all times, having all that you need, you will abound in every good work. . . . You will be made *rich in every way* so that you can be generous on every occasion" (2 Corinthians 9:8, 11).

It's important to note that neither Jesus nor Paul was teaching that God guarantees to multiply our material possessions if we are faithful givers. God has never promised that he will give us *more* than we need. However, he has promised to give us *what* we need.

This principle raises two important questions. Does God ever give Christians more than they need because they're faithful in using their material possessions to glorify God? It appears that he does. We'll explore this more thoroughly in later chapters. On the other hand, are there Christians whose basic needs are not met, even though they are faithful stewards of their material possessions? Visit impoverished countries, and you'll discover that Christians are starving along with non-Christians.

We must remember, however, that in most circumstances God fulfills his divine promises through Christians. Consequently, situations occur in which people's needs may not be met because followers of Christ have not been obedient in applying the principles God has outlined in his Word. For instance, sometimes the basic needs of Christian workers (e.g., pastors, missionaries, teachers) are not met as they should be because the people they've ministered to haven't responded and shared their material blessings as God intended.

But God's normal plan is that believers, when possible, should meet their own needs through hard and diligent work. Some of the Thessalonian Christians violated this principle, and Paul wrote that "if a man will not work, he shall not eat" (2 Thessalonians 3:10).

These are strong words, but they demonstrate that God does not tolerate laziness. When it's possible for us to provide for our own material needs, we are to do so.

# BIBLICAL BASIS

*Do not worry about tomorrow, for tomorrow will worry about itself.*
—Matthew 6:34

Jesus was not teaching his followers to be unconcerned about their material needs. In fact, as he was teaching these people not to worry about tomorrow, his earthly father was probably hard at work in his carpenter shop earning a living in order to support the rest of the family. And as we'll see, several of Jesus's parables emphasized diligent planning, hard work, and being responsible citizens.

In Matthew 6:34, Jesus was dealing with the human tendency to devote all of our energies to worrying about our life on earth— what we'll eat or drink or what we'll wear (Matthew 6:25). He encouraged his listeners to look at the birds of the air and the lilies of the field (Matthew 6:26, 28). If our Father in heaven takes care of the birds, and if he takes care of the flowers, will he not take care of his own children? After all, Jesus said, "The pagans run after all these things, and your heavenly Father knows that you need them" (Matthew 6:32).

## *The Church in Jerusalem*

The early church in Jerusalem is a glowing example of practicing what Jesus taught. They didn't worry about tomorrow. As they were obedient to what was being modeled and taught directly by the apostles, they discovered that God did take care of them: "There were no needy persons among them" (Acts 4:34).

## *Supracultural* Principle 19

### TRUSTING GOD

*Don't worry about the future or how your
material needs will be met.*

This principle offers no conflict with Paul's exhortation to be diligent in earning a living (2 Thessalonians 3:6–10). If we are *continually anxious*, we probably haven't yet arrived at that important balance between trusting God to meet our needs and, at the same time, doing our part to be responsible. Or it may be that we're not applying another basic principle in Scripture: the principle of prayer. This is why Paul told the Philippians, "Do not be anxious about anything, but in everything, *by prayer and petition, with thanksgiving* present your requests to God" (Philippians 4:6). When we follow this principle and apply it in our lives, God promises that "the peace of God, which transcends all understanding, will guard our hearts and our minds in Christ Jesus" (Philippians 4:7).

There's another perspective regarding worry and concern. At times Christian leaders become anxious about meeting the needs of others (e.g., paying salaries, providing funds for needy people, paying operating expenses in the ministry). Often the primary reason for this anxiety is that those who are being ministered to from the Word of God are not, in turn, responding generously, as God has instructed them. Such disobedience makes it difficult for

Christian leaders to avoid anxiety and concern.

Once again we see that God has ordained that all of his divine principles work in harmony. As each part does its work, the body of Christ builds itself up in love (Ephesians 4:16). Certainly Paul's words to the Ephesians include what God has said regarding the way we use our material possessions. When we do God's work in God's way, wonderful things can happen.

## Chapter 5
# More Teachings from Jesus
## (Matthew)

In addition to the teachings in the Sermon on the Mount, Matthew also recorded several other penetrating statements Jesus made about material possessions at other times and in other places. Again, it's not accidental that the Holy Spirit chose a former tax collector and materialist to record these biblical truths.

## BIBLICAL BASIS

*If anyone gives even a cup of cold water to one of these little ones because he is my disciple, I tell you the truth, he will certainly not lose his reward.* —Matthew 10:42

The context for this teaching involves the charge Jesus gave to the twelve disciples when he sent them out to teach and "to drive out evil spirits and to heal every disease and sickness" (Matthew 10:1). Jesus had instructed them, "Do not take along any gold or silver or copper; . . . take no bag for the journey, or extra tunic, or sandals or a staff." Why? Jesus made it clear: "The worker is worth his keep" (Matthew 10:9–10).

When Jesus taught that whoever gives a cup of cold water will be rewarded, he was definitely referring to those who ministered to the apostles materially while they were ministering to these people spiritually. They would receive a reward because they had not neglected Christ's representatives—no matter how unimpressive they may have appeared. When Jesus commissioned them on this particular occasion, the apostles didn't wear colorful robes like the religious leaders in Israel. Neither did they arrive in these cities with pomp and circumstance. They had no money in their pockets and did not even carry a suitcase with extra clothes. From the world's point of view, they were poor and unworthy. Thus, Jesus identified them as "little ones."

What a contrast compared with the priestly class in Israel. Jeremias, in his book Jerusalem in the Time of Jesus, describes "the various extravagances of the rich in Jerusalem in their houses, their clothing, their servants, as well as their rich offerings and bequests to the Temple."[1] More specifically, he relates,

> According to tradition there was great luxury in the Houses of the high-priestly families. . . . It was reported that Martha of the high-priestly family of Boethus was so pampered that she carpeted the whole distance from her house to the Temple gate because she wanted to see her husband Joshua b. Gamaliel officiate on the Day of Atonement, on which day everyone had to go barefoot.[2]

## The Church in Jerusalem

When the apostles were leading the new church in Jerusalem, their lack of prestige and wealth was in stark contrast to the religious leaders who graced the temple courts in Jerusalem. This was dramatically illustrated the day Peter and John went up to the temple to pray and met the poor beggar who asked them for money. They had no silver or gold (Acts 3:6). Consequently, the new believers considered it a rare privilege to support the apostles and to meet their physical needs. These twelve men had no excess property to sell, like Barnabas or Ananias and Sapphira, and no padded bank accounts like their religious counterparts in the temple. They were dependent from day to day on those who would provide them with sustenance. Indeed, it must have been the apostles' example of sacrifice that helped motivate these new believers to unselfishly make their resources available to carry out the work of the kingdom of God.

## *Supra*cultural Principle 20

### SPECIAL BLESSINGS

*God will reward us when we help meet*
*the material needs of others who serve God.*

This principle is frequently reinforced with illustrations and directives in the Scriptures. God designated the first tithe in Israel to be used to care for the physical needs of the Levites who ministered in the tabernacle (Numbers 18:21–29). Paul and other writers of the New Testament letters emphasized the importance of taking care of spiritual leaders who devote a lot of time and energy to the ministry. But one important principle to remember from Jesus's teaching is that Christians who care for their spiritual leaders will not only encourage these people; they will also be blessed themselves, even if they can only give "a cup of cold water" (Matthew 10:42).

# BIBLICAL BASIS

*Honor your father and mother.* —Matthew 15:4

Though this injunction—which was originally given by God at Mount Sinai—was comprehensive in terms of application (Exodus 20:12), Jesus's reiteration related to a certain way in which the Pharisees and teachers of the Law were violating this commandment. Jesus followed this exhortation with the following explanation: "You say that if a man says to his father or mother, 'Whatever help you might otherwise have received from me is a gift devoted to God,' he is not to 'honor his father' with it" (Matthew 15:5–6).

The Pharisees and teachers of the Law had devised a set of human rules whereby people could classify their material possessions as being devoted to God. By making certain religious decisions, the Jews were legally freed up from having to take care of their parents. Sadly, the Pharisees developed these traditions to receive more money themselves.

Jesus directed some of his sharpest barbs toward this kind of hypocrisy. He told these men in no uncertain terms that they had violated the law of God, which says they must honor their fathers and mothers. By quoting Isaiah, Jesus applied Old Testament words directly to the religious leaders: "These people honor me with their lips, but their hearts are far from me. They worship me in vain; their teachings are but rules taught by men" (Matthew 15:8–9).

## The Church in Jerusalem

What Jesus taught about honoring father and mother would certainly have motivated these new believers to take care of their parents and other family members. They were well aware of the hypocrisy and selfishness of their religious leaders. But more generally, Jesus's teaching set the stage for believers to understand that the church is to function like an extended family—a larger body of believers where individual members should be concerned about one another's earthly welfare. Paul later taught: "Be devoted to one another in brotherly love" (Romans 12:10).

This was happening in Jerusalem. "Selling their possessions and goods, they gave to anyone who had need" (Acts 2:45). What a witness the believers' conduct must have been to the unbelieving Jewish community and particularly to their religious leaders who violated this principle regularly. It's not surprising that they were "enjoying the favor of all the people" and that "the Lord added to their number daily those who were being saved" (Acts 2:47).

## *Supracultural* Principle 21

### FAMILY RESPONSIBILITY

*Those who are able should care for their*
*parents' material needs.*

Paul enunciated this principle in his first letter to Timothy: "If anyone does not provide for his relatives, and especially for his immediate family, he has denied the faith and is worse than an unbeliever" (1 Timothy 5:8).

Cultures vary in terms of economic structures devised to care for people who have reached old age. Today in American society, we have retirement pensions, unemployment benefits, Social Security, Medicare, and senior-citizen discounts. These private and government programs must be factored into the way we apply this biblical principle. If our parents' needs are being met in other ways, this enables us to use excess funds more creatively in caring for needs within the larger family—the church. But these governmental provisions for the elderly must never be used as a rationalization to neglect parents or to keep more for ourselves when we could use these resources to further God's eternal work.

Conversely, applying this principle does not mean children should allow parents to be selfish or to take advantage of them. But it does mean that children should assist parents when they have bona fide needs—whether they're Christians or non-Christians. In fact, even if our parents are resentful of what we have and who we are, this should not be the deciding factor in whether we assist them in a material way.

# BIBLICAL BASIS

*Many who are first will be last, and many who are last will be first.*
—Matthew 19:30

To understand this teaching by Jesus, we must look again at the larger context, which definitely relates to the promise that those who have given up land, homes, and family for the sake of Christ will receive a hundredfold in God's eternal kingdom. Further, some of those who from a human perspective seemingly deserve to be honored first will be honored last.

Jesus's remarks regarding the extremely poor widow who put two small copper coins into the temple treasury illustrates this truth graphically. What she gave was worth only a fraction of a penny (Mark 12:42). Jesus, after observing what she gave in comparison with many offerings of the rich, gathered his disciples around and used her gift as a demonstration: "This poor widow has put more into the treasury than all the others. They all gave out of their wealth; but she, out of her poverty, put in everything—all she had to live on" (Mark 12:43–44).

With this observation, Jesus explained what he meant when he said that many who have given much, even as believers, will be last while many who are last will be first (Matthew 19:30). In God's scheme of things, a hundredfold in the eternal kingdom of God would be measured not in terms of the *quantity* but of the *proportional nature* of the gift. The widow would receive much more from the Lord, according to his accounting system, than those who gave a lot and had a lot left over. As author Alan Cole stated, "God measures giving, not by what we give, but by what we keep for ourselves; and the widow kept nothing, but gave both coins, all that she had."[3]

## The Church in Jerusalem

Jesus's remarks regarding the poor widow must have impacted the apostles in an unusual way. Perhaps they had repeated this story often in Jerusalem during the early days of the church.

This perspective on giving also must have given the apostles increased motivation to make sure the widows who had been neglected in the daily distribution of food would be cared for.

Though they couldn't get involved in the distribution itself, they developed a system to make sure the needs of these women were met.

## *Supra*cultural Principle 22

### SACRIFICIAL GIVING

*God will reward us in his eternal kingdom based
on the degree of sacrifice in our giving.*

To understand this principle and how it works from God's perspective, consider the following example. Many Christians tithe (that is, give at least 10 percent of their income) regularly to their church. However, some of these tithers give more sacrificially. In other words, they give up some things they would like to have but cannot buy because of their financial commitment to God's work. Others who tithe could give much more in terms of material possessions. In order to give to the *same degree of sacrifice*, these people would need to give a much higher percentage of their total income and resources.

The Bible calls this giving "in keeping with" one's income (1 Corinthians 16:2)—it's proportional giving. In fact, some Christians could easily give as much as 50 percent or more of their income and still be able to secure for themselves many luxuries that others who give 10 percent cannot.

These observations are not being used to set a specific standard for giving that all believers must follow to be in the will of God. Compare, for example, the poor widow's resources to those of Philemon. It's clear that this wealthy man did not give in the same proportion as the widow. Jesus stated that "she, out of her poverty, put in everything—all she had to live on" (Mark 12:44). Not so with Philemon. And yet Paul did not make this man feel guilty because of his abundance. But the facts are, the widow and others like her will probably be more greatly rewarded in God's eternal kingdom than Philemon and the majority of us who live in an affluent society.

Knowing what we do about Philemon from the biblical record, he likely applauded the poor widow in heaven and rejoiced in her eternal rewards. I consider myself a generous Christian, but I'm looking forward to seeing those honored by God who will be front and center because of what they've sacrificed that exceeds my own generosity many times over.

## *Evaluating Our Giving Patterns*

Only God can judge the hearts of men and women who fall into the categories just discussed. We are responsible, however, to evaluate ourselves and the way in which we use our material possessions in the light of *all* of God's principles (see chapter 27).

- Are we giving unselfishly?
- Are we giving proportionately?
- Are we giving generously?
- Are we ministering materially to those who are ministering to us spiritually?

Though we cannot provide definitive answers for all of these questions—particularly as they relate to others—one thing is sure: "Many who are first will be last, and many who are last will be first"

(Matthew 19:30). Compared with many American Christians, some believers from other cultures and other moments in history (including New Testament Christians) will be more richly rewarded in God's kingdom. Many, like the widow, have given out of their poverty. In some instances, they've given all they had.

Though not always the case, many American Christians have given out of *plenty* rather than out of *poverty*. All of us will receive eternal life, but some will receive more rewards and greater prominence in Glory because of their sacrificial spirit. Some of us will have received our rewards on earth (Matthew 6:2), but the rewards of those who give sacrificially will last throughout eternity.

## BIBLICAL BASIS

*You give a tenth of your spices—mint, dill and cummin. But you have neglected the more important matters of the law—justice, mercy and faithfulness. You should have practiced the latter, without neglecting the former.* —Matthew 23:23

Again Jesus directed his teaching at the Pharisees and teachers of the Law (Matthew 23:23). Referring to the laws of God regarding tithing as outlined in the Old Testament (Deuteronomy 14:22–29), he accused these men of straining out a gnat while swallowing a camel (Matthew 23:24). The religious leaders were giving a tenth of the small aromatic herbs from their gardens—which actually was going beyond the requirements given in the law of Moses. As Hendriksen explained, "Careful examination of *the context* shows that what the law really meant—at least emphasized—was that, as far as products of the field were concerned, the three 'great' crops of the land, namely, grain, wine, and oil, should be tithed. Scribes and Pharisees were always illegitimately over-extending or over-stretching the law."[4]

But Jesus's point was this: Though they were giving beyond what God required, they didn't have their spiritual lives in order. They were not treating others with grace and love.

## The Church in Jerusalem

Most of those who became Christians in Jerusalem were God-fearing Jews. Consequently, they would have understood the three-tithe system described in the Old Testament. In fact, most of them would probably have been faithful in practicing this requirement. (The three-tithe system is described in detail on pages 129 and 165.) However, many wealthy believers in Jerusalem did not allow the three-tithe concept to restrict their giving to this amount. For example, when Barnabas "sold a field he owned and brought the money and put it at the apostles' feet" (Acts 4:37), he did not give only a tenth of the proceeds. He gave it all. We can assume that many others who owned land or houses and who from time to time sold them also brought the entire amount and laid it at the apostles' feet for distribution to those who had a need (Acts 4:34–35).

As we've learned from the account of Ananias and Sapphira, they were not obligated to bring the total amount from these sales. They had a choice. The example of the individuals who had previously given the total amount of their property sales apparently motivated Ananias and Sapphira to give the impression that they too had given the total price of their land.

When the need was there, and when the Jerusalem Christians had the resources to do so, many gave 100 percent of certain transactions. In a literal sense, "no one claimed that any of his possessions was his own, but they shared everything they had" (Acts 4:32). However, the important point is that most of these believers were motivated to give because of their love for God and for their fellow Christians. They were not neglecting the more important matters of the Law. They had only one "outstanding debt"—the "continuing debt to love one another" (Romans 13:8).

## *Supracultural* Principle 23

### INVALID OFFERINGS

*We invalidate our gifts to God when we deliberately
withhold our love from him and from one another.*

Some Christians seem to believe that if they give away a lot of money, this benevolent act compensates for the unethical way in which they've made that money—or for other sins in their lives. Not so, Jesus said. Being generous will never compensate for dishonesty, insensitivity, or selfishness. Giving will never cancel out the results of a lifestyle that conforms to this world's system. God wants us to do his will *in all respects*—including the way we view, use, and give our material possessions (Romans 12:1–2).

### Chapter 6
# Jesus's Use of Economic Illustrations

At least 25 percent of Jesus's parables relate to money and other material possessions. However, Jesus's purpose was not necessarily to teach people how they should view these possessions or what they should give but rather to tap into their economic experiences. He used what is a significant part of all of our lives—no matter what our cultural setting—to teach dynamic spiritual truths and eternal values.

More specifically, when Jesus began his ministry, he demonstrated a keen awareness of all kinds of economic activities in his culture—which is illustrated in the following chart.

## BIBLICAL BASIS

*The disciples came to him and asked, "Why do you speak to the people in parables?" He replied, "The knowledge of the secrets of the kingdom of heaven has been given to you, but not to them. . . . Blessed are your eyes because they see, and your ears because they hear. For I tell you the truth, many prophets and righteous men longed to see what you see but did not see it, and to hear what you hear but did not hear it. Listen then to what the parable . . . means." —Matthew 13:10–18*

# The Parables of Jesus

| The Economic Illustrations | The Spiritual Applications |
|---|---|
| Investments in jewels and treasures | The importance of investing in the kingdom of God (parable of the hidden treasure and the pearl, Matthew 13:44–46) |
| Saving new treasures as well as old treasures | The importance of storing up both old and new truth (parable of the net, Matthew 13:52) |
| Indebtedness | The importance of forgiveness (parable of the unmerciful servant, Matthew 18:23–35) |
| Hiring procedures and wage structures | God's sovereignty and generosity in treating all with equality, forgiving sins, and rewarding people with eternal life (parable of the workers in the vineyard, Matthew 20:1–16) |
| Leasing property | Rejecting God and his Son (parable of the tenant, Matthew 21:33–46; Mark 12:1–12; Luke 20:9–19) |
| Capital, investments, banking, and interest | Our human responsibility to use God's gifts in a prudent and responsible way (parable of the talents, Matthew 25:14–30; parable of the ten minas, Luke 19:11–27) |
| Money lenders, interest, and debt cancellation | The importance of love and appreciation to God for canceling our debt of sin (Luke 7:41–43) |

| The Economic Illustrations | The Spiritual Applications |
|---|---|
| Building barns to store grain for the future | The foolishness of neglecting to store up spiritual treasures (parable of the rich fool, Luke 12:16–21) |
| Architectural planning, building, and cost analysis | The importance of planning and counting the cost before we make decisions in building our spiritual lives (Luke 14:28–30) |
| Human joy that comes from finding lost money | The joy in the presence of angels when a lost soul believes in Christ (parable of the lost coin, Luke 15:8–10) |
| Wealth, dividing up an estate, irresponsible spending, and a change of heart | Repentance and forgiveness (parable of the prodigal son, Luke 15:11–32) |
| Bad financial management and dishonest debt reduction | Dishonest business people sometimes wiser in their worldly realm than honest followers of Christ in the spiritual realm (parable of the shrewd manager, Luke 16:1–12) |
| A rich man and a poor beggar | How money can affect our decisions regarding our eternal destiny (parable of the rich man and Lazarus, Luke 16:19–31) |
| A proud Pharisee who fasted and tithed regularly and a humble tax collector who acknowledged his sin of dishonesty and greed | Fasting and tithing unacceptable when associated with dishonesty and greed (parable of the Pharisee and tax collector, Luke 18:9–14) |
| A grain-ripened field and harvesters | Spiritually ripened hearts in Samaria and the part the apostles would have in "harvesting" people's souls (John 4:34–38) |

It's clear from these references that when Jesus told these parables, his purpose was not to evaluate or attack various aspects of the economic policies and procedures in Palestine. Rather, he was using what was familiar in order to teach spiritual truth. He was tapping into what was uppermost in people's minds at all economic levels in an effort to capture their attention.

## *Supra*cultural Principle 24

### ECONOMIC AWARENESS

*We should develop an awareness of the economic
structures and practices in every culture in which
we're attempting to communicate God's truth
so we can use these economic experiences
to teach people spiritual truths.*

When we're called upon to teach the Word of God or to witness one on one, we can learn a valuable principle of communication from Jesus. Since material needs, worldly possessions, and making a living are important to all people, we can use these needs and concerns as Jesus did to teach spiritual truth. This was the rationale for much of the content in more than a fourth of his parables.

This supracultural principle is particularly applicable to those of us who devote most of our time to ministry. Sometimes we're unable to identify in practical ways with men and women who live and function in the marketplace. But if we don't understand their language or their particular set of problems, we may end up teaching the Bible and trying to make applications in naive or unrealistic ways.

If these people are going to respect us and listen to our message, we must not only understand their world but also be able to touch their world with biblical truth. And we must be able to do this with realistic applications, without compromising the principles of Scripture.

Unfortunately, some Christian leaders tend to cater to wealthy people and, at the same time, avoid tough ethical issues. On this point we can learn another valuable lesson from Christ. He uncompromisingly taught the values of integrity, honesty, and morality in business without attacking the overall economic structures that formed the bulwark of society.

For example, Jesus didn't ask all tax collectors to give up their businesses because of the cheating that had become an integral part of the political value system in Roman society. However, he taught these individuals to be honest and fair and not to steal from people.

The story of Zacchaeus illustrates this. We have no evidence he gave up his business as a tax collector. Rather, he changed his values and paid back those he had cheated and began sharing his wealth with those in need. What an example it must have been to others when he cleaned up his act and became an honest businessman!

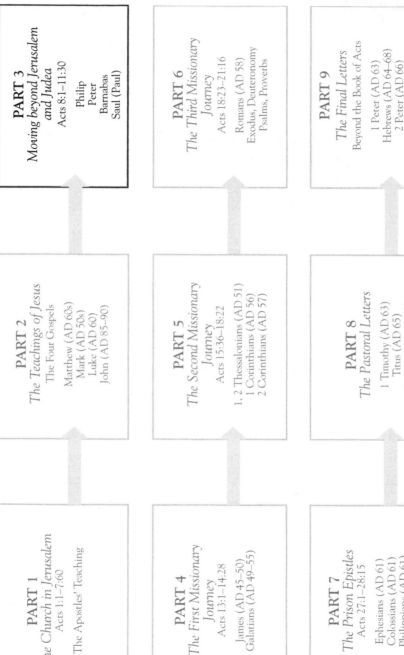

**PART 1**
*The Church in Jerusalem*
Acts 1:1–7:60

The Apostles' Teaching

**PART 2**
*The Teachings of Jesus*
The Four Gospels

Matthew (AD 60s)
Mark (AD 50s)
Luke (AD 60)
John (AD 85–90)

**PART 3**
*Moving beyond Jerusalem and Judea*
Acts 8:1–11:30

Philip
Peter
Barnabas
Saul (Paul)

**PART 4**
*The First Missionary Journey*
Acts 13:1–14:28

James (AD 45–50)
Galatians (AD 49–55)

**PART 5**
*The Second Missionary Journey*
Acts 15:36–18:22

1, 2 Thessalonians (AD 51)
1 Corinthians (AD 56)
2 Corinthians (AD 57)

**PART 6**
*The Third Missionary Journey*
Acts 18:23–21:16

Romans (AD 58)
Exodus, Deuteronomy
Psalms, Proverbs

**PART 7**
*The Prison Epistles*
Acts 27:1–28:15

Ephesians (AD 61)
Colossians (AD 61)
Philippians (AD 61)
Philemon (AD 61)

**PART 8**
*The Pastoral Letters*

1 Timothy (AD 63)
Titus (AD 65)
2 Timothy (AD 66)

**PART 9**
*The Final Letters*
Beyond the Book of Acts

1 Peter (AD 63)
Hebrews (AD 64–68)
2 Peter (AD 66)
Jude (AD 70–80)
1,2,3 John (AD 90)
Revelation (AD 90s)

A Research Paradigm (For studying the subject of material possessions as described in the biblical story.)

# PART 3
## PRINCIPLES FROM THE EARLY CHURCH — MOVING BEYOND JERUSALEM AND JUDEA

For approximately five years, the church expanded and grew in Jerusalem and Judea. Jewish believers became such a dynamic force that they posed a threat to the unbelieving Jewish leaders. This led to Stephen's martyrdom and a great outbreak of persecution. From a human perspective, these disciples of Jesus were practicing their Christianity in incredible ways. There probably has never been a period in Christian history when believers in a particular locality have been such a dynamic witness in the world, using their material possessions to glorify God and build his kingdom.

But God's plan for the church was much broader than its influence in Jerusalem and Judea. It was to begin there and then expand to the ends of the earth (Acts 1:7–8). In God's providence, he allowed persecution to become a major factor in causing various leaders to move from this center of Judaism to carry out the Great Commission.

Chapter 7
# The Gospel in Samaria

A young, zealous Pharisee named Saul took the lead in organizing and fanning the flames of hatred toward Jews who acknowledged that Jesus Christ was their savior and Messiah. He stood by when Stephen was stoned, "giving approval to his death" (Acts 8:1). Apparently on that same day, "a great persecution broke out against the church at Jerusalem" (Acts 8:1).

Saul's hatred was fanatical. Motivated by his strong personal conviction that Christians were heretics and deserved death according to his view of Old Testament law (see Paul's personal account in Philippians 3:4–6 and Galatians 1:13–14), he went "from house to house" and "dragged off men and women and put them in prison" (Acts 8:3). During this period of intense persecution, according to Luke, "all except the apostles were scattered throughout Judea and Samaria" (Acts 8:1).

It may appear that Luke was referring to all believers in Jerusalem, but a careful look at the context indicates he may have been referring specifically to the other six men (other than Stephen) who were appointed to serve the Grecian widows (Acts 6:1–7). If so, they along with Philip were "scattered throughout Judea and Samaria" (Acts 8:1). But their movement didn't stop here. As we'll see, Luke picked up the story later, stating that "those who had been scattered by the persecution in connection with Stephen traveled as far as Phoenicia, Cyprus and Antioch" (Acts 11:19).

# BIBLICAL BASIS

*Philip's Miraculous Display and Simon's Perverted Desire—*Acts 8:4–25

Following Stephen's death, "Philip went down to a city in Samaria and proclaimed the Christ there" (Acts 8:5). The city was probably Samaria itself, which bore the same name as the larger territory.

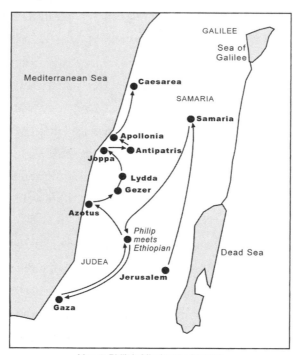

Map 1: Philip's Missionary Journey

## A Mixed Race

Samaritans were a mixed race of Jews and Gentiles—a social situation that had its roots in the dispersion that took place when the Northern Kingdom of Israel was taken captive by the Assyrians in 721 BC Though they still acknowledged Jehovah as God (2 Kings 17:24–33), they continued to include aspects of paganism in their worship. Merrill Tenney points out that "the tension between the two peoples was so strong that the Jews who traveled between Judea and Galilee usually avoided Samaria by crossing the Jordan and by using the roads on its eastern bank."[1]

It was natural for Philip to travel to Samaria. He was a Grecian Jew who lived in Caesarea, a city that bordered the Mediterranean. Philip probably traveled back and forth between Jerusalem and Caesarea, especially after the church was born. Caesarea was inhabited not only by Samaritans but also by Gentiles. As a Grecian Jew who lived in this city, Philip knew the people and understood their culture, which helps explain why the Samaritans listened to him and welcomed his message. A number of them responded to his ministry, believed in Jesus Christ, and were baptized (Acts 8:12).

When the apostles in Jerusalem heard that the people in Samaria had responded to the Word of God, they sent Peter and John to assist Philip. When they arrived, they prayed for these new Christians, and when they placed their hands on them, the Samaritan believers experienced what had happened on the Day of Pentecost approximately five years earlier: "They received the Holy Spirit" (Acts 8:15–17). We are not told specifically what happened when the Spirit came on them in this special way, but

evidently there were—as at Pentecost—some unusual manifestations of power. God was demonstrating that the gospel was not
a message exclusively for Jews.

### Twin Temptations: Power and Money

Luke tells about a sorcerer named Simon who had been a popu-
lar leader in Samaria before Philip arrived on the scene. A
number of Simon's followers shifted their allegiance to Jesus.
Intrigued and amazed by the miracles Philip was performing,
Simon also had professed belief in Christ and had been baptized
(Acts 8:13).

Watching the supernatural manifestations triggered the sorcerer's vain imagination. He wanted the same power as the
apostles. Operating from selfish motives, he offered Peter and
John money for this supernatural ability (Acts 8:19). Peter's
response was straightforward and uncompromising: "May your
money perish with you, because you thought you could buy the
gift of God with money!" (Acts 8:20).

Simon wanted to cash in on a good thing. Though people had
identified him as "the Great Power" (Acts 8:10), probably
because of his magic, the kind of supernatural power Peter and
John had would give him a position of prominence beyond anything he had ever experienced. His monetary investment—no
matter how much the apostles demanded—would pay off in terms
of more prestige and more income for him.

Peter expressed great concern for Simon's spiritual welfare
when he told him that his heart was not right before God. He
went on to exhort him, "Repent of this wickedness and pray to

the Lord. Perhaps he will forgive you for having such a thought in your heart" (Acts 8:22). Simon responded by asking Peter to pray for him in order to avoid God's judgment (Acts 8:24).

## *Supra*cultural Principle 25

### SELFISH MOTIVES

*There will always be people who will try to
use the Christian message to benefit themselves.*

This happened again and again throughout the New Testament. As soon as the church of Jesus Christ was born, it was viewed as "big business" by men and women with selfish intentions. Whenever we practice a positive spiritual principle—such as financially supporting Christian leaders (1 Timothy 5:17)—Satan will attempt to exploit the situation and misuse and abuse that biblical truth. For example, when Paul wrote to Titus, whom he had left in Crete to establish the churches, he warned him against "many rebellious people" who were "ruining whole households by teaching things they ought not to teach—and that for the sake of dishonest gain" (Titus 1:10–11).

This kind of exploitation and abuse is one of the reasons Paul determined at times to preach the gospel free of charge to people who might misinterpret his motives (1 Corinthians 9:12). It's also why he insisted that any person who was appointed as a spiritual leader in the church should not be "a lover of money" (1 Timothy 3:3) or an individual who was guilty of "pursuing dishonest gain" (1 Timothy 3:8; Titus 1:7). Peter affirmed the same concern when he exhorted the elders in various churches to "be shepherds of God's flock . . . not greedy for money, but eager to serve" (1 Peter 5:2).

## *Supra*cultural Principle 26

### GOD'S PATIENCE

*God is sometimes more patient with uninformed people who are materialistic than with people who have more direct exposure to the truth.*

Consider the way God (through Peter) dealt with Simon versus the way he dealt with Ananias and Sapphira. Peter exhorted Simon to repent. However, by contrast, he pronounced the judgment of death on the Jerusalem couple.

Why was God's approach different in these two situations? Wasn't Simon's desire to exploit God's gift of the Spirit to further his own position just as flagrant as Ananias and Sapphira's desire to gain prominence by lying about their gift of money for the work of the church? The difference seems to be related to their personal experience with Christ as well as the amount of knowledge they had regarding the will of God. Ananias and Sapphira were believing Jews who had access not only to Old Testament truth but to the Holy Spirit–inspired teachings of the apostles regarding the Good News of Jesus Christ. They may have even been among those who saw the resurrected Christ. On the other hand, Simon was likely uninformed regarding God's revelation and not a true believer.

We see this principle at work in other situations in Scripture as well. For example, when Jonah went to preach to the pagan

Ninevites, who were ignorant regarding the will of God, they responded in repentance. "When God saw what they did and how they turned from their evil ways, he had compassion and did not bring upon them the destruction he had threatened" (Jonah 3:10).

God's discipline is definitely for his children. Those who are not disciplined are "illegitimate children and not true sons" (Hebrews 12:7–8). Furthermore, the more we know about God's will, the more accountable we are to live up to the light of knowledge we have. It shouldn't surprise us if God disciplines us in ways he may not discipline others who don't have the same understanding. But ignorance isn't always an excuse. God's expectation is higher not only for those of us who *have* more knowledge of his will than others but also for those who have the *opportunity* to know more about his will and yet refuse to take advantage of that opportunity (Hebrews 10:26–27).

This truth is illustrated in one of Jesus's parables. In his absence, a certain master entrusted his servants with a variety of responsibilities. When he returned, he expected them to be busy doing what he had ordered them to do. Jesus then applied this truth: "From everyone who has been given much, much will be demanded; and from the one who has been entrusted with much, much more will be asked" (Luke 12:48). As American Christians, we have been entrusted with much—particularly when it comes to opportunities to accumulate material possessions.

The apostle Paul took this teaching seriously in his own life. Writing to the Corinthians, he said, "Those who have been given a trust must prove faithful" (1 Corinthians 4:2). As

Christians we have been given a trust. The challenge we face is that we too must prove faithful. The more we know, the more responsible we are. The more opportunities we have to learn God's will, the more we are accountable for the way we use those opportunities. This certainly applies to what the Bible teaches regarding our material possessions.

## Chapter 8
# Work and Ministry

## BIBLICAL BASIS

*Philip's Encounter with the Ethiopian Eunuch—Acts 8:26–39*

Following Philip's experience in Samaria, he had another special assignment on a desert road that led from Jerusalem to Gaza. An angel of the Lord instructed him to leave Samaria and head south toward Gaza (see Map 1 on page 90) to meet an Ethiopian eunuch, "an important official in charge of all the treasury of Candace, queen of the Ethiopians" (Acts 8:27). Several things were significant about this encounter.

First, this man was from an African nation. Philip's missionary tour illustrates graphically his willingness to be a witness "in Jerusalem, and in all Judea and Samaria," but also "to the ends of the earth" (Acts 1:8).

Second, this man was a black Gentile. The message of Christianity knows no boundaries in terms of ethnic background or race.

Third, the Ethiopian was interested in Judaism, for Luke

recorded that he "had gone to Jerusalem to worship" (Acts 8:27).

Fourth, though interested in the Old Testament, he did not understand the gospel of Jesus Christ (Acts 8:30–35).

Fifth, when Philip explained from Isaiah's prophetic statements who Jesus was (Acts 8:32–33; cf. Isaiah 53:7–8), the man responded in repentance and faith and asked to be baptized (Acts 8:36–38).

Sixth, and most important for this study, this man was a prominent and wealthy individual. He was in charge of all the wealth of the queen of Ethiopia.

Why did the Holy Spirit inspire Luke to record this event? The reason seems rather transparent. God wants us to know that wealthy people can and do respond to the gospel. When another man whose wealth was great walked away from Jesus sorrowfully, the Lord turned to his disciples and said, "How hard it is for the rich to enter the kingdom of God!" (Luke 18:24). When the disciples asked Jesus, "Who then can be saved?" Jesus answered that it *is* possible.

Though people tend to love their material possessions and to put them ahead of God, a rich person *can* respond to the gospel of Jesus Christ (Luke 18:25). The Ethiopian eunuch demonstrated this truth. Luke, under the inspiration of the Holy Spirit, chose this event to balance the response of the rich young ruler, which Luke had recorded in his gospel record.

## *Supra*cultural Principle 27

### A GOSPEL FOR ALL

*Though it's often difficult for wealthy people to respond to the gospel, God wants us to reach out to rich and poor alike.*

Think of the influence the Ethiopian eunuch must have had throughout his country once he responded to the gospel and returned to his homeland. Wealth and power usually go together.

As we continue our study, we'll observe a number of other prominent people who came to Christ and became influential in helping to spread the gospel. Not only were these individuals able to speak of Christ directly, but they were also able to support Christian leaders financially as they carried out the Great Commission.

# BIBLICAL BASIS

*Philip's Ministry Style—Acts 21:8*

Philip does not appear again in the book of Acts until chapter 21. Following his encounter with the Ethiopian eunuch, he appeared at Azotus, supernaturally transported to this city (see Map 1 on page 90). He then "traveled about, preaching the gospel in all the towns until he reached Caesarea" (Acts 8:40)—his own hometown. Following his evangelistic tour, Philip may have settled into a more normal schedule, giving attention to his responsibilities as a resident of that city, as a businessman and as a husband and father. But he would likely have continued actively ministering in the church in Caesarea as well as making periodic trips to Jerusalem and to other parts of the New Testament world.

When we meet Philip again, years have passed. Paul was on his way to Jerusalem following his major missionary journeys. When he stopped off in Caesarea, he stayed in Philip's home (Acts 21:8). Like other New Testament missionaries, Philip maintained his home in his original place of residence, even though he traveled for significant periods of time.

Philip evidently was the kind of man who was able to give great segments of time to ministry while maintaining a family life. As we've seen, he had a home and probably a business in Caesarea. However, he spent a great deal of time in missionary work, probably traveling at his own expense.

# BIBLICAL BASIS

*Aquila and Priscilla, a Ministry Team—Acts:18:18–22*

Aquila and Priscilla stand out as a rare biblical example of a husband-and-wife team in ministry together. Paul first met them in Corinth. They had been forced to leave Rome when Emperor Claudius issued an order that all the Jews were to leave the city (Acts 18:1–2). They were tentmakers by trade, a skill Paul also had developed. In the initial days of his ministry in Corinth, he made his living by using this skill and, at some point, joined Priscilla and Aquila in making tents (Acts 18:3).

It's not clear when this couple became Christians, but when Paul left Corinth, this dedicated husband-and-wife team accompanied him until they reached Ephesus (Acts 18:19). They remained there and continued the ministry while Paul went on to his home church in Antioch (Acts 18:21–22). At some point, after the ban on Jews living in Rome was lifted, Priscilla and Aquila went back to the imperial city and opened their home to be used as a house church (Romans 16:3–5).

Earlier, when they had been forced to leave Rome, they likely left that residence in the hands of servants. They traveled to Corinth, bought or rented another home, and established their business there. Then they left Corinth a year and a half later and traveled with Paul to Ephesus. Like Philip, they probably used their own resources to help finance their ministry. In Ephesus they rented or bought another house and used it as a meeting place for the church. When Paul wrote back to the Corinthians from Ephesus, he sent greetings from Aquila and Priscilla, who were with him, and also from "the church that meets at their house" (1 Corinthians 16:19). Clearly, wherever they were, they used their home to carry on ministry.

## Supracultural Principle 28

### SELF-FUNDING MISSIONARIES

*God desires to use people who can give great segments of their time to ministry while still providing for their families.*

Today, God needs people who can devote their full time to the ministry and be supported financially by those to whom they minister. But God also wants more men and women like Aquila and Priscilla. If we follow the model of New Testament Christians, we must believe that God desires to use people who are willing to use their own material resources to support themselves while they give great segments of their time to ministry. This demonstrates in a concrete way what Jesus taught about storing up treasures in heaven rather than treasures on earth (Matthew 6:19). Philip and Aquila and Priscilla are dynamic examples of New Testament Christians whom

God allowed to accumulate more than they needed and who, in turn, used their excess in creative ways to further the kingdom of God.

## Contemporary Priscilla-and-Aquila Teams

When our elders first engaged in this study several years ago, I challenged them to think and pray about their future as they planned their retirement. Would it be possible within our American culture, with its marvelous opportunities, to make enough money to continue giving generously and still retire with sufficient income to travel and minister with their spouses as Priscilla-and-Aquila teams? I threw out the challenge to plan and pray about the possibility of traveling to various mission fields of the world while supporting themselves financially.

Mike and Sharon Cornwall took that challenge and planned their future with this goal in mind. They even took early retirement to begin that ministry. To date, this husband-and-wife team has personally financed eleven trips to countries of the former Soviet Union in order to share the gospel of Jesus Christ. They also have made trips to Holland; to Kiev Theological Seminary, where Mike serves on the board of directors; and to Poland to encourage missionaries our church supports.

Jack and Linda Cole have served as an elder couple since the early 1980s. They took this challenge, as well, and have served in a local Christian teaching, training, and counseling ministry for more than ten years. In fact, even before Jack took early retirement, he called his wife his missionary. Linda has served our church over the years in a ministry capacity, teaching and counseling women and, with her husband, ministering to small groups.

Earl Lindgren applied this principle in yet another way. Since retirement, he has joined the staff of our Center for Church-Based Training and is ministering to other groups of elders in various churches, supplementing his retirement income through honoraria. Earl and his wife, Charlotte, also use their talents and abilities to serve the Lord in our church, ministering to small-group leaders.

Don Logue has served as an elder since the beginning of the first Fellowship church in the early '70s. Though still partially active in the insurance business, Don and his wife, Mary, devote many hours to ministering to other small-group leaders in our church. Their hallmark is hospitality—opening their home on a regular basis for a number of small-group meetings.

Eddie Burford sensed that I was feeling a lot of pressure from an economic recession that impacted church giving throughout the country. He volunteered to help in any way he could to relieve this burden. The elders asked him to lead a special task force to study not only our needs as a church but also what the Bible says about stewardship. Eddie accepted our invitation and led this task force, which we called our Acts 6 Group. Their efforts eventually led to this biblical study on material possessions. Still an active businessman, Eddie and his wife, Maureen, serve our church in a shepherding role.

In addition to all of the ministries, the men who originally participated in this study and those who later became elders (John Craig, Vince Ellwood, Dan Debenport, Dirk Hansen, Jeff Jones, and Dwight Saffel) meet regularly to give overall direction to the church, minister to other small-group leaders, and spend time in prayer for our people. Their wives serve alongside them in carrying out these time-consuming responsibilities. In their own unique ways, each of these couples serve as a dedicated Priscilla-and-Aquila team.

For many Christians in the business world, retirement can be the most productive time in life—especially for those who serve as lay ministers in the church. Seldom in the history of the world has it been as economically feasible for people to plan their future with this kind of ministry in mind. Though many will set different goals based on their personal abilities and resources, it's a window of opportunity for husband-and-wife teams to minister to others and serve Jesus Christ.

## Chapter 9
# Dorcas, an Ordinary Woman

Sometime after Paul's amazing conversion to Christ on the road to Damascus (Acts 9:1–19), the persecution against Christians subsided, and "the church throughout Judea, Galilee and Samaria enjoyed a time of peace." Believers matured spiritually, and the church "grew in numbers, living in the fear of the Lord" (Acts 9:31).

At this point in his narrative, Luke again focused on the apostle Peter, who continued to travel about the country (Acts 9:32). While he was visiting the Christians in Lydda, two men came from Joppa, another well-known seaport about thirty miles from Jerusalem (see Map 2 on page 106). They urged Peter to come to their city to minister in a special way because of the death of a prominent Christian woman named Tabitha, or Dorcas (Acts 9:36). Peter responded to their request and was used by God to work a dramatic miracle: he raised Dorcas from the dead (Acts 9:40–41).

## BIBLICAL BASIS

*Dorcas—a Woman Known for Good Deeds—Acts 9:36–43*

Dorcas was a Christian woman "who was always doing good and helping the poor" (Acts 9:36). Although there's no evidence

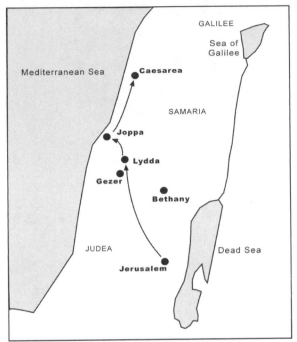

Map 2: Peter's Journey to Joppa and Caesarea

that she was wealthy, she used her talents and what resources she had to make robes and other clothing for women who had needs greater than her own. Evidently, the primary recipients of her gifts were poor widows, for when Peter arrived, a number of these women stood around the apostle and showed him the clothes that Dorcas had made for them (9:39). Note two important things.

First, Dorcas was a deeply loved person in the church in Joppa, so much so that the believers there exerted a great deal of effort to get Peter to come to their city. Obviously, this appreciation was directly related to Dorcas's incredible example of benevolence and love. She was a very unselfish woman.

Second, Dorcas's ministry to the poor evidently involved not only believers but unbelievers. After Peter had raised Dorcas from the dead, "he called *the believers* and *the widows* and presented her to them alive" (Acts 9:41). Luke distinguishes between those who were Christians and those who were widows. It appears there were both believing and unbelieving widows present. If so, Dorcas is a shining example of what Paul would later urge in his letter to the Galatians: "As we have opportunity, let us do good *to all people*, especially to those who belong to the family of believers" (Galatians 6:10).

To this point in our study, the primary focus for benevolence and giving has been within the local family of believers. But Dorcas demonstrated that our concerns, particularly for the poor, should also include those who do not know Christ but do have legitimate needs.

Dorcas's miraculous resurrection impacted the whole city of Joppa. "Many people believed in the Lord" (Acts 9:42), which probably included many of the widows to whom Dorcas had ministered. Obviously, the miracle itself became the primary means whereby people were convinced that Jesus was the living Christ, the Savior of the world (John 20:30–31; Hebrews 2:2–4).

On the other hand, we cannot deny the impact of the less dramatic miracle that laid the foundation for the greater miracle. Dorcas was a transformed person who demonstrated the love of Jesus Christ to many people by "always doing good and helping the poor" (Acts 9:36). Her benevolent and unselfish lifestyle was, in some respects, perhaps a more important miracle. People tend to forget the one-time dramatic events, no matter how miraculous. But they cannot forget the lifestyle of a loving, caring Christian.

## *Supra*cultural Principle 29
### TIME AND TALENT

*God wants to use Christians who may not have an abundance of material possessions but who unselfishly use what they do have, including their skills, to do his work.*

This principle must be applied in concert with the two principles we've just considered. God does not show favoritism toward wealthy people. He simply desires to use their abundance to carry on his work. But he wants to use *all* members of the body of Christ, no matter what their resources. He in no way minimizes the contribution of those with smaller incomes. In fact, as we've seen from the teachings of our Lord, at the judgment seat of Christ, their contributions may be more significant and bring greater reward than the offerings of people who have more but who don't give as sacrificially.

Dorcas exemplified this principle. She may not have been wealthy, but she was skilled in making clothes, and she used that skill to help others who were in need. Note how prominent her story is in the book of Acts! (9:36–42).

## Contemporary Dorcas

Let me share a story about a contemporary Dorcas. I know this story well. It involves my wife's sister, who served as a missionary among an Indian tribe in Brazil. While there she met a fellow missionary, was married, and bore four children. Sadly, her husband abandoned her and the children, leaving them to fend for themselves financially. She had to leave direct mission work in order to survive economically. Yet over the years, Alice has used her basic skills and resources to make ends meet, care for her family, and still serve the larger family of God.

After retiring as a secretary to a doctor, Alice moved to Dallas, primarily to help her youngest daughter, who needed her assistance. Alice helped care for her grandson so her daughter could work and make a living. As a retired person, her resources are minimal, yet she is helping support her family—not only with her time but also financially. In addition to giving to her church, she helps support one of her sons and his family who serve with Wycliffe Bible Translators in Thailand.

As my wife, Elaine, and I were reflecting on this story, she added this comment about her sister: "Alice has always had this special way of doing little things for people that are a real encouragement. She'll send a special card, write a little note that she's praying for someone, or send a gift that's just right for a particular individual. In this way Alice has been a real encourager—both when she was ministering in Brazil as a missionary and afterward, when she had to continue alone with her family."

To my wife and me, Alice is a modern-day Dorcas. She uses what she has to serve others, even when there's barely enough to make ends meet. Based on the story of the widow's mite, we believe her treasure in heaven will far exceed that of many of us who give more quantitatively but also have more left for ourselves. And we'll rejoice with her when she receives her special rewards.

## Chapter 10
# A Gentile Named Cornelius

We come now to what may be classified as one of the most significant encounters recorded in the book of Acts. It's fitting that this event is the last in a series of stories that focus on unusual people before Luke turned his attention to Paul's missionary journeys.

## BIBLICAL BASIS

*Peter's Vision—Acts 10:9–16*

After his experience with Dorcas, "Peter stayed in Joppa for some time with a tanner named Simon" (Acts 9:43). One day about noon, Peter went up on Simon's housetop to pray. "He became hungry and wanted something to eat, and while the meal was being prepared, he fell into a trance" (Acts 10:10).

In Peter's vision he saw a large sheet come down from heaven, holding all kinds of animals—both clean and unclean, according to Jewish law. "Then a voice told him, 'Get up, Peter. Kill and eat'" (Acts 10:13).

Peter's response was negative. "Surely not, Lord! . . . I have never eaten anything impure or unclean" (Acts 10:14). But again he heard the voice, this time saying, "Do not call anything impure that God has made clean" (Acts 10:15).

After offering Peter the opportunity to kill and eat three times, the sheet in Peter's vision was taken back to heaven (Acts 10:16). Needless to say, this was a troubling experience. And while Peter was reflecting on what had happened, another event designed by God coincided with this housetop experience.

# BIBLICAL BASIS

*Cornelius's Vision—Acts 10:1–8*

Approximately thirty-five miles north, in the city of Caesarea (see Map 2 on page 106), a Gentile named Cornelius had an unusual experience the day before Peter's vision. Cornelius was an official in the Roman army. Though no evidence exists that he and his family were proselytes to Judaism in the full sense, his household was "devout and God-fearing" (Acts 10:2). Cornelius was a benevolent man who also was concerned about his relationship with God. We read that "he gave generously to those in need and prayed to God regularly" (10:2).

Cornelius, whether he realized it or not, was a compatriot with a centurion and fellow Gentile in Capernaum who had a direct but unusual encounter with Jesus Christ several years earlier. The centurion had a servant who was deathly ill. Because he had developed a close relationship with the Jews, having built them a synagogue from his own resources, he persuaded several Jewish elders to ask Jesus to heal his servant. These men were delighted to approach Jesus for their friend. Luke recorded that "when they came to Jesus, they pleaded earnestly with him, 'This man deserves to have you do this, because he loves our nation and has built our synagogue'" (Luke 7:4–5).

Both Cornelius in Caesarea and the centurion in Capernaum are examples of wealthy Gentiles who were not satisfied with the pagan religions prevalent in the Roman Empire. They admired the Jews' religious experience and their commitment to the God of Abraham, Isaac, and Jacob.

In some respects, Gentiles like Cornelius had more rapport with God than did God's own chosen people. In fact, when Jesus met the friends of the centurion and heard, through them, his expression of humble respect and childlike trust, Jesus was amazed: "I tell you, I have not found such great faith even in Israel" (Luke 7:9).

Similarly, God honored Cornelius's heart and his desire to please him. The Lord responded in a special way to this man's prayers and his willingness to share his material possessions with those in need: God communicated directly with Cornelius. In a vision, an angel of God appeared to him and called him by name.

"Cornelius stared at him in fear. 'What is it, Lord?' he asked. The angel answered, 'Your *prayers and gifts to the poor* have come up as a memorial offering before God'" (Acts 10:4). He then instructed Cornelius to send for Peter in Joppa.

# BIBLICAL BASIS

*The First Gentile Church—Acts 10:27–48*

Cornelius responded immediately to the heavenly messenger's instruction and sent three men to Joppa. When they arrived, God sovereignly arranged for them to meet Peter at the very moment he was descending from Simon's rooftop, still thinking about his own vision and what it meant. When the men explained their mission, Peter's heart was already prepared to respond. He traveled to Caesarea to meet Cornelius face to face.

When Peter entered Cornelius's large and impressive home, he explained that was an Israelite, he was violating Jewish law by entering the house of a Gentile. But he also explained his own vision from God, which now had become clearer in meaning (Acts 10:28)—not to call anything impure that God had made clean (Acts 10:15).

While Peter was explaining the message of Christ to Cornelius and his household, the Holy Spirit came on those who were listening, just as he had done several years before on the Day of Pentecost. They spoke in various languages and praised God just as the apostles themselves had done as a result of this special baptism in the Spirit (Acts 11:15–16). This was the third such event recorded by Luke: The first was when the Jewish church was born (Acts 2:1–4); the second was when the Samaritan church was born (Acts 8:14–17); the third was when the first Gentile church was born (Acts 10:44–46).

Peter faced an immediate challenge. Word soon spread to Jerusalem "that the Gentiles also had received the word of God" (Acts 11:1). Predictably, the circumcised believers criticized Peter and accused him of violating Jewish law by entering the home of men who were not circumcised (Acts 11:3). Consequently, Peter explained in full detail what had happened to both him and Cornelius (Acts 11:4–17). When the Christians in Jerusalem heard this explanation, "they had no further objections and praised God, saying, 'So then, God has granted even the Gentiles repentance unto life'" (Acts 11:18).

God's heart was drawn to Cornelius even before he became a

Christian. The man didn't know Christ personally, but he prayed and used his material possessions in unselfish ways. This story demonstrates that the way a person who is sincerely seeking to know God uses his material possessions is an important factor in causing the Lord to reach out to him or her. More specifically, Cornelius—though a Gentile—was concerned about God's chosen people, the Jews, and made them beneficiaries of his benevolence. This is not surprising, since God blesses those who bless his people but curses those who mistreat them (Genesis 12:3). This is not only a statement from Scripture but a fact of history.

## *Supracultural* Principle 30

### SINCERE SEEKERS

*God's heart responds to non-Christians who
are sincerely seeking to know and please him
and who express their sincerity by being
generous with their material possessions.*

Cornelius was a rich and influential man. Again, we see the Holy Spirit opening the heart of a strategically important person to the message of Christ. Men like him, who can, for example, build a synagogue with their own private resources (as did the centurion in Capernaum) and who have the authority to do so even in an empire dominated by paganism, were indeed powerful. Once converted, what they could do to help spread the gospel of Christ to the ends of the earth was phenomenal.

This doesn't mean one can be saved by good works. All people are saved by grace, through faith—not by works of any kind (Ephesians 2:8–9). This has always been true, even in Old

Testament days. Paul went to great length in his letters to the Romans and the Galatians to demonstrate that Abraham was made righteous because he *believed* God's promise. He was justified through faith apart from works, just as every person today who finds salvation is justified through faith in Jesus Christ (Romans 4:1–8; 5:1–2; Galatians 3:6).

However, it's clear from Cornelius's experience that God responded uniquely to this man because he and all his family were devout and God-fearing. And the specific way Cornelius demonstrated this devotion to God was that "he gave generously to those in need and prayed to God regularly" (Acts 10:2).

## Chapter 11
# Beyond Judea and Samaria

As Luke unfolded the history of the church in his report to Theophilus, following Cornelius's conversion he picked up again the main storyline. Structurally and grammatically, there is direct continuity between the scattering of the church throughout Judea and Samaria (Acts 8:1–5) and those who continued to travel farther north to begin the process of going to "the ends of the earth":

> Those who had been scattered by the persecution in connection with Stephen traveled as far as Phoenicia, Cyprus and Antioch, telling the message only to Jews. Some of them, however, men from Cyprus and Cyrene, went to Antioch and began to speak to Greeks also, telling them the good news about the Lord Jesus. The Lord's hand was with them, and a great number of people believed and turned to the Lord. (Acts 11:19–21)

As we observed in chapter 7, those who left Jerusalem after Stephen's martyrdom may have been the other six Grecian Jews who were initially chosen to care for the widows in Jerusalem. Luke focused in on Philip's ministry in Samaria while the others who had been scattered preached only to Jews. However, several of them broke rank and went to Antioch in Syria and preached Christ to the Gentiles. Consequently, a church was born in this predominantly Gentile city (see Map 3 below).

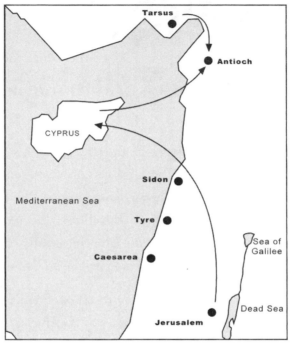

Map 3: Founding of the Church in Antioch

Remember, too, that one of these seven men—Nicolas—was actually a Gentile "from Antioch, a convert to Judaism" (Acts 6:5). It's likely he convinced several of these men—perhaps Procorus, Nicanor, Timon, and Parmenas—to come with him to his home city to preach the gospel to his fellow Gentiles.

When the believers in Jerusalem heard about the response to the gospel in Antioch, they chose Barnabas as their apostolic representative and sent him to evaluate what was happening. When he arrived, there was no question in his mind that what was taking place was the work of the Holy Spirit (Acts 11:23).

Great numbers of people were becoming believers, and he quickly recognized that he needed help. Knowing that his friend Paul was in Tarsus, he went to look for him and convinced him to join hands in ministry at the church in Antioch. There they ministered together for a year. More and more people came to Christ, the church matured, and it was there that the disciples were first called Christians (Acts 11:26).

# BIBLICAL BASIS

*The disciples, each according to his ability, decided to provide help for the brothers living in Judea.* —Acts 11:29

The most significant event that took place in the early history of the church in Antioch involved the famine described in the latter part of Acts 11. Agabus, a prophet who came to this city from Jerusalem, stood up one day and prophesied "that a severe famine would spread over the entire Roman world" (Acts 11:28). The effects of this famine were going to be particularly felt in Judea.

Luke recorded that the Christians in Antioch, "each *according to his ability*, decided to provide help for the brothers living in Judea" (Acts 11:29). They gathered together a special gift of money, and Barnabas and Paul were sent to deliver this gift to the elders in the various churches in Judea (Acts 11:30).

We're not sure of all the details surrounding this famine, but professor Harold Hoehner shed some light on Luke's account. He explained that according to Josephus, "when Helena, the queen of Adiabene, visited Jerusalem she noticed the great famine in Judea and so she sent agents to Cyprus to purchase dried figs and to Egypt to buy grain to relieve the Jews of their dilemma."[1]

However, this provision did not help the Christians, since Jews who had "defected" to Christianity "were outside the economic commonwealth of Judaism."[2]

The problem, then, was not exactly the lack of food but insufficient money to buy food at prices inflated because of scarcity.[3] This explains why the Christians in Antioch sent money and not food to Judea.

This background information is helpful in understanding Luke's succinct account in the book of Acts. He simply recorded that the famine happened and that Christians in the church in Antioch responded out of love and concern. It was their opportunity to express in a tangible way not only their concern for the physical welfare of their fellow Christians, but also their appreciation to these believers for having brought the gospel to Antioch and having sent Barnabas to encourage them in their new faith.

Notice that *each* Christian in Antioch gave to meet this need "according to his ability." As in all the other churches, the people were at a variety of economic levels. Those who could give a lot gave a lot. Those who couldn't give as much gave what they could. It appears, however, that everyone was involved in some way.

## *Supra*cultural Principle 31

### A COMMUNITY EFFORT

*All Christians, according to their ability,
should share their material possessions
to carry on God's work in the world.*

Although we cannot prove conclusively from Luke's statement that *every* individual Christian in Antioch participated, it appears they did—at least as family units. This harmonizes with Paul's exhortation to the Corinthians when he said, "On the first day of every week, *each one of you* should set aside a sum of money in keeping with his income" (1 Corinthians 16:2).

Experience, of course, teaches us that some Christians cannot give *anything*—particularly during certain periods in their lives. For example, no one would expect the Christians in Jerusalem who were suffering because of the famine to give to others when they didn't even have enough to meet their own needs. However, the time would come when they could reciprocate to meet the needs of other believers.

Generally speaking, all Christians can and should participate in using their material possessions to carry on God's work. Though this may not always be possible during certain crises in our lives, we must remember the example of some New Testament believers who actually gave out of their poverty (2 Corinthians 8:2). Though their gifts may have been similar to that of the poor widow's in size, in God's sight, they represented incredible generosity. Just so, as Christians today we must not hesitate to give merely because we cannot give a lot.

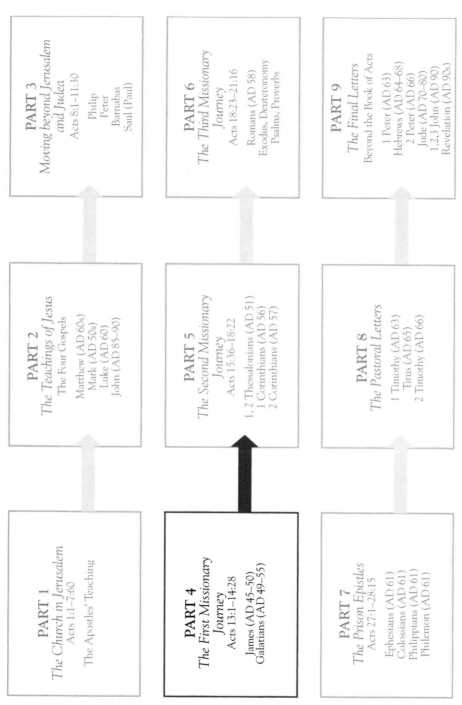

**PART 1**
*The Church in Jerusalem*
Acts 1:1–7:60

The Apostles' Teaching

**PART 2**
*The Teachings of Jesus*
The Four Gospels

Matthew (AD 60s)
Mark (AD 50s)
Luke (AD 60)
John (AD 85–90)

**PART 3**
*Moving beyond Jerusalem
and Judea*
Acts 8:1–11:30

Philip
Peter
Barnabas
Saul (Paul)

**PART 4**
*The First Missionary
Journey*
Acts 13:1–14:28

James (AD 45–50)
Galatians (AD 49–55)

**PART 5**
*The Second Missionary
Journey*
Acts 15:36–18:22

1, 2 Thessalonians (AD 51)
1 Corinthians (AD 56)
2 Corinthians (AD 57)

**PART 6**
*The Third Missionary
Journey*
Acts 18:23–21:16

Romans (AD 58)
Exodus, Deuteronomy
Psalms, Proverbs

**PART 7**
*The Prison Epistles*
Acts 27:1–28:15

Ephesians (AD 61)
Colossians (AD 61)
Philippians (AD 61)
Philemon (AD 61)

**PART 8**
*The Pastoral Letters*

1 Timothy (AD 63)
Titus (AD 65)
2 Timothy (AD 66)

**PART 9**
*The Final Letters*
Beyond the Book of Acts

1 Peter (AD 63)
Hebrews (AD 64–68)
2 Peter (AD 66)
Jude (AD 70–80)
1,2,3 John (AD 90)
Revelation (AD 90s)

A Research Paradigm (For studying the subject of material possessions as described in the biblical story.)

# PART 4

## PRINCIPLES FROM THE FIRST
## MISSIONARY JOURNEY

At this point in the biblical story, Luke launches us into a new phase in history—an explosive expansion of the church into the Gentile world. Following Jesus's statement that the apostles and their representatives would become witnesses first "in Jerusalem,

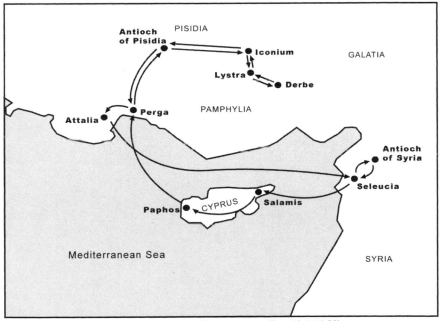

Map 4: Paul's First Missionary Journey (Acts 13:1–14:28)

and all Judea and Samaria," they were now beginning the process of taking the message of Christ "to the ends of the earth"—a process, of course, that is still ongoing two thousand years later (Acts 1:8).

Paul and Barnabas emerge as the primary leaders God chose to launch the first phase of this significant missionary outreach (Acts 13:1–3). But it's at this point that the Holy Spirit also introduces us to another means of communication. New Testament leaders began to write letters to those who had put their faith in Christ. Among other early doctrines, these letters contain additional and expanded teachings on how Christians are to use their material possessions. In this unit of study, we'll look at what many consider to be the first of these letters.

Chapter 12

# The Letter from James

James, the half brother of Jesus, became the primary leader of the elders in the Jerusalem church. He may have written this epistle about the same time a famine spread throughout the Roman world sometime between AD 45 and 47 (Acts 11:27–30). If so, this helps explain why James emphasized that true faith results in good works, particularly in sharing our material possessions with those who are in serious need (James 2:14–17).

Since the recipients of this letter are identified as "the twelve tribes scattered among the nations" (James 1:1), James may have been writing to a core of believers who had come to Jerusalem from all over the New Testament world to celebrate the Feast of Pentecost (Acts 2:5–11). If so, when these people put their faith in Jesus as their Messiah, they eventually returned to their homes and started churches in their local communities.

## BIBLICAL BASIS

*The brother in humble circumstances ought to take pride in his high position.* —James 1:9

When the Grecian Jews who became believers on the Day of Pentecost returned to their homes bearing the message of Christ—hoping their Messiah would soon return and restore the kingdom to Israel—they discovered rather quickly that becoming Christians did not automatically solve their economic problems. Those who became believers in the midst of humble circumstances often remained so the rest of their lives. Jesus did not return, and they knew nothing of the prosperity theology so frequently taught today in affluent societies.

One major thing did change, though. These people gained a new perspective on life. They had eternal hope. James encouraged anyone in "humble circumstances . . . to take pride in his high position" (James 1:9). In many respects, this sounds like what Jesus taught in the Sermon on the Mount: "Blessed are the poor in spirit, for theirs is the kingdom of heaven" (Matthew 5:3).

James reminded them that in God's sight, their lack of material things had nothing to do with their position in Christ. They may not have had much by this world's standards, but they were exceedingly rich in God's sight. They were "heirs of God and co-heirs with Christ" (Romans 8:17).

## *Supra*cultural Principle 32

### EQUALITY IN CHRIST

*Christians who have few material possessions should
not feel inferior to those who have more.*

All believers, no matter what their economic standing, are equal in Jesus Christ. Poor Christians are just as rich as well-to-do Christians in terms of the way God views their position in his church. Together we form one body with one hope, serving one God (Ephesians 4:4–6). Consequently, spiritual leaders have a responsibility to encourage believers not to feel intimidated by wealthier members. Neither must Christians with few material possessions judge, criticize, or question the motives of those more affluent.

# BIBLICAL BASIS

*The one who is rich should take pride in his low position, because he will pass away like a wild flower.* —James 1:10

James directed these words to affluent Christians. As we've already seen, the Scriptures do not teach that having wealth is sinful. But the Bible clearly warns of temptations and difficulties associated with riches. People who are wealthy tend to rely on their material possessions for their security and happiness. They may become materialistic in attitudes and actions, wanting more and more. Wealth also can lead to arrogance.

Paradoxically, James warned wealthy Christians to boast about their "low position" rather than about their possessions. To make his point, he elaborated on his flower analogy and its application: "The sun rises with scorching heat and withers the plant; its blossom falls and its beauty is destroyed. In the same way, the rich man will fade away even while he goes about his business" (James 1:11).

All people will someday fade away. Those without many earthly possessions will enter into their position in Jesus Christ forever. Rich Christians, likewise, even though their material possessions pass away, will also inherit eternal life. At that moment, however, those who were blessed with wealth will discover whether they had stored up treasures in heaven or treasures on earth.

## *Supra*cultural Principle 33

### NO ROOM FOR PRIDE

*Christians who have a lot of material possessions should demonstrate humility, realizing that their only true treasures are those they've stored up in heaven.*

All Christians need to understand this principle, particularly those of us who live in affluent cultures. No matter what our resources, we should remember Paul's words to the Philippians and Corinthians:

> Your attitude should be the same as that of Christ Jesus; Who, being in very nature God, did not consider equality with God something to be grasped, but made himself nothing, taking the very nature of a servant. (Philippians 2:5–8)

> You know the grace of our Lord Jesus Christ, that though he was rich, yet for your sakes he became poor, so that you through his poverty might become rich. (2 Corinthians 8:9)

## BIBLICAL BASIS

*Religion that God our Father accepts as pure and faultless is this: to look after orphans and widows in their distress.* —James 1:27

There are many indications that a person is deeply religious. But James reminds us that nothing is more basic than how we relate to children without parents and women without husbands whose needs are not being met. This is not a new concern in God's plan. He designed the third tithe in Israel to meet this need (Deuteronomy 14:28–29; 26:12). And when the Grecian widows were cut off from the welfare system in Judaism, the church devised a plan to care for them. Years later Paul also addressed this issue when he wrote his first letter to Timothy. He gave detailed instructions as to how worthy widows should be properly cared for by the church (1 Timothy 5:3–16).

But caring for the poor encompasses more than widows and orphans. It includes all believers who have true material needs and who have difficulty meeting those needs on their own. This principle is clearly illustrated in the church in Jerusalem. Luke recorded: "There were no needy persons among them. For from time to time those who owned lands or houses sold them, brought the money from the sales and put it at the apostles' feet, and it was distributed to anyone as he had need" (Acts 4:34–35).

As we'll see, James continued this emphasis later in his letter when he broadened his concern for people who are unable to put bread on their tables because of economic crises (James 2:15–17).

## *Supra*cultural Principle 34
### CARING FOR THE POOR

*People who are in need — and the Christians who help meet those needs — have a special place in God's heart.*

God is definitely concerned about the poor, and he notices Christians who share his concern by meeting these human needs. When we respond to these needs with generous and open hearts and hands, God accepts these acts of kindness as being pure and faultless. We can be sure that God keeps accurate records and will someday reward believers who have been faithful in this respect (Philippians 4:17).

# BIBLICAL BASIS

*Don't show favoritism.* —James 2:1

Favoritism ran rampant in Israel, particularly among religious leaders. Social politics permeated the hierarchy. Among wealthy Jews, extravagant living, prejudice, arrogance, and insensitivity were common.

When both rich and poor in the Jewish community were converted to Jesus Christ and began to fellowship together in the same place, they were thrown together in a new social mix, and the old attitudes about social hierarchy had spilled over from Judaism into the church. But the message of Christianity cuts across this kind of sinful behavior and must continue to do so in every culture of the world.

Since James eventually served as the lead elder or pastor in Jerusalem, he faced these carry-over attitudes regularly, and he addressed them. So everyone would understand his concerns, he used a hypothetical example:

> Suppose a man comes into your meeting wearing a gold ring and fine clothes, and a poor man in shabby clothes also comes in. If you show special attention to the man wearing fine clothes and say, "Here's a good seat for you," but say to the poor man, "You stand there," or "Sit on the floor by my feet," have you not discriminated

among yourselves and become judges with evil thoughts? (James 2:2–4)

## *Supra*cultural Principle 35

### AVOIDING FAVORITISM

*Never show favoritism toward people who
are wealthy or prejudice against people who
have few material possessions.*

James wasn't saying it's wrong to honor those worthy of honor. Barnabas and Philemon are classic illustrations of men honored for faithfully serving God with their material possessions. However, while honoring some, these New Testament Christians were dishonoring others. They were allocating the poor to a lower position because of their economic status. This, James made clear, is sinful. It's discriminating and out of harmony with Christian truth.

In most cases, people change slowly. It takes time for positive, Christlike attitudes and actions to replace sinful habits that have been an integral part of the very fabric of our society and even our personalities. But if people are truly born again, these changes *will* come, which is the next issue James addressed.

## BIBLICAL BASIS

*Faith by itself, if it is not accompanied by action, is dead.* —James 2:17

This is a major theme in James's epistle, and it's significant that he chose the subject of material possessions to illustrate faith that produces good works. To focus the issue, James asked two questions: "What good is it, my brothers, if a man claims to have faith but has no deeds?" (James 2:14) and "Can such faith save him?" (James 2:14).

To make his point, James used the same technique he employed earlier to illustrate the sin of showing favoritism (compare James 2:2). He posed another hypothetical situation, probably based on reality: "Suppose a brother or sister is without clothes and daily food. If one of you says to him, 'Go, I wish you well; keep warm and well fed,' but does nothing about his physical needs, what good is it? In the same way," James concluded, "faith by itself, if it is not accompanied by action, is dead" (James 2:15–17).

## *Supracultural* Principle 36

### A Test of Faith

*The way we view and use our material
possessions is one of the most significant
ways our saving faith is tested for validity.*

When evaluating whether a person's relationship with Jesus Christ is real, I've seldom heard anyone attempt to answer the question based on how a person uses material possessions. I've frequently heard people refer to a professing Christian's morality or ethics, but never materialistic and selfish behavior. Yet the way we use our material possessions is the very illustration James used to test whether a professing Christian is truly saved.

This is a sobering thought. Again, we must understand that changes take place over time—in all aspects of a Christian's life. Believers must be taught what God expects, including the way they should use material blessings. Authentic Christians will eventually respond to what they learn about God's will. If they don't, it's possible they're not legitimate children of God.

## BIBLICAL BASIS

*You ought to say, "If it is the Lord's will, we will live and do this or that."* —James 4:15

This exhortation can apply to many aspects of doing the will of God. Yet James once again illustrated this truth by referring to the way Christians conduct their affairs economically: "Listen, you who say, 'Today or tomorrow we will go to this or that city, spend a year there, carry on business and make money.' Why," James warned, "you do not even know what will happen tomorrow. What is your life? You are a mist that appears for a little while and then vanishes" (James 4:13–14). James's point is that Christians ought to consider the Lord's will in all they do. To do otherwise is to "boast and brag"—and that, he said, "is evil" (James 4:16).

James certainly wasn't saying we shouldn't plan ahead. That would be in contradiction to numerous other statements in Scripture. It's not inappropriate to go to another city to conduct business, and he wasn't teaching that it's wrong to make money. Rather, he was outlining what we'll coin as the next supracultural guideline for all Christians.

## *Supra*cultural Principle 37

### A BIBLICAL PRIORITY

*Do all economic and financial planning with an intense desire to be in God's will in every respect.*

All of our future planning should be done with one question in mind: am I living in the will of God? In terms of our economic perspective, whatever business we transact and whatever amount of money we make, all should be done for one ultimate purpose—to glorify God and to store up treasures in heaven. This, of course, does not exclude meeting our personal needs and providing for our families. In essence, James was saying that we should always do business with a sense of humility, recognizing that it is only because of God's grace that we can do anything.

# BIBLICAL BASIS

*Listen, you rich people, weep and wail because of the misery that is coming upon you.* —James 5:1

Here James switched audiences. He began speaking to those who were *not* believers—though what he wrote certainly can apply to Christians. The shift demonstrates that James expected Jewish people who had not accepted Jesus as their Messiah to hear this letter read as well. Since James was a well-known Jew in Jerusalem before he became a believer, it's understandable why unbelieving Jews would be interested in the content of this epistle. James anticipated that this would happen and addressed some rather pointed statements to them.

## Three Principles

First, material things do not provide ultimate happiness. In fact, James warned against misery that will come upon the wealthy (James 5:1).

Second, *material things are not enduring.* They "rot." Even our finest clothes deteriorate. James said that even gold and silver corrode or rust (James 5:2–3).

Third, *gold and silver that is hoarded will testify against us* and eat our "flesh like fire" (James 5:3).

*Three Temptations*

First, materialism entices us *to accumulate more and more:* James said, "You have hoarded wealth in the last days" (James 5:3).

Second, there is the temptation *to be unfair and dishonest.* Not only did these rich people accumulate more and more for themselves, but they also failed to pay the workmen they hired to take care of their fields (James 5:4). They were unethical and dishonest.

Third, there is the temptation *to be self-indulgent.* James accused these rich people of having "lived on earth in luxury and self-indulgence" (James 5:5). They had "fattened" themselves in the "day of slaughter." They had prepared themselves for a tragic end.

## *Supra*cultural Principle 38
### GOD'S DISPLEASURE

*Non-Christians who put faith in their material possessions and who abuse and misuse other people in order to accumulate wealth must be warned that God will judge them severely.*

Many people have the potential to accumulate wealth and live in luxury. The day is coming, however, when all material things will vanish. They have no eternal significance, and people who do not know Christ will not only lose everything they have on earth, but they also will live in lonely isolation, suffering eternal consequences separated from God.

## *Supra*cultural Principle 39

### Being on Guard

*Accumulating wealth brings temptations for both Christians and non-Christians.*

Though James was addressing his warnings to non-Christians in this section of the letter (5:1–6), certain aspects of what he wrote also apply to Christians. When we accumulate wealth, we must be on guard against the same temptations everyone faces. We, too, will be tempted to be unfair and dishonest, to be self-indulgent, and to hoard what we have—to store up treasures on earth rather than in heaven.

The picture is clear. All Christians who have been, or who are, in a position to accumulate wealth must acknowledge that being a Christian does not eliminate these temptations. In fact, Satan may launch a special attack on wealthy Christians, just as he did on Jesus Christ. He offered Jesus the kingdoms of the world in all their splendor if Jesus would only bow down and worship him. Jesus's response is a divine model for all of us who are tempted to abuse our wealth. We too must say, "Away from me, Satan! For it is written: 'Worship the Lord your God, and serve him only'" (Matthew 4:10).

The apostle Paul also recognized that these temptations would come to people who acquire wealth. He wrote to Timothy when this young missionary was in Ephesus and encouraged him to warn these believers: "People who want to get rich fall into temptation and a trap and into many foolish and harmful desires that plunge men into ruin and destruction" (1 Timothy 6:9).

This, of course, is not a foregone conclusion. It *is* possible to become wealthy and to serve Jesus Christ wholeheartedly. In fact, wealthy Christians who are dedicated to building God's kingdom are important gifts to the church. However, if we are among those with wealth, we must make sure we don't store up treasures here on earth but rather in heaven. Jesus's warning must be a constant reminder in our hearts and lives—"Where your treasure is, there your heart will be also" (Matthew 6:21).

Chapter 13

# The Letter to the Galatians

Paul probably wrote his letter to the Galatians from Antioch shortly after he and Barnabas returned from the first missionary tour through southern Galatia (Acts 13:1–14:28). Furthermore, he evidently composed this epistle sometime prior to the Jerusalem council meeting described in Acts 15. The fact that Paul said nothing in this letter about the conclusions reached at the Jerusalem council (which relate so directly to his teachings regarding law and grace) seems to indicate that this historic meeting had not yet taken place.

It should not surprise us then that Paul wrote little about how Christians should use their material possessions. That was not his primary concern. However, as he concluded this letter, he did have two important things to say about this matter.

## BIBLICAL BASIS

*Anyone who receives instruction in the word must share all good things with his instructor.* —Galatians 6:6

Paul wasn't concerned about himself when he wrote this statement. Rather, he was concerned that elders and pastors who devote themselves to the ministry of God's Word should be cared for financially. Assuming an early date for this letter, Paul and Barnabas would have just returned from the first missionary journey. On this tour they had appointed elders in the Galatian churches in Lystra, Iconium, and Pisidia Antioch (Acts 14:21–23). Paul was concerned that these new believers understand their financial responsibilities to those who minister to them spiritually. This correlates with what Paul wrote to Timothy in a later epistle: "The elders who direct the affairs of the church well are worthy of double honor [remuneration], especially those whose work is preaching and teaching" (1 Timothy 5:17).

## *Supra*cultural Principle 40

### SUPPORTING SPIRITUAL LEADERS

*Local church leaders whose primary ministry is to teach the Word of God should be given priority consideration in receiving financial support.*

The principle of caring for the economic needs of people who serve Jesus Christ vocationally—particularly for those who teach—appears frequently throughout the Scriptures. To communicate God's will effectively takes a great deal of time and effort, especially if it is done in a manner pleasing to God. In that sense, Paul was simply saying—as Jesus did—"The worker deserves his wages" (1 Timothy 5:18; Luke 10:7).

## BIBLICAL BASIS

*As we have opportunity, let us do good to all people, especially to those who belong to the family of believers.* —Galatians 6:10

Since Paul included "all people" in this injunction to the Galatians, he was probably referring specifically to the way these believers were to use their material possessions to assist both Christians and non-Christians. He made clear, however, that their priority should be the needs of "the family of believers"— that is, those in the church. But they were to do good to everyone when they had opportunity.

## *Supracultural* Principle 41
### HELPING ALL PEOPLE

*Plan ahead so you can be prepared to minister
economically, first and foremost to fellow Christians
who are in need but without neglecting non-Christians.*

Practically speaking, as Christians we should not only set aside money regularly to support our spiritual leaders, but we should also save money to help with emergency needs. Opportunities always come our way to support worthy causes. If we don't have money in escrow for God's work, it won't be possible to experience the joy that comes from giving when those unforeseen situations present themselves.

This doesn't mean we should give to every cause that comes our way—or even every worthy one. We have to establish priorities. For example, my wife and I give a minimum of 10 percent (a tithe) to our local church. However, there are more opportunities even within the church. We enjoy supporting young people who go on short-term mission trips. But we have to establish priorities: if we're going to be able to share in these opportunities, we have to make sure we're setting aside money for that purpose.

## Being a Generous Tipper

My wife has modeled for me in many ways what it means to be a generous Christian. One area in which she has taught me generosity is an important opportunity for Christian witness, especially in our culture. Tipping those who serve us in special ways is part of our economic structure. This applies particularly in restaurants. Waiters and waitresses are dependent upon tips to make an adequate living. Since my wife is a former waitress, she understands this dynamic well.

To be honest, I grew up with a somewhat negative attitude toward this custom. When I paid the bill at a restaurant, I was not a generous tipper. But I noticed one day that my wife was watching what I left on the table—and when she thought I was distracted, she reached into her purse and discretely added to the tip from her own resources.

Another time I saw an ad in the paper advertising a special lecture. I don't remember the exact subject, but it had to do with being a successful person. The man speaking was not a Christian, but one thing he said gripped me: "If you're going to be successful financially, you must become a generous person, willing to share what you have with others."

God spoke to my heart through this unbeliever. After all, I was the one who should be teaching and practicing that principle—being generous. I began to think about opportunities to help others: the man who fixes my furnace, those who change the oil in my car—and the person who serves me in a restaurant or delivers pizza to my front door. Rather than resenting the fact that I had to pay someone something, I began to see this as an opportunity to help someone else care for their own needs. I'm not talking, of course, about people who rip others off but about those who are trying to make a legitimate living—just as you and I are.

I began to see tipping as a unique opportunity to do good to all people—to be a witness to those who serve me. After all, if we bow our heads and thank God for the food before we eat—which we should—it becomes clear to the average waiter or waitress that we at least claim to be religious. Think of the negative message it sends to people who serve us when Christians either leave a stingy tip (far below what is expected in our culture) or, worse yet, leave nothing at all. What a tragedy when believers leave inadequate tips but leave a gospel tract on the table! We're giving non-Christians exactly what they look for in Christians in order to discount the gospel—hypocrisy.

I know of one Bible-believing church where after the Sunday service, members descended on several restaurants in the area. Talk among restaurant employees centered around the "Christian crowd" and the small tips they left on the tables. In fact, the reputation of this particular church became so damaged in the community that the pastor had to address the issue from the pulpit.

This is a sad commentary on how some Christians think and act. In some respects, we've become more materialistic than our secular counterparts. I saw this reality in my own life when God convicted me years ago and pointed out my carnal and selfish attitudes in this area of my life. It's a confession I've made from my own pulpit. I now believe firmly and state publicly that if Christians in our culture cannot afford to be generous tippers, they cannot afford to eat out. It's far better to eat at home than to be a poor witness to unsaved people working hard like the rest of us to make a living.

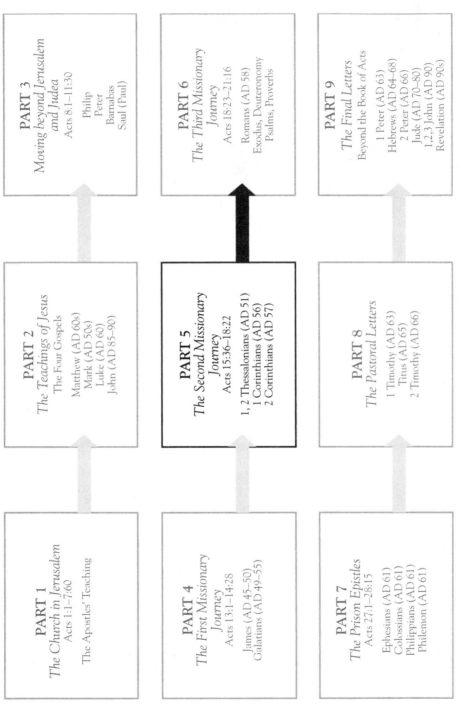

**PART 1**
*The Church in Jerusalem*
Acts 1:1–7:60

The Apostles' Teaching

**PART 2**
*The Teachings of Jesus*
The Four Gospels

Matthew (AD 60s)
Mark (AD 50s)
Luke (AD 60)
John (AD 85–90)

**PART 3**
*Moving beyond Jerusalem and Judea*
Acts 8:1–11:30

Philip
Peter
Barnabas
Saul (Paul)

**PART 4**
*The First Missionary Journey*
Acts 13:1–14:28

James (AD 45–50)
Galatians (AD 49–55)

**PART 5**
*The Second Missionary Journey*
Acts 15:36–18:22

1, 2 Thessalonians (AD 51)
1 Corinthians (AD 56)
2 Corinthians (AD 57)

**PART 6**
*The Third Missionary Journey*
Acts 18:23–21:16

Romans (AD 58)
Exodus, Deuteronomy
Psalms, Proverbs

**PART 7**
*The Prison Epistles*
Acts 27:1–28:15

Ephesians (AD 61)
Colossians (AD 61)
Philippians (AD 61)
Philemon (AD 61)

**PART 8**
*The Pastoral Letters*

1 Timothy (AD 63)
Titus (AD 65)
2 Timothy (AD 66)

**PART 9**
*The Final Letters*
Beyond the Book of Acts

1 Peter (AD 63)
Hebrews (AD 64–68)
2 Peter (AD 66)
Jude (AD 70–80)
1,2,3 John (AD 90)
Revelation (AD 90s)

A Research Paradigm (For studying the subject of material possessions as described in the biblical story.)

# PART 5

## PRINCIPLES FROM THE SECOND
## MISSIONARY JOURNEY

In the previous section, we began a new phase in our study. In addition to using the activities and functions described by Luke in the book of Acts as our main source for deriving principles to guide us in the use of our material resources, we began to look at

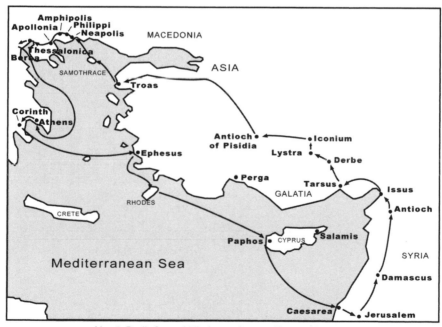

Map 5: Paul's Second Missionary Journey (Acts 15:36–18:22)

the literature written by various New Testament leaders.

In the epistles of Galatians and James, we noted how the unique theological circumstances and cultural issues at that time affected what both Paul and James said about material possessions. This helps clarify the importance of following God's unfolding revelation in determining his will in all aspects of Christian doctrine and living. This process gives unusual insight and an enlarged perspective on God's plan for believers of all time, no matter what our cultural or ethnic backgrounds.

The observations and conclusions in this next section take us a step further into the world of the New Testament as we follow Paul and his companions on his second missionary journey. Paul planted churches in Europe, including the church in Thessalonica and the church in Corinth. Paul's subsequent letters to these churches provide biblical material that confronts all of us with some of the most specific supracultural principles in the whole New Testament on how to use material possessions.

Chapter 14

# The Letters to the Thessalonians

After being forced to leave Thessalonica, Paul was deeply concerned about the spiritual welfare of the believers he had left behind. So when he arrived in Athens, he sent Timothy back to see how they were doing (1 Thessalonians 3:1–5). Paul had moved on to Corinth when Timothy brought good news about the faith, hope, and love that existed among the believers in Thessalonica (1 Thessalonians 1:3). Apparently, Paul was so encouraged with their spiritual growth that he immediately penned a letter to these believers (1 Thessalonians 3:6–8). But he also expressed some concerns regarding the way they viewed their material possessions. He addressed two important issues.

## BIBLICAL BASIS

*Surely you remember, brothers, our toil and hardship; we worked night and day in order not to be a burden to anyone while we preached the gospel of God to you.* —1 Thessalonians 2:9

This statement comes from the autobiographical section of the letter. Beginning in chapter 2, Paul reflected on his experience when he and his missionary companions (Silas and Timothy) first arrived in Thessalonica. They had come from Philippi, where he and Silas were severely beaten and imprisoned (Acts 16:22–24). When they arrived in Thessalonica, they were still feeling the trauma of their suffering (1 Thessalonians 2:2).

By sharing this personal experience, Paul was emphasizing a principle that consistently governed his life and ministry. "We are not trying to please men but God," he wrote (1 Thessalonians 2:4). "You know we never used flattery, nor did we put on a mask to cover up greed" (1 Thessalonians 2:5). Had they been motivated by impure motives (1 Thessalonians 2:3), they never would have subjected themselves to the persecution they encountered in Philippi, nor would they have taken the same risks in Thessalonica.

Having disclosed to the Thessalonians their true motive, Paul reminded them that he and his fellow missionaries were apostles of Christ (1 Thessalonians 2:6). Because of this divine appointment and divine mission, they had a right to ask the Thessalonians to care for their physical needs. Note that while Paul, Silas, and Timothy were ministering in Thessalonica, they gratefully received material gifts from the Christians they left behind in Philippi (Philippians 4:14–18).

The issue then is not whether Christian workers should or should not receive financial assistance for serving Christ. Paul later clarified this matter in his letter to the Corinthians: "The Lord has commanded that those who preach the gospel should receive their living from the gospel" (1 Corinthians 9:14; see context in 1 Corinthians 9:7–18 and exposition on 1 Corinthians 9:14–15 in chapter 15).

But while in Thessalonica, Paul and his companions did not use this apostolic privilege. Rather, they "worked night and day" to provide for their needs by some other means, such as making tents (Acts 18:1–3) so they wouldn't burden the Thessalonians with this responsibility.

Paul didn't want the people he was reaching for Christ to falsely accuse him of being in the ministry to benefit himself. Most importantly, he was concerned that these people clearly understand that salvation is a free gift and not something that can be earned or bought (Ephesians 2:8–9). Conversely, once believers understood that salvation was purely by grace, and once they had come to know Paul well enough to understand his pure motives, he never hesitated to teach them their responsibility to give, and in turn receive, gifts of money to care for his and others' daily needs.

## *Supracultural* Principle 42
### DEMONSTRATING PURE MOTIVES

*Christian leaders should look to fellow believers for financial support, not to the unbelievers they're attempting to reach with the gospel.*

This principle can also be applied when ministering to new believers who may be immature and who may misinterpret our motives. However, it's important that those who are new in the faith be taught their responsibility to those who have led them to Christ and nurtured them in the faith—especially if those who have ministered to them are depending on financial support to be in a full-time ministry. Supporting those God has used to bless us will bring great blessing in return.

# BIBLICAL BASIS

*Make it your ambition to lead a quiet life, to mind your own business and to work with your hands, . . . so that your daily life may win the respect of outsiders and so that you will not be dependent on anybody.*
—1 Thessalonians 4:11–12

When Paul and his associates went to Thessalonica, he taught the people about Christ's overall redemptive plan—including the Second Coming of Christ. They responded with such commitment and dedication that their faith was spoken about all over Macedonia and Achaia (1 Thessalonians 1:8). Everywhere people were discussing the way in which these people had "turned to God from idols to serve the living and true God, and *to wait for his Son from heaven*" (1 Thessalonians 1:9–10).

No doubt the Thessalonian believers had heard about the Jerusalem Christians and how they had cared for each other. Perhaps in their own poverty they, too, had received gifts from benevolent believers but had used this as an opportunity to take advantage of others' unselfishness. Or perhaps they were just so excited about the prospect of being delivered from their earthly circumstances that they were spending all of their time talking about the Second Coming of Christ and not working to earn a living. Whatever the circumstances, Paul had to admonish some of them for being lazy.

First, Paul addressed some believers who had incorrectly interpreted the doctrine of the Second Coming of Christ and were using their spare time—of which they had a lot—to get into trouble. Consequently, Paul wrote, "Make it your ambition to lead a quiet life, to mind your own business and to work with your hands" (1 Thessalonians 4:11).

Second, Paul reminded the Thessalonians that he had already instructed them to work and not to use their Christian experience as an excuse for laziness (1 Thessalonians 4:11).

Third, Paul told them that Christians who refuse to work to make an adequate living are bad examples to unbelievers— particularly when they take advantage of others. Paul exhorted them to "win the respect of outsiders" by not being "dependent on anybody" (1 Thessalonians 4:12).

This final observation is particularly important in evaluating the way the Thessalonians lived compared with the Jerusalem Christians. The believers' behavior in Jerusalem won the respect of unbelievers and served as a means to help bring people to faith in Christ. By contrast, the Thessalonians' behavior brought disrespect.

## *Supra*cultural Principle 43

### AN EXEMPLARY WORK ETHIC

*Work hard to provide for your economic needs*
*so you're not criticized by unbelievers for*
*being lazy and irresponsible.*

Again it's clear that following God's unfolding revelation gives us balance. We're to be unselfish and generous with what we have, but we shouldn't allow our Christian love to encourage irresponsibility in others. Neither should other Christians take advantage of our generosity. We are all to be diligent, seeing the opportunity to make a living as a gift from God. As we do, we will also positively impact non-Christians.

# BIBLICAL BASIS

*Keep away from every brother who is idle and does not live according to the teaching you received from us. —2 Thessalonians 3:6*

Paul wrote a follow-up letter to the Thessalonians just a couple of months after his first letter. He clarified some issues regarding the Second Coming of Christ and addressed again the problem of idleness (1 Thessalonians 4:11–12). As has been true in most churches throughout the centuries, some believers in Thessalonica did not respond to the will of God. Consequently, Paul had to take more extreme measures. He issued two more exhortations regarding how to handle Christians who were deliberately disobedient. Paul's words reflect seriousness and apostolic authority. The Greek word for "command" was often used to describe a general in the army who was giving orders to his troops. The word *ataktous* (translated "idle" or "unruly") was used to describe soldiers who were not maintaining rank.

Paul's word picture is clear. He was deeply disturbed. Initially, he had exhorted them regarding this matter while he was with them (2 Thessalonians 3:10). Then he reminded them of his own example, along with that of Silas and Timothy (1 Thessalonians 2:7–9). He also repeated in writing the exhortation he had given them face to face (1 Thessalonians 4:11). Finally, he had ended his first letter by asking all the Christians in Thessalonica to "warn those who are idle" (1 Thessalonians 5:14).

Obviously, some of these believers had persistently and blatantly ignored Paul's exhortations and God's will in the matter. They were without excuse. It was time to take action. Paul issued an order for the Christians in Thessalonica to disassociate themselves from every believer who continued to live such an irresponsible life. They were no longer to tolerate this kind of behavior in the Christian community.

## Supracultural Principle 44

### CHURCH DISCIPLINE

*Separate yourself from other believers who
are persistently irresponsible, not providing
for their own economic needs.*

This scriptural example demonstrates dramatically how displeased God is when Christians won't work to earn a living but rather take advantage of others. In a sense, Paul grouped lazy Christians in the same category with immoral Christians. When writing to the Corinthians, he'd had to deal with a man who was engaging in immorality with his father's wife, a sin that did not occur "even among pagans" (1 Corinthians 5:1). Paul himself was astounded. "And you are proud!" he wrote. "Shouldn't you rather have been filled with grief and have *put out of your fellowship* the man who did this?" (1 Corinthians 5:2).

Christians are not to fellowship with believers who, after being warned, continue to live in flagrant sin of *any* kind. Paul considered laziness and taking material advantage of others flagrant sins.

We must remember, however, that church discipline is necessary for two basic reasons. First, we need to maintain purity in the church. We are not to allow continual flagrant and open sin to be practiced among believers. Not only does it hurt the testimony of a local body of believers, but it also tends to corrupt the church. Other individuals will begin taking similar liberties.

The second purpose for church discipline is to bring about godly sorrow in the one who has been disciplined. Though Paul was very direct in his dealings with the sinful man in Corinth (he exhorted the church to "expel the wicked man," 1 Corinthians 5:13), he was quick to encourage these believers to restore the man and reaffirm their love for him once he had turned from his sin (2 Corinthians 2:8). Paul underscored this purpose for discipline when he wrote to the Galatians: "Brothers, if someone is caught in a sin, you who are spiritual should restore him gently. But watch yourself, or you also may be tempted" (Galatians 6:1).

Church discipline should be administered with a great deal of sensitivity and humility, but it must be done if we intend to obey God. Since some of the Thessalonian Christians had been repeatedly taught what was proper and right regarding work habits, and since they refused to respond, they were to be excluded from the fellowship of believers.

Paul's exhortation, of course, does not apply to believers who want to work but cannot—only to those who can work but will not. Hopefully, when this principle is applied in love, those disciplined will respond by beginning to live in the will of God. When they do, they should be completely forgiven and quickly restored.

# BIBLICAL BASIS

*If a man will not work, he shall not eat.* —2 Thessalonians 3:10

Paul's words, taken out of context, may seem harsh and insensitive. But these people needed tough love. They were not responding to the apostle's gracious reminders and exhortations. He had already warned them that believers who will not work should not be given food (2 Thessalonians 3:10). To keep providing them with the necessities of life would only encourage their irresponsibility.

Paul's intention was not to kick these people out. He was trying to get their attention and to bring needed changes in their lives. Thus he concluded by saying, "If anyone does not obey our instruction in this letter, take special note of him. Do not associate with him [or her] *in order that he [or she] may feel ashamed*" (2 Thessalonians 3:14).

To make sure the Thessalonian Christians really understood his motives, Paul clarified that they should not regard this person as an enemy but as a brother (2 Thessalonians 3:15). In other words, they were to approach individuals—even those who were sinning—as members of the family of God, dealing with each person lovingly but firmly.

Paul had already modeled this parental approach. He said of himself and his fellow missionaries, Silas and Timothy, "You know that we dealt with each of you *as a father deals with his own children,* encouraging, comforting and urging you to live lives worthy of God" (1 Thessalonians 2:11–12). Paul was simply asking the more mature Christians in Thessalonica to continue this nurturing process with those who needed discipline.

## *Supra*cultural Principle 45

### WITHHOLDING ECONOMIC ASSISTANCE

*Christians who can but won't work for a living should not be given economic assistance.*

This principle is to be practiced only after Christians have been thoroughly taught that they are out of the will of God and after they persistently refuse to respond. But it must be applied eventually. Lazy people who are given economic assistance will continue to take advantage of others' generosity. This is affirmed again and again in our culture. People think of all kinds of ways to misuse and abuse a welfare system. Unfortunately, Christians are not exempt from this kind of behavior.

Few biblical principles are more difficult to apply. Manipulative Christians can easily make others feel guilty. It's difficult to resist someone who cries out, "How can you do this to me and call yourself a Christian?" But a hungry stomach will do wonders for a lazy person. As in other aspects of Christian living where believers refuse to behave according God's will, it sometimes takes a traumatic experience to motivate people to break out of their sinful habits.

This principle is perhaps most difficult to apply when other parties are involved. Paul didn't intend for us to be insensitive to innocent family members who become victims because of a lazy father or mother. We must develop an approach to discipline that will deal with the offender without making the innocent suffer. For example, at times when a father will not provide sufficiently for his family to afford groceries, we as a church will provide food—but not money. An irresponsible parent can quickly squander cash on cigarettes, alcohol, and other nonessentials.

All of the instructions about being diligent in economic matters in the letters to the Thessalonians are reinforced in other places in Scripture. The book of Proverbs particularly supports what Paul taught and provides Christians with divine wisdom about being diligent in our work habits. For example, we read:

> I went past the field of the sluggard, past the vineyard of the man who lacks judgment; thorns had come up everywhere, the ground was covered with weeds, and the stone wall was in ruins. I applied my heart to what I observed and learned a lesson from what I saw: A little sleep, a little slumber, a little folding of the hands to rest—and poverty will come on you like a bandit and scarcity like an armed man. (Proverbs 24:30–34; see also 6:9–11; 13:4; 16:26; 19:15; 20:13)

The opportunity to work is one of God's greatest gifts to mankind. Note that before sin entered the world, he placed Adam "in the Garden of Eden to work it and take care of it" (Genesis 2:15). True, the Fall affected all creation. The ground was cursed and began producing thorns and thistles (Genesis 3:18). Since the day Adam and Eve were banished from the Garden, someone has had to bear the burden of hard work to provide for our daily needs. But sin did not remove the blessing that comes when we are responsible human beings. To violate God's ordained work ethic is to bring more hardship and to miss the opportunity, as Paul wrote, to do "something useful" with our hands so that we "may have something to share with those in need" (Ephesians 4:28).

Chapter 15
# The First Letter to the Corinthians

To understand the setting of Paul's first letter to the Corinthians, we need to re-create some events that are only alluded to and not spelled out in the biblical record. Evidently, Paul wrote a letter to the Corinthians that is no longer in existence. He referred to that letter in 1 Corinthians 5: "I have written you in my letter [commonly called the lost letter] not to associate with sexually immoral people" (verse 9). It seems what he had shared in that first letter had been misunderstood, and Paul felt it necessary to clarify what he actually meant—which he does in 1 Corinthians 5:10–12.

When Paul wrote this lost letter, he probably was in Ephesus, the same city in which he composed 1 Corinthians. Three men from Corinth—Stephanas, Fortunatus, and Achaicus (1 Corinthians 16:17)—came to Ephesus and delivered a written response to this lost letter. Paul made reference to this epistle in 1 Corinthians 7:1.

Stephanas, Fortunatus, and Achaicus reported some of their own concerns as well, and in addition, they brought a gift of money to help meet Paul's needs (1 Corinthians 16:17–18). Since the Corinthians as a church had been remiss in using their material possessions to further the gospel of Christ, these three men apparently took on themselves the responsibility to assist Paul.

Paul spoke to a number of concerns when he wrote 1 Corinthians: immorality, inappropriate lawsuits, marriage issues, misuse of spiritual gifts, and inappropriate behavior during the Lord's Supper. He even had to address some believers who were questioning the resurrection of Jesus Christ.

Paul hit all of these problems and concerns head on. Not surprisingly, the Corinthians also were failing to measure up to God's standards regarding how they used their material possessions. Though Paul didn't speak as comprehensively to this issue in 1 Corinthians as he did in his follow-up epistle, he did address three important concerns.

## BIBLICAL BASIS

*Those who preach the gospel should receive their living from the gospel. But I have not used any of these rights.* —1 Corinthians 9:14–15

Perhaps the most painful issue for Paul was that some of the Corinthians were questioning his apostolic calling. More particularly, they were scrutinizing his motives regarding how he handled financial matters. What made this so vexing was that Paul had gone so far as to give up his rights in order to demonstrate pure motives—and now his ethics were being called into question.

To answer these charges, Paul explained his personal approach to finances. The example he used at length involved his rights as an apostle to receive material support. To demonstrate that he indeed had this right, he asked three questions (1 Corinthians 9:7):

- "Who serves as a soldier at his own expense?"
- "Who plants a vineyard and does not eat of its grapes?"
- "Who tends a flock and does not drink of the milk?"

Paul continued building his case by quoting from the law of Moses: "Do not muzzle an ox while it is treading out the grain" (1 Corinthians 9:9). He applied this Old Testament teaching to his ministry among the Corinthians. Posing another question, he asked: "If we have sown *spiritual seed* among you, is it too much if we reap a *material harvest* from you? If others have this right of support from you, shouldn't we have it all the more?" (1 Corinthians 9:11–12).

It's difficult to conclude specifically what the Corinthians were complaining about. Perhaps some were upset that Paul hadn't accepted financial support, and some probably were upset that he did, when he received a gift of money from the Macedonians. Initially, he put bread on his table by being a tentmaker, but "when Silas and Timothy came from Macedonia, Paul devoted himself exclusively to preaching" (Acts 18:5). But the Corinthians' criticisms are not surprising, since Christians who are living outside the will of God in other areas of their lives—as the Corinthians certainly were—often are the first to be critical of leaders who address money issues.

As hurtful as the situation must have been for Paul, he didn't back off. He reminded them that he had not initially accepted financial support, even though he had that right. He appealed again to God's plan in the Old Testament, reminding the church that in Judaism, "those who work in the temple get their food from the temple, and those who serve at the altar share in what is offered on the altar." He concluded, "In the same way, the Lord has commanded that those who preach the gospel should receive their living from the gospel" (1 Corinthians 9:13–14).

Why such a lengthy explanation and defense of his position?

Under the inspiration of the Holy Spirit, Paul wanted all Christian leaders to know the importance of maintaining pure motives, unselfish attitudes, and nonmaterialistic goals. To give up rights in the realm of time and convenience is one thing. It's another to give up rights to material possessions. Few Christians have ever been able to measure up to Paul's sterling character in this area.

## *Supracultural* Principle 46

### BEING ABOVE REPROACH

*Though God has commanded that spiritual leaders be cared for financially by those to whom they minister, at times it is wise to give up that right.*

When Paul applied this principle to his own life and ministry, he was not suggesting that other spiritual leaders were out of the will of God if they chose to exercise this right. He was saying, however, that no action on the part of a Christian leader demonstrates more dramatically a pure motive and concern for God's reputation than giving up money that belongs to you by divine decree.

### *Honor in Honoraria*

A number of years ago, when I began receiving a lot of invitations to speak at conferences, I became concerned about falling into that insidious trap known as a conflict of interest. After all, I'm a pastor receiving an adequate salary from the church based on a full-time position. Was it right for me to take time to speak elsewhere and receive honoraria? If my invitations had been few and far between, I could have used vacation time. Surely no one would accuse me of taking advantage of the church if I accepted a few additional engagements. After all, the elders all knew my work ethic and that any time away would be made up with additional hours ministering and shepherding my own people.

I sensed, however, that I was facing a potential problem. As opportunities multiplied, I could easily become guilty of neglecting my primary responsibilities and receiving additional income in the process. Consequently, I proposed a plan to the elders suggesting that all the income I generate from speaking would go into a special fund that would be reported regularly in the monthly financial reports. I asked that I might utilize these funds for special ministry projects. I was particularly interested in accepting invitations to minister on mission fields to missionaries and national ministers, where they had no funds for travel expenses and certainly none for honoraria.

The elders approved this plan, which I've implemented for a number of years. For me, there have been several significant benefits.

First, I'm never tempted to accept speaking engagements based on the amount of money I might receive.

Second, I'm free from any conflict of interest, though I still have to maintain my priorities as a full-time pastor, never neglecting my primary responsibilities.

Third, this arrangement allows me to speak knowing that the money I receive is monitored and goes into ministry projects—not to me personally. This way, my ministry *outside* the church becomes a ministry *of* the church.

I've often hesitated to share this personal experience because I don't want to be guilty of the Corinthians' sin—judging the motives of fellow pastors who accept honoraria for speaking engagements beyond their regular full-time ministry. God knows that many pastors are woefully underpaid and certainly deserve the extra income. But I'm concerned about what I perceive is a materialistic mind-set in our culture. I believe we can all take a lesson from the apostle Paul, giving up what may be our rights at times in order to be above reproach in the eyes of our fellow Christians— and particularly among others in the watching world.

# BIBLICAL BASIS

*On the first day of every week, each one of you should set aside a sum of money in keeping with his income, saving it up, so that when I come no collections will have to be made.* —1 Corinthians 16:2

After addressing a number of serious issues in the Corinthian church, in the closing section of his letter, Paul reminded the Corinthians of another spiritual failure. He was speaking here of a collection of money that he was taking for the needy Christians in Jerusalem.

Sometime earlier he had shared this special need. The Corinthians' initial response was positive and even enthusiastic (2 Corinthians 8:10–11). But they had not followed through on their commitment.

Paul tried to help them resolve this issue with a specific plan. He exhorted every family unit in Corinth to "set aside a sum of money" for a special offering each week when they met to worship. He didn't specify the amount, only that all were to participate and that what they gave was to be determined by their income (1 Corinthians 16:2).

Though Paul didn't mention a percentage, he spoke in terms of percentages. Not to do so is a pragmatic impossibility. The believers were to determine a certain amount in light of how God had prospered each of them. Furthermore, that percentage was to be predetermined. They were not to simply give from what they had left over or what they felt like giving from week to week. It's clear from this passage that this was to be a carefully designed program of stewardship.

## *Supra*cultural Principle 47

### SYSTEMATIC AND PROPORTIONAL GIVING

*Set aside a percentage of your income on just
as regular a basis as you are paid so you
can give systematically to God's work.*

The Word of God, from beginning to end, teaches that our giving to his work should be systematic and regular. Just as physical needs are ongoing among all people, causing us to have to work and earn a living from day to day, so the needs for carrying on God's work are consistent and regular. Christian leaders who earn their living serving Christ and the body of Christ have regular material needs just as those who earn a living in other vocations.

This leads to an important question. What percentage should Christians set aside on a consistent basis from their regular income? The children of Israel were to give 10 percent of their resources to support their spiritual leaders (Leviticus 27:30–34). They were to set aside another 10 percent to be able to worship God as a family—to make a trip to Jerusalem (Deuteronomy 14:22–27). And every third year, they were to set aside another 10 percent to meet the needs of others (Deuteronomy 26:12;

14:28–29).[1] Yet the Holy Spirit did not lead New Testament writers to specify certain amounts and percentages.

### Old Testament Influence on the Early Church

Those who first came to Christ in Jerusalem were God-fearing Jews—many men and women who would have been faithful in giving at least three tithes. They were committed to keeping the Old Testament laws. Without doubt, this three-tithe pattern in Israel became an influential factor in helping Jewish Christians determine their giving patterns in the church of Jesus Christ. If this was what God expected under law, they would tend to at least use this as a basis for evaluating how much they should give in view of God's saving grace. In fact, at times, these New Testament Christians gave more than designated in the three-tithe system—particularly in the early days of the church as it functioned in Jerusalem. Some sold properties, like Barnabas, and gave the entire proceeds to the church.

Does this mean Christians are obligated to follow the three-tithe system? The answer is no, since God does not reiterate this system as an absolute form or method for Christians. Furthermore, the annual trip to Jerusalem to worship in the temple became an impossibility. Believing Jews were no longer welcome. Nevertheless, what the Israelites practiced at God's command provides us with a strong model for evaluating our own giving patterns.

First, if we're going to give *systematically* and *regularly*, we must predetermine a percentage or amount.

Second, if we're going to give *according to our ability* (as the Christians in Antioch did), and if we're going to give *proportion-*

*ately* (as Paul exhorted the Corinthians to do), we must carefully and honestly determine how much we can give, even beyond a tithe (10 percent).

Third, if we're going to make sure God's work gets done in God's way, we must also look at why God gave us specific giving measurements.

In other words, why did God designate certain amounts to carry on his work in the Old Testament? Is there something special about 10 percent as it relates to supporting those who carry out the Great Commission on a full-time basis? Is there something important about 10 percent to make sure family members worship God and learn his will as they should? Is there something unique about the 10 percent specified to help meet the needs of others who are not as fortunate as we are?

These are questions we must carefully consider when determining how much we should give on a regular and systematic basis. From a pragmatic point of view, one thing is clear: if all Christians simply gave one tithe on a regular basis, every church would be able to generously support Christian leaders in the ministry.

## An Act of Obedience

I grew up in a family where no form of regular systematic giving was modeled or taught. In fact, I never considered making it a part of my Christian lifestyle until I graduated from college and married Elaine. Her family experience was just the opposite. Though her parents were small-time farmers who basically lived from hand to mouth, they still gave 10 percent of what they had and taught their children to do the same. Consequently, when I married their youngest daughter, I married a tither.

Before we were married, we decided Elaine would handle the family finances—depositing checks, paying bills, keeping records, etc. Well, you can guess what happened when I brought home my first paycheck. Elaine immediately set aside 10 percent from my gross monthly salary so we could give it to our church.

Frankly, I was concerned—even somewhat irritated. I couldn't see how we were going to make ends meet. Prior to the wedding, I had saved $750 and promptly spent it on a car—something we desperately needed. So we began our married life together with a rented apartment, a car, and a few hand towels Elaine brought, along with our wedding gifts.

But we began to tithe regularly. All of our financial decisions from that point on were made accordingly. God received our first fruits, and after that we planned our other expenditures.

In those early years as our family grew to include three children, we had virtually nothing left over at the end of each month, and the living room in our home had very little furniture (it made a great gymnasium for the kids). But there was never a day that went by that we didn't have what we *needed*—food on our table, clothes on our backs, and a car to drive. And when our children were old enough to receive an allowance, we showed them how to tithe. I remember laying out ten pennies and showing them how to set aside one for Jesus and his work in the world. I then took ten dimes and did the same—and then ten dollars, etc. Our children grew up understanding and practicing this concept of regular, systematic giving, and it's a part of their lives today.

I believe this is one reason God designed the tithe system. It's easy to understand in every culture of the world, and it's easy to teach our children. The facts are, if we don't model and teach giving, our kids will grow up (as most do in our materialistic culture today) giving next to nothing from their resources. In many cases, Christians have become just as materialistic as their secular counterparts.

That's why it has become imperative for church leaders to teach the principles of giving—even to adults who have grown up in Christian homes. It's quite possible they never learned it from their parents.

As I reflect back on my experience as a new husband and father, I'm deeply grateful to Elaine's parents for what they taught her—and that she taught me about this important part of Christian life. Though I began tithing reluctantly, fearful we wouldn't have enough to meet our daily needs, God was never unfaithful in rewarding our obedience.

Over the years, God has honored that obedience and has enabled us to give beyond a tithe. Our goal now is proportional giving—trusting God to enable us to use any excess beyond our tithe in creative ways to help build his kingdom. To us, giving is a joyful worship experience—one that began years ago with obedience.

## Proportional Giving

If all Christians gave proportionately—which God says we should—many Christians in our affluent society would be giving much more than a single tithe. There are believers in America who could easily set aside 50 percent or more of their income for God's work and still have more than enough to meet their own needs. Thankfully, some believers *are* this generous.

A Christian friend of mine inherited a successful business. If you're a reader, you may be familiar with his book *Halftime*. Being an astute and highly motivated businessman, he made his inheritance even more successful—in fact, very lucrative. At age thirty-one, Bob Buford became president of his company and immediately set some lofty goals. His chief ambition was to grow his company and himself. He soon had all the money he needed—and much more!

Then, about ten years later, something dramatic happened. Bob felt convicted about his "slavish devotion to the art of the deal and thrill of the kill. How much was enough?"

This question led Bob to what he calls his halftime experience—and to ask himself some penetrating questions: Where should I invest my talents, time, and treasures? What are the values that give purpose to my life? What is the overarching vision that shapes me? Who am I? Where am I? Where am I going? How do I get there?

Strange as it may seem, the Lord used an atheist—a strategic planning consultant—to change Bob's focus. After hearing Bob tell of his jumbled dreams and desires, the consultant asked a pointed question: "What's in the box?" He told Bob he would have to make a choice between money and Jesus Christ as his priority—a rather startling statement coming from an unbeliever. "If you can't tell me which it is," the consultant continued, "you are going to vacillate between these two values as I've seen you do for years and be confused."

Since Bob is a Christian, he knew in his heart the answer to that question. Jesus Christ had to become his primary loyalty—but "not my exclusive loyalty," Bob explained in his book. He still had his loyalties to his wife, his work, his friends, and to various projects. But he put Christ at the center of all these things in order to have balance and wholeness in his life. He established his priority in terms of his wealth.

Bob eventually began devoting 75 percent of his time, talent, and treasures to "serving those who serve others, helping them to be more effective in their work." Bob made a decision to take Christ's words seriously—to "seek first his kingdom and his righteousness" (Matthew 6:33). He has become one of a growing number of Christians who have determined not to allow financial success to control their lives.

Today Bob encourages other men and women of means to think about the second half of their lives and how they can use their resources to build the kingdom of God. When they do, they become great encouragers—a significant "Barnabas team" within the body of Christ (Acts 4:34–37).

# BIBLICAL BASIS

*I will give letters of introduction to the men you approve and send them with your gift to Jerusalem. If it seems advisable for me to go also, they will accompany me. —1 Corinthians 16:3–4*

Though Paul was doing the planning regarding this collection, he would not handle the money personally. He exhorted the Corinthians to raise the funds and to store the gift until he arrived. Then they were to choose people they trusted to transport the offering. True to form, Paul wanted to be above reproach in all respects so no one could accuse him of raising this money to benefit himself.

Not only would he never take what did not belong to him, he would never engage in any activity that could be misinterpreted—either by Christians or non-Christians. What a powerful lesson for all Christian leaders today.

## *Supra*cultural Principle 48

### LEADERSHIP ACCOUNTABILITY

*Those who handle and distribute money given to God's work should be above reproach and should be held accountable.*

What an important principle in today's world, when some prominent leaders in the church have been guilty of misappropriating funds. In applying this principle, we would do well to follow Paul's model:

First, Christian leaders who receive money directly to meet their own needs should set up a plan whereby they do not handle the money personally without a careful reporting and accounting system. They should never make decisions on their own regarding the amounts they receive.

Second, more than one person should be selected to handle the money for God's work. These people should be approved by those who know them to be men and women of integrity. God established this principle early in Israel's history, when leaders were appointed to assist Moses. The people were to "select capable men from all the people—men who fear God, trustworthy men who hate dishonest gain" (Exodus 18:21; see also Deuteronomy 1:13). Later, those selected to be deacons in the church (men and women in serving roles) were to be individuals who did not and would not pursue "dishonest gain" (1 Timothy 3:8). They were to be "worthy of respect" (1 Timothy 3:8).

In our own church, we have set up a system whereby multiple trustworthy individuals process and record our offerings. These reports, with the money, are sealed in a locked bag and delivered to our bookkeeper, who again counts the offerings and compares those totals with the initial reports. All reports are then filed in a permanent record, and the income is deposited in our local bank. No staff pastor handles offerings directly, and the staff person who does the final processing is protected from any accusation of dishonesty.

Whatever system your church sets up, this supracultural biblical principle should be applied: those who handle and distribute money should be above reproach in all respects and should be held accountable.

Chapter 16
# Second Corinthians 8

Paul wrote 2 Corinthians from somewhere in Macedonia (perhaps Philippi). He had just received a report from Titus, who had returned from Corinth, informing him that these immature and carnal believers had responded positively to his first letter. Paul was encouraged, since he had spoken bluntly about their sinful attitudes and actions and what to do about them.

As Paul wrote his second letter, he commended the Corinthians for their repentant responses (2 Corinthians 7:5–16). However, Titus had reported that there was one major area in which they still needed to reshape their attitudes and take more positive action: how they used their money. Some were confused, frustrated, and negligent regarding Paul's exhortations in the first letter. We can reconstruct why this was so from the letter itself.

Even in their carnal state, the Corinthians had been the first church to respond to Paul's request for money to help the needy Christians in Jerusalem (2 Corinthians 8:10). They had meant well. In fact, their enthusiastic response had motivated the churches in Macedonia—even though these believers were needy themselves—to also participate in this project (2 Corinthians 8:1–2; 9:1–2). But even when Paul wrote 1 Corinthians, they had not followed through on their financial commitments. Paul had exhorted each of them to immediately set aside a sum of money each week, based on their personal resources (1 Corinthians 16:1–2).

Predictably, this exhortation created some negative reactions. Like many twenty-first–century Christians, these believers had not been putting God first in their financial planning, and to begin to "seek first his kingdom and his righteousness" would cause an economic crunch. When Titus reported these less-than-positive reactions, Paul penned 2 Corinthians and elaborated extensively on what he had told them to do in 1 Corinthians. Consequently, in this letter we have more supracultural principles for using our material possessions for the glory of God than in any other section of the New Testament.

# BIBLICAL BASIS

*We want you to know about the grace that God has given the Macedonian churches. Out of the most severe trial, their overflowing joy and their extreme poverty welled up in rich generosity.* —2 Corinthians 8:1–2

Since some of the Corinthians reacted negatively to Paul's instructions to give regularly, systematically, and proportionately (1 Corinthians 16:1–2), Paul called their attention to the Macedonian churches (probably the Philippians and Thessalonians, and possibly the Bereans). He reminded the Corinthians that the believers in these churches had given generously in spite of their own economic needs. In fact, Paul used the phrase "extreme poverty" to identify the Macedonians and stated that they "gave as much as they were able, and even *beyond their ability*" (2 Corinthians 8:2–3).

Nowhere in Scripture are Christians commanded to give away what is absolutely necessary for their own existence. But the believers in Macedonia gave anyway. There was no coercion. Their decisions were "entirely on their own" (2 Corinthians 8:3). In fact, Paul said, "They urgently pleaded with us for the privilege of sharing in this service to the saints" (2 Corinthians 8:4). They were eager to help meet other Christians' material needs. Frankly, in all my years of ministry, I've never met Christians with this kind of generous heart—including myself. What a rewarding experience this must have been for Paul!

Their response was far beyond what he had expected. But a more significant reason than human need prompted this sacrificial generosity. They gave "themselves first to the Lord"—which is the larger context in which Christians are to use their material possessions (2 Corinthians 8:5). It involves, first of all, presenting our bodies as "living sacrifices, holy and pleasing to God" (Romans 12:1). Once we take this step, it follows naturally that we'll view everything we have as belonging to God. And it's this perspective that makes our material gifts "a fragrant offering, an acceptable sacrifice, pleasing to God" (Philippians 4:18).

## *Supra*cultural Principle 49

### CORPORATE MODELS

*Every local body of believers needs real-life examples of other churches that are positive models of giving.*

Initially, the Corinthian believers' eager response to the financial needs of the poor Christians in Jerusalem had motivated the Macedonians to participate (2 Corinthians 9:2). But the

Corinthians hadn't matched their walk with their talk. In an ironic reversal, Paul used the *Macedonians* as a positive model for the *Corinthian* church (2 Corinthians 8:1–5, 8).

Many of us in the Western church today have no concept of truly sacrificial giving. And yet there are groups of Christians in Third World countries in the twenty-first century that are Macedonian in nature. Many are giving out of *poverty*, and American churches, generally speaking, are not even giving out of *plenty*. We need to know about such believers. It will help activate us to greater commitment, and if it doesn't, we're more in bondage to materialism than any of us realize.

## A Contemporary Illustration

On one occasion I was impressed with the story of a small, struggling church in northern Chile. Most of the believers were very poor with large families. Initially, the monthly offerings in that church totaled no more than six dollars.

A missionary involved in planting this church was concerned about its financial condition. How could he help this small body of Christians become self-supporting and indigenous? He began to pray about the matter.

About six weeks later, the missionary stopped to visit a middle-aged couple who had recently become Christians. They had begun reading the Bible on their own and had discovered the concept of tithing. They began asking questions. It didn't occur to the missionary immediately that this was an answer to his prayers. In fact, he tried to dodge the tithing question. The man was a carpenter and had been without work for months. He and his wife had somehow managed to care for themselves and their twenty-five Rhode Island

Red hens on the income from the eggs laid each day. The missionary was certain it would be a waste of time to talk to them about tithing.

But the couple would not be denied, so the missionary showed them the classic passages regarding regular giving in 1 Corinthians 16 and 2 Corinthians 8 and 9. Here's the rest of the story as told by this missionary. It's remarkable and challenging!

The following Sunday at the end of the service, Manuel handed me an envelope. When he saw the puzzled look on my face, he said with a note of pride, "That's our tithe!"

I could scarcely believe it and stood for a long moment with the envelope in my hand. When he had gone, I opened the flap and saw two or three small bills equaling about 19 cents.

The next Sunday afternoon I was passing their house on my bicycle when they waved me down. They had some exciting news. The Tuesday morning after they had given their tithe, there wasn't a crumb of bread in the house for breakfast, nor money to buy more.

Their first impulse was to take the few pesos that had accumulated in the tithe box. But on second thought, Manuel said, "No, we won't. That's God's money. We will go without breakfast this morning."

There wasn't anything to do but attend to the chickens. Much to their amazement, several of the hens had already laid eggs—at 6:30 in the morning! Never before had they laid before noon.

They gathered up the eggs, and Manuel hurried to the corner store. Eggs brought a good price, so he came back with enough bread for the entire day.

That same afternoon, a little old man with a pushcart knocked on their door, asking if they might have any fertilizer to sell. They hadn't cleaned out the chicken house for some time, so they were able to gather 20 sackfuls.

That, too, brought a good price. They bought feed for the hens, staple groceries for themselves—and had money left over.

They decided the wife should buy a pair of shoes with the extra money. The next afternoon, she got on a bus and rode 12 kilometers around the bay to a bigger town.

As soon as she got off the bus, she bumped into a nephew she had not seen for five years. They greeted each other affectionately, and he asked what she might be doing in his town. When she explained, he said, "Well, I've got a shoe store right behind you. Come on in and see what you can find."

She soon found just what she needed, at the exact price she dared spend. The nephew wrapped up the package, and she handed him the money. "Oh no, Aunt, I can't take your money. These shoes are a gift from me."

"No, no, Nephew! That wouldn't be right. Please take the money."

When the argument ended, she found herself out in the street with both the shoes and the money.

The following week, Manuel got a job on a project that would last for two years. The workmen were paid every 15 days. And sure enough, after each payday, this couple arrived at church with their tithe, which now amounted to more than the offering of the rest of the congregation.

Word got around the church, and others began to experiment in giving. I had been paying the rent on the old building, along with the light and water bills, but soon there was money in the treasury to cover all three.

The congregation continued to grow, and so did the income. Each month our books showed more surplus in the treasury. I knew that one of the mission's national pastors working among the Indians was not receiving the support he needed and deserved, so I suggested that we designate some money for him. The congregation agreed, and we sent him the equivalent of $20 each month.

Before long, the church was ready to have its own pastor, and an invitation went to that same man. When he arrived, my wife and I were free to move to a new location and start another church.

The next two years brought continued good news. As the congregation continued to grow, they bought the old building and lots I had rented for them. They began remodeling, and soon they had an attractive, modern structure with Sunday school rooms and an auditorium seating 200.

On our last visit, they had just completed a house for the pastor, solidly built of cement blocks, with a living room-kitchen, bath, and four bedrooms, and they had started a branch church in a housing area a mile away.

We had offered up a little bit of prayer and 19 cents, and God did the rest.[1]

# BIBLICAL BASIS

*We urged Titus, since he had earlier made a beginning, to bring also to completion this act of grace on your part.* —2 Corinthians 8:6

This special project had been in progress for some time, having been initiated by Paul even before he wrote his first letter to the Corinthians. On Titus's first return visit, he helped the Corinthians get started. On his second visit, he was following Paul's instructions to bring the project to completion. This is probably what brought some negative response.

## *Supra*cultural Principle 50

### PERSONAL ACCOUNTABILITY

*All Christians need accountability when making financial commitments to God's work.*

When it comes to giving, many Christians have good intentions. Like the Corinthians, we may respond enthusiastically when we hear about special needs. However, also like the Corinthians, it's easy to forget our commitments. Notice how many steps Paul took to make sure the Corinthians followed through:

- He sent Titus to help them complete the project (2 Corinthians 8:6).
- He wrote a personal letter encouraging them to "finish the work" (2 Corinthians 8:10–11).
- He sent a group of brothers ahead of time to make sure they had collected the money before he arrived (2 Corinthians 9:3).

- He alerted them to his personal plans to arrive with some Macedonian Christians so that they would be prepared and not be embarrassed (2 Corinthians 9:4).

Paul's plan illustrates a system of accountability. The situation in Corinth demonstrates how easy it is for all of us to conveniently forget what we've set out to do, especially when our own desires overshadow the needs of others. Consequently, we, too, need constant reminders.

# BIBLICAL BASIS

*Just as you excel in everything—in faith, in speech, in knowledge, in complete earnestness and in your love for us—see that you also excel in this grace of giving.* —2 Corinthians 8:7

When the Corinthians were converted to Christ, they were given an abundance of "grace gifts" (1 Corinthians 1:4–5, 7). Paul returned to this subject in his second letter and reminded these believers that they *did* "excel in everything" (2 Corinthians 8:7). However, as Paul enumerated the ways in which this grace was manifested—"in faith, in speech, in knowledge"—he broadened the concept beyond spiritual gifts. He referred to complete earnestness and love (1 Corinthians 8:7), qualities that are comprehensive and reflect spiritual maturity among *all* members of the body of Christ. In other words, Paul wasn't simply referring to a spiritual gift of giving bestowed on certain individuals in the Corinthian church (see also Romans 12:6–8). He was exhorting the members to grow in the *spiritual quality* all believers must develop if they're going to remain in the will of God.

## *Supra*cultural Principle 51

### EXCELLING IN GENEROSITY

*Be generous in sharing your material possessions.*

We must never rationalize away our responsibility to give because we don't have a desire to do so, concluding that God has not "gifted" us in the area of sharing what we have. It's God's will that all of us be generous Christians, just as he wants all of us to give ourselves to him as a living sacrifice (Romans 12:1–2). Giving regularly, systematically, and proportionately is the will of God for *every* Christian.

## BIBLICAL BASIS

*I am not commanding you, but I want to test the sincerity of your love by comparing it with the earnestness of others. For you know the grace of our Lord Jesus Christ, that though he was rich, yet for your sakes he became poor, so that you through his poverty might become rich.*
—2 Corinthians 8:8–9

Paul did not command the Roman Christians to offer their bodies as living sacrifices to God; rather, he urged or beseeched them. He made clear that they certainly *owed* this response "in view of God's mercy" (Romans 12:1). But Paul knew God wanted their response to be from their own willingness to do so. Here again we see the correlation between sharing our material possessions and presenting our bodies to God. Though we certainly owe it to the Lord to be generous people because of his generosity to us, he wants our gifts to come from willing hearts.

Paul had a second motive when he penned these words: "I want to test the sincerity of your love by comparing it with the earnestness of others" (2 Corinthians 8:8). This is why he began this section of his letter by illustrating what the Macedonian churches had done. How sincere were the Corinthians?

## Supracultural Principle 52
### GRACE GIVING

*God wants us to share our material possessions not in response to a command but rather out of love, reflecting sincere appreciation for his gift of salvation.*

When Paul reminded the Corinthians that he didn't want them to respond to a command to share their material possessions, he at the same time reminded them of Jesus Christ, who willingly became poor so they (and all believers) might become rich (2 Corinthians 8:9). Jesus Christ is our example in every respect. What he, "who, being in very nature God," did for the world in giving his life as a humble servant, even unto death (Philippians 2:6–7), should constantly motivate all of us as Christians to joyfully give our material possessions in a generous way. That's "grace giving!"

## BIBLICAL BASIS

*If the willingness is there, the gift is acceptable according to what one has, not according to what he does not have. —2 Corinthians 8:12*

Paul reminded the Corinthians that in the previous year (probably sometime in AD 56) they had taken the lead in this project. Now, it seems, they had stopped giving to the project altogether because they didn't feel they had the resources to do so. Paul did not accept this rationale as valid. He encouraged them: "Finish the work, so that your eager willingness to do it may be matched by your completion of it, according to your means" (2 Corinthians 8:11).

This was a sensitive subject. Paul didn't want to issue a command, putting the Corinthians under additional pressure. He was realistic. He knew the believers wouldn't be able to collect money they had already spent. He also recognized that because of this negligence on their part, they would not be able to give what they had hoped and originally planned to give. So he reminded them that what they set aside *now*, according to what they had, was acceptable. God would not evaluate their giving on the basis of what they did *not* have. In other words, Paul realized that money spent is money spent. He encouraged the believers to begin where they were at that moment in their lives and to collect the money week by week on the basis of what they could do. God would then recognize and honor their willingness.

## *Supracultural* Principle 53

### RESPONDING IMMEDIATELY

*God accepts and honors our gifts once we begin giving
regularly and systematically, even if we're not yet
able to give as proportionately as we will
once our economic lives are in order.*

God wants all of us as Christians to begin immediately to organize our financial affairs so we can put God first in the use of our material possessions. Though we may not be able to give in a proportional way at this point in our lives, we should make a start. God will honor us based on our willingness. Many Christians have discovered, however, that once they take this step of faith and obedience, God often makes it possible for them to give proportionately and in a generous way much sooner then they ever imagined.

## BIBLICAL BASIS

*Our desire is not that others might be relieved while you are hard pressed, but that there might be equality.* —2 Corinthians 8:13

Paul evidently was speaking to concerns that the Corinthians themselves had voiced as a result of his first letter when he instructed them to give regularly and systematically (1 Corinthians 16:1–2). If they followed through, it would put them under financial pressure. It was their own negligence, of course, that had caused this problem. But it's understandable why they would not be eager to share their possessions to meet others' needs when they themselves would be inconvenienced.

The apostle didn't want to make life difficult for the Corinthians while they were helping others who were in need. He wasn't advocating a socialist system. Rather, he was dealing with a specific situation in which Christians were experiencing unusual trials and were in deep economic need. As a result, he approached those he knew had *more* in order to help those who had *less*. "Equality" here simply refers to mutual sharing in the midst of a crisis.

## *Supracultural* Principle 54
### BIBLICAL EQUALITY

*God is not pleased when Christians with*
*abundance refuse to help others in need.*

As we've already observed, the Bible never teaches that it's wrong to have an abundance of material possessions. Neither does it teach that Christians should give away everything they have to help others in crisis, putting themselves in a state of need. Rather, Scripture simply teaches that God wants Christians who have sufficient material possessions to share with other Christians who do not, and at times to do so sacrificially.

What Paul was teaching the Corinthians was also a temporary solution. From what he taught the Thessalonians and Corinthians, we can see that he wanted all Christians to be free from having to rely on others to meet their economic needs. On the other hand, Paul recognized that some needs would be ongoing—such as those who had no family to help them and who were unable to work because of age or illness. But the totality of Scripture—including Proverbs—teaches that in the majority of situations, God's people *will* be able to work and earn their own living and "not be dependent on anybody" (1 Thessalonians 4:12).

## BIBLICAL BASIS

*As for Titus, he is my partner and fellow worker among you; as for our brothers, they are representatives of the churches and an honor to*

*Christ. Therefore show these men the proof of your love and the reason for our pride in you, so that the churches can see it.* —2 Corinthians 8:23–24

In this final paragraph of 2 Corinthians 8, Paul let the believers know that when he arrived in their city, he would be accompanied not only by Titus but by two other brothers who were chosen by the Macedonian churches because of their honesty, integrity, and faithful service in God's work.

It seems Paul never handled monetary gifts by himself. He knew how easy it was to be accused of having false motives and being dishonest. This is why he later required that all local church leaders be above reproach when it comes to financial integrity.

## *Supra*cultural Principle 55

### TEAM EFFORT

*No one Christian leader should handle the financial needs of the Christian community alone.*

Handling money in God's work is an awesome responsibility. One reason is the emotional risk involved. Rejection and criticism will come to those who are either carnal or selfish. There will be criticism from those who simply don't understand—or don't want to understand. And there will always be potential accusations of dishonesty or selfishness from both Christians and non-Christians.

Paul faced all of these problems, even though his motives were pure. He faced emotional reactions from Christians because he was teaching an aspect of God's will that makes people feel guilty and uncomfortable when they are, at that moment, living outside the will of God. Every Christian leader who is faithful in trying to care for the economic needs of doing God's work and who at the same time teaches what God has to say about faithful stewardship will face similar challenges. No Christian leader should have to carry out this responsibility alone.

Chapter 17
# Second Corinthians 9

As Paul waited for the Macedonian and Corinthian churches to complete their collections, he also anticipated that once offerings were ready, some of the Macedonian Christians would accompany him to Corinth. Since Paul had been trumpeting the Corinthians' initial response (2 Corinthians 9:2), he wanted to make sure that they were prepared so they wouldn't embarrass him or themselves (2 Corinthians 9:4). The apostle was being pragmatic and realistic.

As Paul concluded this opening paragraph in 2 Corinthians 9, he also introduced us to another important supracultural principle.

## BIBLICAL BASIS

*I thought it necessary to urge the brothers to visit you in advance and finish the arrangements for the generous gift you had promised.*
—2 Corinthians 9:5

Since it would take a lot of money to meet the needs of the poor Christians in Jerusalem, Paul knew the necessary amount could not be generated with a one-time offering. So as he visited various churches, he presented the need, asking people to make a long-range commitment to this project by setting aside money every week from their income to fulfill a "faith promise."

The Corinthian problem was not their promise but their failure to follow through on that commitment. If they had encountered circumstances beyond their control, Paul surely would have put them at ease. But he knew their unpreparedness was a result of negligence and so corrected their thinking with proper instruction and challenged them to fulfill their promise immediately to the best of their ability.

## *Supra*cultural Principle 56

### Faith-Promise Giving

*Take a step of faith and trust God to enable you
to give based on your future earnings.*

Some common-sense rules must be applied in this kind of financial planning. First, we must project what we believe we can give based on our potential performance—which must be evaluated realistically by both our past and present income. Most of us use this practical guideline regularly in terms of making purchases, planning business ventures, and working out budgets that cover many areas of our personal and vocational lives.

The second rule relates to faith. God wants his children to trust him for the future. He doesn't want us to be unrealistic and foolish in our projections, but neither does he want us to be so reserved and hesitant that we don't trust him to provide beyond what may be a human possibility. It takes wisdom, advice, and prayer to maintain a proper balance between planning and trusting God to provide.

# BIBLICAL BASIS

*Then it will be ready as a generous gift, not as one grudgingly given.*
—2 Corinthians 9:5

Paul became more specific as to why he was sending Titus and the two brothers ahead of time. He wasn't being redundant. Rather, he was introducing them to another concern. They had promised to give a generous gift. If Paul arrived in Corinth and the money had not been collected as they had promised, it would create greater pressure because it would be more difficult to come up with the money. What the Corinthians would try to gather together after Paul and his traveling companions arrived would be given in a grudging manner, and the apostle wanted to avoid this.

## *Supracultural* Principle 57

### JOYFUL GIVING

*Organize and plan your giving so you*
*can give generously, not grudgingly.*

When money is available because we've planned our giving, it becomes a joyful experience to share it with others. We've not only prepared our hearts for that moment, but we've prepared our hearts in a broader way ahead of time, because we've arranged our giving together with our overall financial plans. In other words, we've prepared a budget.

Conversely, when we don't plan our giving, we usually don't have money to give. Many of us tend to allow our standard of living to rise to our present level of income. Then, when we're asked to give (either regularly to meet the ongoing needs of the ministry or through special gifts for special needs), we respond reluctantly. This is understandable, since we've already spent our excess funds on our own needs and desires or laid aside that excess for our future benefit.

Under such circumstances, negative emotions are predictable. Often we not only have no excess to give to God's work, but we're worried that we won't even have enough money to meet what we believe are our own needs. Yet, as with the Corinthians, this problem often is not God's but ours—the result of not becoming systematic planners and givers.

## BIBLICAL BASIS

*Whoever sows sparingly will also reap sparingly, and whoever sows generously will also reap generously.* —2 Corinthians 9:6

Any farmer knows that if he sows seeds sparingly, he'll reap a small harvest. But if he sows seeds generously, he'll reap an abundant harvest. Paul used this agricultural fact to illustrate a truth about Christian giving. The analogy must be carefully interpreted and applied, however, since Paul was referring not to quantity but quality. When it comes to giving, God doesn't measure the seed by how much is sown. Rather, he measures how much is sown by what is *available* to sow. Paul was applying the same principle Christ taught when he talked about the widow in the temple whose coin was counted as more than other larger gifts because she had given sacrificially rather than out of plenty.

Serious error can arise from misinterpreting Paul's statement. Some believe he was teaching that God promises material prosperity. Yet nowhere in the New Testament are Christians taught that if we *give*, we will automatically and always *gain* earthly abundance. Rather, our giving is to be motivated by an unselfish heart that is willing to share *unconditionally* with those in need, regardless of the monetary return.

## *Supracultural* Principle 58

### GENEROUS BLESSINGS

*If we give generously, we will receive generous blessings; if we're not generous in our giving, we won't receive generous blessings.*

Biblical generosity involves proportional and sacrificial giving. The Macedonians gave out of their poverty, which was very little in terms of quantity. But in God's sight, it was indeed generous.

God's blessings in response to generous giving also include more than material possessions. The blessing may be, for example, seeing others respond generously because we've been an example. There's always joy and satisfaction in knowing we've helped someone else draw closer to God and walk in his will more faithfully.

The greatest blessing, however, will come in eternity when we hear our Savior say, "Well done, good and faithful servant!"

(Matthew 25:21). When we take our crowns and the rewards we've received for our faithfulness and place them at the feet of Jesus—expressing our love for God all over again—we will be rewarded beyond anything we can anticipate or comprehend while on earth.

# BIBLICAL BASIS

*Each man should give what he has decided in his heart to give, not reluctantly or under compulsion, for God loves a cheerful giver.* —2 Corinthians 9:7

Paul wanted to make sure the Corinthians prepared their *hearts* as well as their *gifts*—not only to gather the money in a systematic fashion but to do so happily. When the time came for them to present their gift publicly to Paul and his coworkers, they would be able to give cheerfully because the money was in hand. In fact, if we're giving "reluctantly or under compulsion," God's heart is not as responsive to our act of worship.

## *Supra*cultural Principle 59

### A CHEERFUL GIVER

*Each of us is responsible to give to God
on the basis of our heart's decision.*

Does this mean we shouldn't give if we can't give cheerfully? If this were true, Paul would not have encouraged the Corinthians to give when they had negative attitudes. His hope, of course, was that careful planning would revive their sense of worship.

## BIBLICAL BASIS

*God is able to make all grace abound to you, so that in all things at all times, having all that you need, you will abound in every good work.*
—2 Corinthians 9:8

We've noted that most of God's promises for being faithful with material possessions relate to eternity and not to our life here on this earth. However, Paul also talked about temporal blessings. He reminded the Corinthians that if they were faithful and generous in helping others, God would take care of them. They would have all they needed in all things and at all times. And with what God provided, they would be able to "abound in every good work."

## *Supracultural* Principle 60

### GOD'S PROVISION

*When we're faithful in our giving,
God will meet our material needs.*

God never promised to give us everything we want or desire. But he has promised to meet our needs. The apostle Paul knew what this meant by personal experience. This is why he wrote to the Philippians—who sacrificed significantly to help him—reassuring them, "My God will meet all your needs according to his glorious riches in Christ Jesus" (Philippians 4:19).

We must note, however, that part of God's grace may be the strength to endure difficult economic times and to learn "the secret of being content in any and every situation" (Philippians 4:12).

Paul's personal testimony was that he had learned that secret. And Christians can claim the same promise today.

# BIBLICAL BASIS

*You will be made rich in every way so that you can be generous on every occasion.* —2 Corinthians 9:11

Probably no verse has been more misinterpreted and misused. If you want to accumulate material possessions, some say, then sow your seed and it will grow and multiply one hundredfold.

What did Paul mean? It may be he wasn't speaking of material possessions at all but rather of spiritual riches. But probably Paul had both in mind. If he were not speaking of material possessions, how could he say the Corinthians would be able to "be generous on every occasion"? Furthermore, his agricultural analogy (2 Corinthians 9:10) implies that he was talking about material blessings as a result of being generous with their material gifts.

It seems, then, that Paul *was* teaching that if the Corinthians were generous, based on their own resources, God would provide them with material blessings so they could continue to invest in the kingdom of God and see people come to Christ and grow in Christ. In this sense, they would be enlarging the harvest of their righteousness. The focus, then, is not on what they would *receive* but on what they could *give* in order to do God's work in the world.

Paul was also speaking of being rich in grace, meaning that because of God's gift of grace, the Corinthian believers would be able to be generous no matter what their economic situation. They would be able to respond like the Macedonians, who gave in spite of poverty, which in God's sight was generous. This leads us to another principle.

## *Supra*cultural Principle 61

### CONTINUED GENEROSITY

*When we're generous, God will enable
us to continue being generous.*

One of the promises God gives us is, when we're faithful in helping others, our own needs will be met and we'll be able to continue helping others. The emphasis in Scripture is not on the amount we give or receive but simply on giving from what we have—whether little or much.

## BIBLICAL BASIS

*Through us your generosity will result in thanksgiving to God. This service that you perform is not only supplying the needs of God's people but is also overflowing in many expressions of thanks to God. Because of the service by which you have proved yourselves, men will praise God for the obedience that accompanies your confession of the gospel of Christ, and for your generosity in sharing with them and with everyone else.* —2 Corinthians 9:11–13

Paul reminded the Corinthians that not only would their generous gift meet the needs of God's people, but it would also cause many people to praise God. People would thank God for these material blessings. They would also thank God for the Corinthians and the Macedonians and all of the other Christians who contributed to meet their needs. And they would thank and praise God for who he is.

## *Supracultural Principle 62*

### PRAISE AND THANKSGIVING

*Generous Christians cause others to
praise and worship God.*

Nothing brings a more positive response among Christians than to see other believers being faithful stewards of their material possessions. Though it may create appropriate guilt in the lives of those who are not obeying God as they should, it will bring a response of thanksgiving and praise in the hearts of those who want to respond to God's Spirit in all things.

True, there will always be those who are critical and negative because of their carnality and worldliness. But for the most part, these people are simply unhappy with those who give because it reveals their own lack of response to God.

## BIBLICAL BASIS

*In their prayers for you their hearts will go out to you, because of the surpassing grace God has given you.* —2 Corinthians 9:14

Paul wanted to demonstrate to the Jerusalem believers in a tangible way that the Corinthians, as well as other Gentile Christians, were truly born again. Thus he wrote that these Christians in

Jerusalem would "praise God for the obedience that accompanies your confession of the gospel of Christ" (2 Corinthians 9:13). In other words, here was proof that their faith was real. Paul said, "You yourselves are our letter, written on our hearts, known and read by everybody. You show that you are a letter from Christ, the result of our ministry, written not with ink but with the Spirit of the living God, not on tablets of stone but on tablets of human hearts" (2 Corinthians 3:2–3). This was the visual message Paul was excited about communicating to the Jerusalem Christians through the Corinthians' generosity.

## *Supracultural* Principle 63

### RESPECT AND LOVE

*People respect and love Christians who are unselfish and generous.*

It has often been said that people cannot hate people who truly love. So it can also be said that people cannot resent Christians who are unselfish and generous with their material possessions. Paul was confident that the generosity among Gentile Christians in the first-century world would break down the theological and cultural barriers that existed because of Jewish prejudice. Just so, Christians today who are unselfish and generous will break down the social and cultural barriers that exist in the twenty-first–century world.

No one can improve upon Paul's final declaration to this extensive section on Christian giving. "Thanks be to God for his indescribable gift!" (2 Corinthians 9:15). Jesus Christ is the "indescribable gift." God the Father is the giver. It was he who "so loved the world that he gave his one and only Son, that whoever believes in him shall not perish but have eternal life" (John 3:16). And it is because of this indescribable gift that all Christians can respond to each other and share what they have materially in order to further the work of God's eternal kingdom!

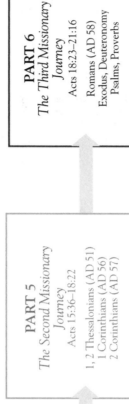

**PART 1**
*The Church in Jerusalem*
Acts 1:1–7:60

The Apostles' Teaching

**PART 2**
*The Teachings of Jesus*
The Four Gospels

Matthew (AD 60s)
Mark (AD 50s)
Luke (AD 60)
John (AD 85–90)

**PART 3**
*Moving beyond Jerusalem and Judea*
Acts 8:1–11:30

Philip
Peter
Barnabas
Saul (Paul)

**PART 4**
*The First Missionary Journey*
Acts 13:1–14:28

James (AD 45–50)
Galatians (AD 49–55)

**PART 5**
*The Second Missionary Journey*
Acts 15:36–18:22

1, 2 Thessalonians (AD 51)
1 Corinthians (AD 56)
2 Corinthians (AD 57)

**PART 6**
*The Third Missionary Journey*
Acts 18:23–21:16

Romans (AD 58)
Exodus, Deuteronomy
Psalms, Proverbs

**PART 7**
*The Prison Epistles*
Acts 27:1–28:15

Ephesians (AD 61)
Colossians (AD 61)
Philippians (AD 61)
Philemon (AD 61)

**PART 8**
*The Pastoral Letters*

1 Timothy (AD 63)
Titus (AD 65)
2 Timothy (AD 66)

**PART 9**
*The Final Letters*
Beyond the Book of Acts

1 Peter (AD 63)
Hebrews (AD 64–68)
2 Peter (AD 66)
Jude (AD 70–80)
1,2,3 John (AD 90)
Revelation (AD 90s)

A Research Paradigm (For studying the subject of material possessions as described in the biblical story.)

# PART 6
## PRINCIPLES FROM THE THIRD MISSIONARY JOURNEY

At some point on the third missionary journey, the Holy Spirit led the apostle Paul to pen a letter to the believers in Rome. In many respects, this letter is his magnum opus in terms of biblical theology. Paul described God's mercy and grace in providing

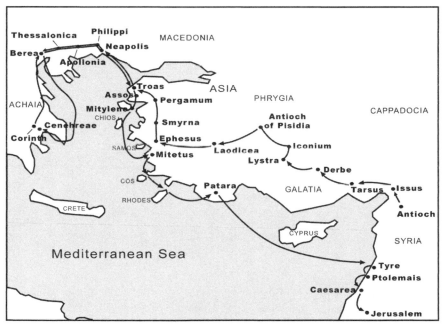

Map 6: Paul's Third Missionary Journey (Acts 18:23–21:16)

salvation for all mankind and then urged all true believers to continuously live in the good, acceptable, and perfect will of God (Romans 12:1–2).

Paul then addressed the subject of debt in Romans 13—a section of Scripture that often has been misinterpreted and mis-applied. We'll look at some important references to material possessions in the Old Testament that also have been taken out of context and inappropriately related to Paul's teaching in Romans. Chapter 19 of this book has been written to help clarify what the Bible actually teaches about borrowing money and going into debt and about loaning money and charging interest.

Chapter 18
# The Letter to the Romans

Paul was concerned that the believers in Rome show respect to government leaders, particularly by paying taxes and revenues. What he taught them was especially pertinent, since they lived in the city where all major governmental decisions were made regarding the vast Roman Empire. Some of these Christians probably lived a stone's throw away from the emperor's palace, and one of Paul's exhortations introduces us to the subject of a Christian's financial responsibility to government.

## BIBLICAL BASIS

*Give everyone what you owe him: If you owe taxes, pay taxes; if revenue, then revenue; if respect, then respect; if honor, then honor.*
—Romans 13:7

Paul outlined two areas of obligation. The first is *financial*, and the second is *attitudinal*. In the financial area, Paul probably was referring to the tax on persons and property, a levy similar to federal, state, and local taxes in America. This was what the Pharisees and Herodians referred to when they asked Jesus if it was right to pay taxes to Caesar. Jesus responded by telling them, "Give to Caesar what is Caesar's, and to God what is God's" (Matthew 22:21).

In addition to taxes, Paul made reference to paying "revenue." This probably referred to the tax on goods. It would correspond in part to state sales tax in certain parts of the United States.

Paul also dealt with an *attitudinal* obligation. Not only are Christians to pay taxes, they're to do so with a proper spirit. If we owe respect—which we do—we are to give respect. If we owe honor—which we do—we are to give honor.

This poses a problem for some Christians. How can we respect those who may not deserve it because of their behavior? How can we honor government leaders if they disqualify themselves from being honorable?

Jesus set the example in this matter. He disagreed with Herod Antipas, the ruler in Galilee, and Tiberius Caesar, the ruler of the Roman Empire. In many respects, their values were in complete opposition to his. But Christ still paid respect to these men because of their God-ordained positions. And one way he demonstrated that respect was by paying taxes.

## *Supra*cultural Principle 64

### Respectful Citizens

*Be a responsible and honest citizen by paying
all governmental taxes and revenues.*

From an eternal perspective, our true citizenship is in heaven (Philippians 3:20). We are "aliens and strangers on earth" (Hebrews 11:13). However, we are also citizens of our earthly society. Consequently, we have a responsibility to help maintain law and order by providing money to support people in leadership and various governmental programs.

Dishonesty is a strong temptation for Christians in today's society. There are many ways to cheat the government without being detected. Unfortunately, some Christians fall prey to this kind of behavior in direct violation of the will of God. Rather than taking advantage of the government, we are to pray "for kings and all those in authority, that we may live peaceful and quiet lives in all godliness and holiness" (1 Timothy 2:2). Significantly, the Greek word *semnotes*, translated "holiness" in the NIV, could be better translated "honesty." In other words, there's no room for rationalization. Whether we are honest should *not* depend on the ethics of our government leaders. No form of dishonesty on their part makes it right for Christians to engage in the same kind of sinful behavior.

## BIBLICAL BASIS

*Let no debt remain outstanding, except the continuing debt to love one another, for he who loves his fellowman has fulfilled the law.*
—Romans 13:8

Some people use this verse to teach that it's always wrong to borrow money. Most Bible commentators disagree. Douglas J. Moo is representative when he says, "This command does not forbid a Christian from ever incurring a debt (e.g, to buy a house or a car); it rather demands that Christians repay any debts they do incur promptly and in accordance with the terms of the contract."[1]

It may, of course, be unwise and even out of God's will in certain circumstances to borrow money, but that's not what Paul was referring to in the above verse. He was simply saying that if we owe money, we should pay it. In context, this includes taxes and every kind of revenue required by the government (Romans 13:7).

The Scriptures broaden our responsibility to be free of financial obligation to include *any kind of debt*. In the New Testament world, it involved wages. James wrote, "Look! The wages you failed to pay the workmen who mowed your fields are crying out against you. The cries of the harvesters have reached the ears of the Lord Almighty" (James 5:4). It is utterly sinful to hire people to perform tasks with no intention of paying them a fair and equitable salary.

The command to "let no debt remain outstanding" includes any borrowed money. And certainly, there should be repayment of anything stolen. Paul was so conscientious about this obligation that after he led the runaway slave Onesimus to Christ, he personally offered to repay Philemon (Onesimus's owner) anything this man had taken illegitimately (Philemon 18).

## *Supracultural* Principle 65

### PAYING DEBTS

*Whether money, goods, or services,*
*always pay what you owe.*

As a pastor, I've known Christians who borrow money from friends and associates seemingly without intending to repay it. Or if they do make payments, they're frequently late or woefully behind. But such behavior is even more deplorable when it comes from pastors and other Christian leaders. I've heard tragic stories of ministers who have transferred to churches in other cities, leaving behind a string of personal unpaid debts. Fortunately, these situations seem the exception rather than the rule. But a single instance among those who claim to be spiritual leaders is one too many.

Most Christians don't set out to violate this principle. Still, little by little they get into debt beyond their ability to repay on the pre-determined and agreed schedule. They're guilty of poor planning or impulsive buying. For these people, easy credit is a curse rather than a blessing. Either they need to use credit cards cautiously and only as a convenience for not carrying cash or writing checks, or they need to destroy them. In fact, if they cannot use them within their budgeted guidelines, they need to avoid credit buying altogether.

There are, of course, economic crises that affect all people, including Christians. We may have entered into financial agreements with every potential ability to make our payments on time. Everyone involved in the contract is satisfied that the debt is a good risk. But circumstances arise beyond everyone's control.

What should a Christian do when this happens? We'll look at some important guidelines in the next chapter, but it's important to emphasize here that all Christians need wise financial counsel as to the best approach to faithfully applying the principle in Romans 13:8. People caught in an unexpected financial crisis should communicate with their creditors to indicate their desire to meet their obligations and to work out an acceptable plan to do so.

## BIBLICAL BASIS

*They were pleased to do it, and indeed they owe it to them. For if the Gentiles have shared in the Jews' spiritual blessings, they owe it to the Jews to share with them their material blessings.* —Romans 15:27

When Paul wrote to the Romans, he was preparing to leave for Jerusalem with a group of men to deliver the gift of money for use among needy Christians. In fact, he reported that he was already on his way (Romans 15:25), which probably means he was ready to leave as soon as he finished his dictation. The money was finally in hand, having been collected over a period of time (1 Corinthians 16:1–4).

As Paul concluded this letter, he explained the spirit and motivation that had caused the Macedonian and Achaian Christians to gather this monetary gift. First, "they were *pleased* to do it" (Romans 15:27). In spite of the challenges he had faced in Corinth, Paul could now share the concern and compassion those Christians demonstrated toward the Jewish believers in Jerusalem who were suffering from economic deprivation. Apparently, the Corinthians had responded maturely to the exhortations in his second letter (2 Corinthians 8:1–9:15).

Paul went on to state *why* a Christian should share his material possessions with others. Though the churches in Macedonia and Achaia responded out of concern, Paul made clear that they also had an *obligation* to help the Jewish Christians in Jerusalem. "They owe it to . . . them," he wrote and then explained why (Romans 15:27).

The gospel first came to the Jews through Jesus Christ, who was a Jew. The apostles were all Jews, and so were the first converts to Christianity. And it was the Jewish Christians in Jerusalem who first brought the message of Christ to the Gentiles, primarily because of persecution (Acts 8:1, 4; Acts 11:19–21).

As we've seen in the biblical story, the Jewish believers in Jerusalem were deeply affected by the famine in the Roman world. They had been cut off from the welfare system in Judaism because of their faith in Jesus Christ, and inflated prices made it virtually impossible for them to buy even staple foods.

Frederick Louis Godet explains the challenge these Jewish believers faced: "The indigence of those first believers must have been increased day by day by the violent hatred of the Jewish authorities and of the upper classes; comp. Jas. ii. 4–6. What easier way for rich and powerful families than to deprive poor artisans, who had become the objects of their reprobation, of their means of subsistence!"[2] Godet further points out that this is not an unusual phenomenon among Christians: "This is an event which is reproduced everywhere when there is a transition from one religious form to another; so in Catholic countries where Protestantism is preached; among the Jews, among the heathen of India or China, etc., when one of their own becomes a Christian."[3]

Paul made it clear that Gentile Christians had a responsibility to care for those who had sacrificed and made it possible for them to hear the gospel of Jesus Christ and to respond in faith. He wrote, "They owe it to the Jews to share with them their material blessings" (Romans 15:27).

## *Supra*cultural Principle 66

### OUR OBLIGATION

*All Christians have an obligation to support*
*God's work in material ways.*

Earlier we noted two important corollary principles from Paul's second letter to the Corinthians. First, God does not want Christians to share their material possessions because of a command but rather to respond out of love, reflecting sincere appreciation for the gift of salvation in Christ (2 Corinthians 8:8–9; see Principle 52 on page

185. Second, every Christian is responsible to give to God on the basis of his or her own heart's decision (2 Corinthians 9:7; see Principle 59 on page 196). It may seem that this third principle from Romans, which focuses on obligation, contradicts the two principles from 2 Corinthians. But the three principles are complementary, not contradictory.

To understand this apparent tension more fully, we need to gain a wider perspective on Christian commitment. We are all *obligated* to present ourselves to God because of his gift of eternal salvation in Christ (Romans 12:1–2; Titus 2:11–14). To not understand that this action on our part is obligatory is to be ignorant of what God has done for us through his sovereign and elective grace. At the same time, however, we should present our lives to God *freely* in response to his mercy, love, and grace.

Just so, we have an obligation to give to God's work. However, we should also give freely, voluntarily, from hearts of love. In Christ, it is possible for these two concepts to be in alignment. Once we understand God's grace, it becomes a *blessed obligation* to give, not an oppressive burden.

This paradox can be illustrated with the concept of being a slave to Christ and yet experiencing freedom. How can this be? There is only one way to be truly free in our hearts and lives, and that is to live in harmony with God's will. Then and only then can we experience the reality of this antinomy in all aspects of our lives, including the way we use our material possessions. True *freedom* to give comes once we understand and appreciate how *indebted* we are to Jesus Christ for his gift of eternal life.

## Chapter 19
# Borrowing, Loaning, and Debt

What Paul said in Romans 13:8 raises some questions. What guidelines are there in Scripture regarding borrowing money? When is it wrong? When is it unwise? When is it appropriate?

## Jesus's Perspective

It's not necessary to review all Jesus had to say about borrowing and debt, except to say that he never addressed the issue as being right or wrong. Rather, he acknowledged the practice of borrowing and loaning money in the Roman Empire without making value judgments. Furthermore, as we noted earlier in our study, he often used these economic settings as illustrative material to teach spiritual truths. As in all free-enterprise systems, the economy of the Roman Empire was highly integrated, with financial systems that involved indebtedness. Jesus understood this and taught people how to live an upright and spiritual life in that kind of society.

## An Old Testament Perspective

To understand God's will regarding financial indebtedness, it's important to look carefully at some teachings in the Old

Testament. Interpreting these teachings accurately means we must understand the cultural, economic, and spiritual differences that existed in Israel, both before the nation went into captivity and later before it became a part of the Roman Empire.

## The Cultural and Economic Setting

A. E. Willingale gives us some helpful insights when speaking of the time Israel occupied their own land and determined their own economic destiny as a nation:

> Loans in Israel were not commercial but charitable, granted not to enable a trader to set up or expand a business but to tide a peasant farmer over a period of poverty. Since the economy remained predominately agricultural up to the end of the Monarchy, there developed no counterpart to the commercial loan system already existing in Babylonia in 2000 BC. Hence the legislation contains not mercantile regulations but exhortations to neighbourliness.[1]

Initially there was no need for the people of Israel to purchase property, since they had received it at no cost from God himself. Before they entered Canaan, Moses reminded them that they would receive large, flourishing cities they hadn't built, houses filled with all kinds of good things they hadn't provided, wells they hadn't dug, and vineyards and olive groves they hadn't planted (Deuteronomy 6:10–11).

Because of God's material provisions, there was no need for the Israelites to establish businesses based on free enterprise. They were able to make a living from the land they had received free from indebtedness. Initially, at least, business loans of any kind were unnecessary.

## The Spiritual Setting

God had also promised his people that he would provide unusual blessings if they obeyed him. Note these words from Moses: "The LORD will open the heavens, the storehouse of his bounty, to send rain on your land in season and to bless all the work of your hands. *You will lend to many nations but will borrow from none*" (Deuteronomy 28:12).

If Israel obeyed God, it would be a nation free from any need for economic assistance from other nations. It would be able to lend money to other nations in distress, which would be a dynamic witness to its pagan neighbors. By contrast, if Israel disobeyed God, it would deteriorate economically. Not only would the people be unable to meet their own needs, they would have to borrow from their pagan neighbors in order to survive (Deuteronomy 28:47–48).

When Jesus walked among the children of Israel, this economic setting had changed. Israel now existed in a totally different environment, and in order to survive, the people had to adapt their laws to a commercial economy. Jesus recognized and accepted this reality.

## Interpretation and Application Today

Our challenge as Christians living in our own twenty-first–century culture is to interpret and apply certain Old Testament teachings without transplanting Old Testament laws into our cultural world in a literal or legalistic fashion. At the same time, we must not bypass the spirit of these laws. Though designed for Israel, they yield timeless principles that are supracultural.

## BIBLICAL BASIS

*If you lend money to one of my people among you who is needy, do not be like a moneylender; charge him no interest.* —Exodus 22:25

When the people of Israel came into the Promised Land, God would bless them materially as a nation; and if they obeyed him, he would give them even more. Yet the Lord recognized there would always be poor people in Israel (Deuteronomy 15:11). Thus he prefaced the law on lending money in Exodus 22:25 by warning, "Do not take advantage of a widow or an orphan. If you do and they cry out to me, I will certainly hear their cry. My anger will be aroused" (Exodus 22:22–24; see also Leviticus 25:35–38).

The picture is clear. How could people who had received everything as a free gift from God turn around and take advantage of the poor and needy? How could they even consider charging interest on loans to fellow Israelites who were already in a desperate financial situation? To do so would be an act of selfishness and sin. God forbade it.

## *Supra*cultural Principle 67

### PROTECTING THE POOR

*Never take economic advantage of poor people.*

We can't establish a universal principle from these Old Testament laws that it's *always* wrong to lend money to fellow Christians or even to charge interest. However, if a Christian takes advantage of others—especially poor people—there's no question but that this is sinful behavior. It's an act of selfishness on our part, and worse, it's an affront to God, who has freely given us the gift of salvation.

# BIBLICAL BASIS

*The wicked borrow and do not repay, but the righteous give generously.*
—Psalm 37:21

Following the flow of God's unfolding revelation in the Old Testament, it's logical to look next at this proverb in Psalm 37. In concise fashion, David interpreted and explained the promises given to Israel relative to the Promised Land. If Israel obeyed the Lord, it would never be necessary for her to borrow money from her pagan neighbors. She would always have enough for herself and plenty left over to give to others. Conversely, those in Israel who do not obey the laws of God will find themselves in a state of desperation. They will have to borrow money to survive and never have enough resources to pay it back.[2]

## *Supracultural Principle 68*
### HELPING OTHERS

*If we obey God's Word, we'll be able not only to meet our own economic needs but also to help others.*

Inherent in David's proverb is a profound principle affirmed in the New Testament, particularly in 2 Corinthians. Paul taught that when Christians are faithful in their giving, God will meet their needs (2 Corinthians 9:8; see also Philippians 4:19).

Furthermore, he taught that when we are generous, God will enable us to continue being generous (2 Corinthians 9:11).

These promises, however, raise a practical question: will faithful and generous Christians ever need to borrow money to meet their needs? The Bible doesn't answer this question directly. Part of God's provision in our culture may be an opportunity to be involved in responsible borrowing to meet special needs, such as buying a car or house or helping a child through college.

But when there are circumstances beyond our control—such as a need for food, clothing, or temporary shelter—the Word of God teaches that if all Christians are generous as God says they should be, there will never be a need for believers to dig themselves into a deeper pit by borrowing money. Paul wrote to the Corinthians, "Our desire is not that others might be relieved while you are hard pressed, but that there might be equality. At the present time your plenty will supply what they need, so that in turn their plenty will supply what you need. Then there will be equality" (2 Corinthians 8:13–14). Every local church needs a system by which these needs are met. In our own church, we have a Love Fund that is monitored carefully but always available to Christians who have serious economic needs during times of crisis.

## BIBLICAL BASIS

*At the end of every seven years you must cancel debts. . . . You may require payment from a foreigner, but you must cancel any debt your brother owes you.* —Deuteronomy 15:1, 3

Understandably, these commands to cancel debts have puzzled a lot of people. But we must examine Israel's unique economic position once they arrived in Canaan. Two important factors need to be considered in explaining these laws.

First, note the context of this statement. Moses was still outlining laws that governed relationships with people who were in a desperate economic situation. He had just reminded Israel of their responsibility to "the aliens, the fatherless and the widows" who lived among them (Deuteronomy 14:29). "At the end of every *three* years, bring all the tithes of that year's produce and store it in your towns" (Deuteronomy 14:28). Then those in need could "come and eat and be satisfied" (Deuteronomy 14:29). Moses went on to explain their responsibility at the end of every *seven* years toward poor people who had borrowed money in order to survive (Deuteronomy 15:1–3).

Second, consider what Moses was actually saying in a still larger context. In the book of Exodus, God had commanded the children of Israel to sow their fields and harvest crops for six years. During the seventh year, God commanded them, "Let the land lie unplowed and unused. Then the poor among your people may get food from it, and the wild animals may eat what they leave. Do the same with your vineyard and your olive grove" (Exodus 23:11).

The command to cancel debts refers to this seven-year period of time (Deuteronomy 15:1–3). God was expressing concern for those who had borrowed money from their fellow Israelites. They too were forbidden to cultivate their fields during the seventh year. Keil and Delitzsch explain: "If no harvest was gathered in, and even such produce as had grown without sowing was to be left to the poor and the beasts of the field, the landowner could have no income from which to pay his debts."[3]

Consequently, Moses outlined a plan for handling these debts. Those who had loaned money to poor people (which was to be loaned without interest, see Exodus 22:25) were not to put pressure on them to pay back what they owed during this seventh year. Keil and Delitzsch translate Deuteronomy 15:2 as follows: "This is the manner of the release. . . . Every owner of a loan of his hand shall release (leave) what he has lent to his neighbour; he shall not press his neighbour, and indeed his brother; for they have proclaimed release for Jehovah."[4] Moses was not issuing a command to cancel debts once and for all. Rather, the debt payment was simply to be postponed. Lenders were not to put pressure on these poor people during this seventh year.[5]

This interpretation also explains the exception that the children of Israel could require payment from a foreigner (Deuteronomy 15:3). Foreigners were not obligated to allow their land to lie uncultivated during the seventh year, so they were not in the same predicament as the poor in Israel. Israel not only had the right to charge interest for loans to foreigners, but they could also insist that those loans should continue to be paid even during the seventh year.

The specific economic conditions and requirements described in this Old Testament passage cannot and should not be duplicated in other cultural situations. However, it contains an important principle that captures the spirit of God's intent and that should be applied universally.

## *Supra*cultural Principle 69

### DEMONSTRATING GRACE

*Be gracious to people who borrowed money with good
intentions but encountered crises beyond their control
that make it difficult to repay their loan on time.*

Clearly, the Bible teaches that it's a poor testimony for Christians to borrow money and then to renege on paying it back. But there will be times when people borrow with good intentions and have difficulty repaying. As Christians, what should we do?

### Personal Loans

If we've made a personal loan, we have more control over the circumstances than if a lending institution is involved. First of all, personal loans to fellow Christians should be made with full awareness that those we're attempting to help may not be able to repay. We should be willing to make the loan a gift if necessary or to postpone payments indefinitely. This decision should be made in one's heart and mind before a personal loan is made.

When making personal loans, is it ever right for a Christian to charge interest? The Scriptures don't give a definitive answer to this question. Though this aspect of Old Testament law doesn't apply in other cultural and spiritual situations, the *spirit* of those laws *does* apply. To loan money to poor people with the intent of making a profit violates both Old and New Testament teachings.

But to loan money to Christians who are expanding their businesses in order to make their own profit is another matter. It's only logical that the borrower should share the income with those who helped make it possible. However, if the business venture fails, leaving the owner in dire straits, it's within the spirit of Old Testament law for every Christian who has invested in the venture to be prepared to either cancel the debt or postpone repayment until the borrower is able to pay the loan.

*Business Loans*

If a loan has been secured through a recognized lending organization, Christian loan officers must function within the guidelines of that agency. If the business operates unethically, a believer should look elsewhere for employment. If Christians own the business, they should set up guidelines that are not only in harmony with government regulations but also reflect the spirit and principles of Christianity.

The principles of grace and forgiveness, however, in no way license a Christian to take advantage of either an individual or an organization. If at all possible, borrowed money should always be paid back. Though certain bankruptcy laws in our society protect the rights of individuals and organizations during times of crisis, these laws should never be used by Christians to justify irresponsibility or to avoid paying back borrowed money on a reasonable and feasible payment schedule.

## BIBLICAL BASIS

*The rich rule over the poor, and the borrower is servant to the lender.*
—Proverbs 22:7

Here is another proverb that must be interpreted in light of Old Testament laws and in view of what was happening in Israel's history.

When people are in such a state of poverty that they don't have enough to meet their needs for food and shelter, they'll often borrow—if they can—out of desperation. When they do, they become servants to the lender.

Unfortunately, this happened in Israel again and again, and people became slaves. Because there was no way to pay back what they borrowed, they lost everything they had. This is why the prophets cried out so vehemently against this unfair treatment of poor people.

One of the most dramatic examples of the way Israel violated God's laws regarding lending and borrowing took place after a number of Israelites returned to the Promised Land, first under the leadership of Zerubbabel (536 BC) and then under Ezra (458 BC). Several years later, when Nehemiah arrived to help rebuild the walls of Jerusalem, he discovered a deplorable situation. Because of a famine, many of the poor people in Israel had mortgaged their fields, their vineyards, and their homes in order to buy grain (Nehemiah 5:3). Others, in order to keep their property, had borrowed money from their Jewish brothers to pay taxes to King Artaxerxes (Nehemiah 5:4). The problem was compounded by the fact that these fellow Jews charged the poor people exorbitant interest rates, which was a direct violation of the laws of Moses.

To make matters even more desperate, those who had borrowed to survive faced a famine and crop failure. At that point their fellow Jews who had loaned them money confiscated their property and sold their children into slavery (Nehemiah 5:5).

Nehemiah confronted this sinful abuse. He rebuked the Jewish nobles and officials: "I told them, 'You are exacting usury [interest] from your own countrymen!'" (Nehemiah 5:7). Nehemiah was so disturbed he called a large meeting to deal with the problem.

> What you are doing is not right. Shouldn't you walk in the fear of our God to avoid the reproach of our Gentile enemies? I and my brothers and my men are also lending the people money and grain. But let the exacting of usury [interest] stop! Give back to them immediately their fields, vineyards, olive groves and houses, and also the usury you are charging them—the hundredth part of the money, grain, new wine and oil. (Nehemiah 5:9–11)

Fortunately, the Israelites responded to Nehemiah's exhortations. Had they not done so, God's judgment would have fallen on them, as it had before, because of their selfish and greedy behavior.

Is there general wisdom in Solomon's proverb for those of us who live in a twenty-first–century culture where lending and borrowing are integral parts of our economic and social structures? The answer is a decided yes, even though the literal message of this proverb may not apply (such as being sold into slavery). It's possible for people in any culture to find themselves in bondage to some degree to those from whom they have borrowed money.

## *Supra*cultural Principle 70
### BORROWING WISELY

*Before borrowing money for any purpose,
seek wisdom from others who can help you
evaluate all aspects of the decision.*

Any form of borrowing brings with it a certain amount of bondage. As Otto Zöckler stated, "Indebtedness always destroys *freedom*, even though no sale into slavery of him who was unable to pay should ever take place."[6]

Certain financial decisions can be made, however, that do not involve high risk. The lower the risk, the less your sense of bondage. The amount of money borrowed when weighed against liquid assets is an important factor in the equation. What will we actually lose if we cannot repay the loan? For example, could we be obligated the rest of our lives? That's a terrible price to pay in order to achieve an economic goal.

# BIBLICAL BASIS

*Do not be a man who strikes hands in pledge or puts up security for debts; if you lack the means to pay, your very bed will be snatched from under you.* —Proverbs 22:26–27 (See also 6:1–5; 11:15; 17:18.)

Solomon was again dealing with a significant problem in Israel when he warned against taking on an obligation for someone else's indebtedness. Those who often put up surety were also poor; for if they were not, they could have easily covered the debt involved.

The Scriptures teach that this is a foolish decision and one a person should attempt to reverse as quickly as possible. Solomon made the issue urgent: "Go and humble yourself; press your plea with your neighbor! Allow no sleep to your eyes, no slumber to your eyelids" (Proverbs 6:3–4). In other words, do everything you possibly can to free yourself from this kind of financial bondage.

## *Supracultural* Principle 71
### GUARANTEEING LOANS

*Before guaranteeing another person's loan based on your own assets, make sure you'd be able to repay the loan without defaulting on other financial obligations, including your indebtedness to the Lord.*

There are times when a Christian may cosign a note without violating the will of God. In fact, it may be a gracious and generous act of love. For example, parents who are financially able may wish to cosign on a loan to help their child build or purchase a home. But, anyone who guarantees a loan should be prepared to assume the entire loan without serious consequences.

Even today it's wise to heed the Old Testament warnings and to encourage others seeking help securing a loan to wait, if possible, until they're in a better financial position so as not to need this kind of guarantee. Though there are exceptions to this rule, they should be made cautiously, considering all of the scriptural principles that relate to how a Christian should view and use material possessions.

## Borrowing within God's Will

If the Scriptures don't teach against borrowing per se, then when does going into debt become an irresponsible decision that leads us out of the will of God and into sinful attitudes and actions? The following biblical principles will help us answer this question.

## *Supracultural* Principle 72

### DECEITFUL BORROWING

*We're outside of God's will when we knowingly*
*borrow money we can't pay back according*
*to a predetermined agreement.*

As we've already acknowledged, all borrowing involves a certain amount of risk. But when we make foolish decisions based on ignorance or arrogance, we're acting irresponsibly and can quickly find ourselves in violation of God's will. Following are several guidelines that will help us avoid irresponsible decisions that may lead us to sin against God:

- We're outside of God's will when we borrow because we're in bondage to materialism—when our treasures are on earth rather than in heaven (Matthew 6:19–21; 24).
- We are outside of God's will when any form of dishonesty is involved in borrowing money.
- We're out of God's will when we use borrowed money to achieve any goals that are outside the will of God.

## *Supracultural* Principle 73

### LEAVING GOD OUT

*We are outside of God's will when we cannot give*
*him the first fruits of our income because we've*
*obligated ourselves to pay off debts.*

Solomon wrote, "Honor the LORD with your wealth, with the *firstfruits* of all your crops" (Proverbs 3:9). Years later Paul exhorted the Corinthians, "On the first day of every week, each of you should set aside a sum of money in keeping with his income" (1 Corinthians 16:2).

It's clear from both Old and New Testaments that when we cannot set aside money to support God's work because we've obligated ourselves financially, we have ceased putting God first in our lives. Obviously, this isn't true if it happens because of economic reversals beyond our control. But in most instances in our western culture, overobligation happens because we have materialistic goals that lead us to make irresponsible decisions.

We should never make decisions to borrow money that make it impossible, even temporarily, to give to God's work regularly, systematically, and proportionately. Unfortunately, many Christians are in bondage to debt on their homes, their cars, their boats, their four-wheelers, and countless other twenty-first–century toys—and are among those who don't have enough money to give their first fruits to the Lord. This is a clear violation of God's will, which will eventually bring serious consequences.

## Corrective Steps

If we're in violation of any of these biblical principles, we should first confess our sins to God and accept his forgiveness (1 John 1:9). We must acknowledge that violating scriptural principles inevitably leads to sinful attitudes and actions. Indeed, in most instances, violating these principles is in itself sin.

Next, we must take steps as quickly as possible to bring our lives into harmony with God's will. If we owe money we can't pay, we need to immediately draw up a plan to correct the situation. We then need to communicate with every creditor in order to let each one know the specific steps we plan to take.

Finally, we must include in this plan a way to give regularly and systematically to God's work. Paul's words to the Corinthians are applicable in these difficult economic circumstances. Because of poor financial planning, those New Testament Christians were in violation of scriptural principles and not able to give as they should.

But Paul's exhortations to the Corinthians raise another question. Should Christians give regularly and systematically to the Lord's work when they have debt payments that are overdue? This is a difficult question to answer, since the Scriptures don't speak directly to this issue. However, we must remember that we're also in debt to God for his gracious provision of salvation.

The late Larry Burkett, to whom we've dedicated this volume, believed that "the first portion of everything we receive belongs to God. It doesn't belong to anybody else, even a creditor."[7] He pointed out that Christians who make the commitment to give regularly to God are "almost always better money handlers, and as a result of their commitment to God, they will honor their commitment to their creditors."[8] It was also his experience that rarely does a creditor object to this arrangement once he understands this kind of commitment.[9]

Burkett advised Christians who are behind in debt payments to contact their creditors with a plan of action, spelling out their plans to repay these debts systematically. They should also include in the plan their intention to give a certain amount of their income regularly and systematically to their church. He found that many creditors feel comfortable with this kind of planning because it indicates honesty and moral integrity. People who have these kinds of values can usually be trusted to pay off their debts over a period of time. Certainly, Christians who establish these priorities will be honored and blessed by God in economic ways that will eventually enable them to not only meet their financial obligations to creditors but also be able to give more proportionately to the work of God.

## Church Debt

Some teach that it's never God's perfect will for a church body to go into debt. The most common reason for assuming debt is building projects, and it's another issue not directly addressed in Scripture. We have no illustrations in the New Testament of special buildings being constructed for worship. This doesn't mean it would have been wrong. It was simply impossible because of the political and economic conditions that existed within the Jewish culture and in the Roman Empire as a whole. Christians met in homes, particularly those owned by wealthier believers.

But in the Old Testament, the Israelites built the tabernacle in the wilderness and, later, the temple in Jerusalem (Exodus 25:1–9; 1 Chronicles 29:1–9). In these instances, the people financed the projects with their own freewill offerings and gifts. They didn't borrow money or any other material substance because there were sufficient resources in Israel. The vast number of family units involved made this possible.

A second reason they didn't borrow money is that they had no commercial loan system. None was necessary, remember, because they operated on an entirely different economic plan.

*Pragmatic Considerations:* Of course it's ideal for a church body never to go into debt, just as it would be ideal for a Christian family never to incur debt when building a home. However, several pragmatic considerations make it virtually impossible for some churches to build without borrowing, just as it usually is not feasible for the average couple to buy a home without taking on a certain amount of debt.

The first consideration is available resources. Small, independent churches face this problem regularly. They have no large denominational structures to look to for assistance. In order to have a permanent facility, it may be necessary to borrow.

The second factor is psychological. In American culture, it's difficult to attract people to a meeting place that doesn't reflect permanence. Generally speaking, people don't take a ministry seriously without a church building. There is a direct correlation between their sense of security and their commitment. Try as we might, we cannot ignore this reality.

This alone puts Christian leaders in a difficult position. On one hand, you can't fund a debt-free building project without a sufficient number of members. On the other hand, it's difficult to attract people to a temporary or makeshift facility. The work may never grow large enough to make it possible to have a permanent facility.

*Practical Guidelines:* Here are some helpful guidelines to follow as you consider taking on debt for a church building project.

They're presented in the form of reflective questions and based on practical considerations as well as on biblical principles.

- Is it possible to use a semipermanent facility until there are enough committed members to fund construction of a permanent building? For example, some churches lease public schools, theaters, office or warehouse space, etc.

- Is the building project designed in phases, making it possible to increase in attendance as you increase the size of the facility?

- Is there a general sense of unity among the people regarding the plans to build? The greater the unity, the easier it will be to fund the project.

- Are the people involved already committed financially? Christians who give regularly, systematically, and proportionately will be amazed at how much money they can generate for this kind of project while still maintaining the ministry as God intended.

- Is it possible to build debt-free? If so, this should be your goal, even if it means postponing the project for a period of time. However, this goal must be realistic, or people will become discouraged.

- Is it possible to secure a church loan and to guarantee that loan without personal signatures? Scripture doesn't say it's wrong for individuals to guarantee a church loan, but it does warn against obligations that could create economic hardships in case of foreclosure. People who are willing to guarantee a loan should be willing and able to pay off the debt if there is an unforeseen crisis. Generally speaking, it's wise to avoid this approach if at all possible.

We live in a debt-oriented culture. But allowing ourselves to be driven by a society permeated with materialism is dangerous. We can easily rationalize our decisions and violate the principles of Scripture. When we do, we'll suffer the consequences. This is why we need to carefully consider all of the principles outlined in this study. God has given us sufficient guidelines to determine his will for our lives when it comes to our material possessions.

**PART 3**
*Moving beyond Jerusalem and Judea*
Acts 8:1–11:30

Philip
Peter
Barnabas
Saul (Paul)

**PART 6**
*The Third Missionary Journey*
Acts 18:23–21:16

Romans (AD 58)
Exodus, Deuteronomy
Psalms, Proverbs

**PART 9**
*The Final Letters*
Beyond the Book of Acts

1 Peter (AD 63)
Hebrews (AD 64–68)
2 Peter (AD 66)
Jude (AD 70–80)
1,2,3 John (AD 90)
Revelation (AD 90s)

**PART 2**
*The Teachings of Jesus*
The Four Gospels

Matthew (AD 60s)
Mark (AD 50s)
Luke (AD 60)
John (AD 85–90)

**PART 5**
*The Second Missionary Journey*
Acts 15:36–18:22

1, 2 Thessalonians (AD 51)
1 Corinthians (AD 56)
2 Corinthians (AD 57)

**PART 8**
*The Pastoral Letters*

1 Timothy (AD 63)
Titus (AD 65)
2 Timothy (AD 66)

**PART 1**
*The Church in Jerusalem*
Acts 1:1–7:60

The Apostles' Teaching

**PART 4**
*The First Missionary Journey*
Acts 13:1–14:28

James (AD 45–50)
Galatians (AD 49–55)

**PART 7**
*The Prison Epistles*
Acts 27:1–28:15

Ephesians (AD 61)
Colossians (AD 61)
Philippians (AD 61)
Philemon (AD 61)

A Research Paradigm (For studying the subject of material possessions as described in the biblical story.)

# PART 7
## PRINCIPLES FROM THE PRISON EPISTLES

Regardless of numerous warnings that trouble lay ahead, Paul was determined to return to Jerusalem following his third missionary journey. When he arrived, he was almost killed in the very city in which he had approved of Stephen's death. In God's providence, Paul's life was spared, and he was transported to Caesarea for trial. He remained incarcerated there for two years.

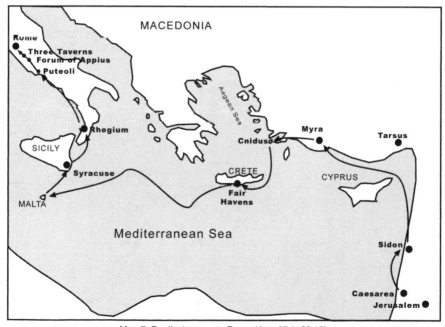

Map 7: Paul's Journey to Rome (Acts 27:1–28:15)

Knowing he had been falsely accused by the Jews and was being held in prison illegally, he eventually appealed to Caesar in Rome. When Paul arrived in the Imperial City and was placed under Roman guard, he was allowed to stay in his own rented quarters.

This two-year period in Paul's life generated some very rich New Testament literature. He penned his four prison epistles—Ephesians, Colossians, Philippians, and Philemon. These letters provide us with additional insights that expand our understanding about the way God wants Christians to view and use their material possessions.[1]

Chapter 20

# The Twin Epistles:
# Ephesians and Colossians

Though written to different churches, the content of Ephesians and Colossians is is often very similar—in fact, almost identical. This is particularly true with Paul's instructions regarding relationships: husbands and wives, parents and children, and servants and masters. Consequently, these letters are often considered twin epistles.

## Ephesians: A Circular Letter

Apparently Paul's letter to the Ephesians was composed to be a circular that would be read in the other churches in Asia.[1] Though most of what Paul wrote dealt with our position in Jesus Christ and how we should live in light of this calling, he made one very powerful statement regarding material possessions.

## BIBLICAL BASIS

*He who has been stealing must steal no longer, but must work, doing something useful with his own hands, that he may have something to share with those in need.* —Ephesians 4:28

Stealing was a common practice in the Roman Empire, and it wasn't unusual for it to carry over into the lives of those who professed Christ. As in other areas of morality and ethics, it took time for these people to know what God expected and to respond obediently to his will.

When exhorting the believers not to steal, Paul didn't stop with a "thou shalt not." He went on to instruct them to actually work harder in order to have money left over so they could share with others (Ephesians 4:28). What an incredible testimony it must have been to others when they saw these people reverse their behavior so dramatically. Rather than being unethical *takers*, they became Christlike *givers*.

## *Supra*cultural Principle 74

### HONESTY AND GENEROSITY

*Work hard to make an honest living, not only to take care of your own needs but also to help others.*

It's no secret that many people in today's world do everything they can to get something for nothing. If they don't steal money outright from their employers, they steal time, which is a form of money. Paul said this should never happen among Christians. Rather, we should be diligent in what we do—not only to take care of our own needs but to help meet the needs of others.

How many Christians begin the day on the job with the objective of working hard to make money to give away? If this were our attitude, our work would definitely take on new meaning. A number of employers may even be overwhelmed with our productivity. Think also of the doors that this would open for a direct Christian witness. This is no doubt one thing Peter had in mind when he wrote, "Live such good lives among the pagans that, though they accuse you of doing wrong, they may see your good deeds and glorify God on the day he visits us" (1 Peter 2:12).

## Colossians: A Local Church Letter

Much of the content Paul wrote to the Ephesians—and the other churches in Asia—is also included in the letter he wrote to the Colossians, though more succinctly. But what he did elaborate on in this letter was what a Christian's work ethic should be.

# BIBLICAL BASIS

*Whatever you do, work at it with all your heart, as working for the Lord, not for men, since you know that you will receive an inheritance from the Lord as a reward. It is the Lord Christ you are serving.*
—Colossians 3:23–24

Paul did not condone slavery. But neither did he attack this social problem directly. If he had, he would have created serious problems for Christians in the Roman Empire. Yet what he taught eventually had the effect of eliminating slavery within the Christian community. As the body of Christ practiced Christlike love, it became clear that slavery was incompatible with biblical principles. In Colossians we see how Paul addressed what was a sensitive issue.

First, he exhorted slaves to obey their earthly masters: "Slaves, obey your earthly masters in everything; and do it, not only when their eye is on you and to win their favor, but with sincerity of heart and reverence for the Lord" (Colossians 3:22). In other words, they were not to be faithful to their masters simply to benefit themselves, just as we are not to serve the Lord only to benefit ourselves.

Then Paul went a step further. He actually reminded these slaves that in reality they were serving the Lord when they served their earthly masters (Colossians 3:24). Consequently, if they did their work as if they were "working for the Lord" and not men, they would receive their ultimate reward from the Lord himself.

## *Supracultural* Principle 75

### WORKING FOR THE LORD

*Work hard to serve your employer (whether Christian or non-Christian) as if you were actually serving the Lord Jesus Christ.*

Though the illustrations in God's Word frequently focus on slave/master interaction, what Paul and others taught applies to any kind of employee/employer relationship. When we faithfully serve those who employ us, God views our effort as *actually serving Jesus Christ*—no matter what our employer's spiritual status. This perspective alone could revolutionize the Christian work force. The sad thing is that many Christians *do* serve their employers as they serve Jesus Christ—halfheartedly. Paul made clear that this should never be.

## BIBLICAL BASIS

*Masters, provide your slaves with what is right and fair, because you know that you also have a Master in heaven.* —Colossians 4:1

Paul addressed masters as authoritatively as he addressed slaves. He commanded them to treat slaves as brothers and sisters in

Christ. In fact, he told the Galatians, "There is neither Jew nor Greek, *slave nor free*, male nor female, for you are all one in Christ Jesus" (Galatians 3:28).

Paul also exhorted masters to provide their slaves with what was "right and fair," which certainly would include proper provisions or wages. Since these *earthly* masters were now servants of their *heavenly* Master, they should be able to understand how a servant should be treated. Paul was telling them to treat their slaves as they themselves wanted to be treated by God.

## *Supra*cultural Principle 76

### EQUITABLE TREATMENT

*Treat employees fairly in every respect, including*
*fair and equitable financial remuneration.*

We've seen that Christian employees should work hard to serve their employers (both Christians and non-Christians), as if they're actually serving the Lord (Colossians 3:23–24). Conversely, Christian employers should always treat their employees fairly—just the way they want God to treat them.

This fairness should be equally applied to both Christians and non-Christians. There should be no prejudice. Furthermore, Christian leaders should do everything they possibly can to encourage their employees. This includes paying a living wage. And when employees work hard and faithfully to increase profits, employers should do whatever they can to share those profits equitably with those who made them possible.

## Chapter 21
# Philippians: An Intimate Epistle

In the epistle to the Philippians, Paul used the personal pronoun *I* at least one hundred times. It's an intimate letter. Paul felt close to these believers for a number of reasons, but one was predominant: they had cared for his needs on a continuing basis. Their acts of love and generosity were the subject of his opening lines in the letter.

## BIBLICAL BASIS

*I thank my God every time I remember you. In all my prayers for all of you, I always pray with joy because of your partnership in the gospel from the first day until now.* —Philippians 1:3–5

When Paul and his missionary team arrived in Philippi, Lydia, a purveyor of purple garments and a proselyte to Judaism, responded first to the gospel. Then her whole household became Christians (Acts 16:13–15). It had to be an emotional moment for Paul. But perhaps the most memorable event in his relationship with Lydia was when she insisted that he and his fellow missionaries (Silas, Timothy, and Luke) stay in her home—using it as a base of operation for their ministry (Acts 16:15). It's also likely that her home became the first permanent meeting place for the new believers in Philippi.

Paul remembered her generosity and was probably referring to it when he wrote that he prayed with joy because of their "partnership in the gospel from the first day" (Philippians 1:5). From the moment Lydia and her household believed in Christ, this group of believers began to fellowship together in her home (Acts 16:15).

But Paul reminded these Christians that their partnership in the gospel was "from the first day until *now*." The fellowship that began in Lydia's home in the early days of the Philippian church was an ongoing experience. Again and again, after Paul left Philippi to start new churches, these believers had sent gifts to meet his material needs (Philippians 4:15–16). And now, once again, they had sent a gift to him while he was in prison in Rome. Epaphroditus, perhaps an elder and pastor in the church at Philippi, had delivered the gift, almost losing his life in the process (Philippians 2:29–30). He then returned to Philippi bearing Paul's letter of deep joy and thanksgiving.

## *Supra*cultural Principle 77

### CAUSE FOR REJOICING

*Faithfully supporting God's servants in material ways*
*brings joy to the hearts of those who receive our gifts.*

Anyone in the ministry whose material needs are faithfully met by fellow Christians can identify with Paul's feeling. He joyfully thanked God every time he remembered these believers in Philippi. All of us who support others financially should give with this in mind. Not only do we cause God's heart to rejoice, but we also bring joy and happiness to those we support. This is why Paul closed his letter to the Philippians by saying, "I *rejoice greatly* in the Lord that at last you have renewed your concern for me" (Philippians 4:10).

## *Supra*cultural Principle 78

### JOYFUL PRAYING

*When you faithfully support God's servants in material ways, you make their prayers a joyful experience.*

Paul prayed with joy every time he remembered these believers, and what he remembered was their partnership in the gospel—from the first time he was welcomed into Lydia's home until the day he received their gift of money as he sat chained to a Roman guard.

Perhaps only Christian workers who receive financial support from those they minister to can fully appreciate this principle. But it's true. As one who has been financially supported in Christian ministry for many years, I'm well aware of how faithful givers have brought joy to my prayer life. This is not only because of the way my own needs have been met but because of the way Christians have helped me meet the economic needs of others. Anyone who receives a paycheck should be able to identify at least somewhat with the joy of receiving the means of your support. Unfortunately, we too often take this for granted and forget to thank God for his daily provision.

## BIBLICAL BASIS

*Welcome him in the Lord with great joy, and honor men like him, because he almost died for the work of Christ, risking his life to make up for the help you could not give me.* —Philippians 2:29–30

When Epaphroditus arrived in Rome, he delivered the Philippians' gift of money to Paul. But when he did, he found a man who needed more than money. Paul needed encouragement and continual economic assistance. Rather than return to Philippi immediately, Epaphroditus decided to stay by his friend's side. He felt such a keen sense of responsibility to Paul that he nearly died fulfilling that duty. We don't know exactly what Epaphroditus did that endangered his life, but there are several clues.

First, it was probably a physical illness, for Epaphroditus "was ill, and almost died" (Philippians 2:27). Though the Greek word for *ill* could refer to either psychological or physical illness, few die from psychological problems, unless the stress is so great that it results in a heart attack or some other physical ailment.

A second clue is that whatever caused Epaphroditus's problem, it involved his efforts to make up for the help the Philippians couldn't give Paul (Philippians 2:30). He may have worked so hard to make additional money that he overexerted his body and mind, leading to some kind of deterioration. Whatever happened, Epaphroditus demonstrated unusual commitment.

In Paul's final words about Epaphroditus, he made clear that this man should be given due recognition for his sacrificial service: "Welcome him in the Lord with great joy, and honor men like him" (Philippians 2:29). It almost seems Paul was afraid the Philippians might not understand why Epaphroditus was gone so long. Or conversely, Paul may have been concerned that they might question his commitment for returning to Philippi because of homesickness (Philippians 2:26). The latter concern is more likely, since Paul clarified that it was his idea for Epaphroditus to return, and he wanted him to be welcomed joyfully and with full awareness of this man's sacrificial service for Jesus Christ.

## *Supra*cultural Principle 79

### HONORING FAITHFUL SERVANTS

*Honor Christians who make special sacrifices to help
meet the material needs of God's servants.*

This principle is similar to the one that emerges from the way the apostles showed their appreciation to Barnabas when he demonstrated unusual generosity in the Jerusalem church (Acts 4:36–37). They evidently changed his name to conform to his generous spirit. There could be no greater honor, for a name that means "son of encouragement" would be a constant reminder to others of the way he reflected the unselfishness of Jesus Christ.

If Barnabas represents Christian leaders in general, Epaphroditus represents spiritual leaders in the local church. He went beyond the call of duty, sacrificing his own needs and desires to help Paul in his time of need, and he did it for those Christians who comprised the church he served.

Many pastors devote most of their lives to helping others, at times neglecting their own families to minister to the larger family of God. They often serve long hours. They're always on call. Their lives are not their own, and they have little privacy. Ministers often work seven days a week, and in many instances are not paid commensurate with their education, experience, and dedication when compared with many of their fellow Christians in the business world. And the majority of pastors I rub shoulders with do all of this without complaining or feeling sorry for themselves. They have voluntarily chosen to be servants of Jesus Christ and others.

And yet these leaders often are the last to be shown appreciation and honor. They are frequently taken for granted. Unfortunately, they're even misunderstood, misinterpreted, and criticized when they try to take some time off. And if pastors dare ask for a raise in salary, they're accused of being materialistic and self-serving. Sadly, Christians are too quick to point to those few spiritual leaders who have abused their sacred role and taken advantage of others as justification for this response. Against the backdrop of a few unfaithful shepherds, they judge their own pastors.

There are exceptions, of course. Some churches practice well the principle of honoring those who serve. But often it is woefully neglected. In these cases, the church should take a careful look at what Paul said about Epaphroditus and how the Philippians were to honor his sacrificial efforts.

I would like to take this opportunity to honor the elders I've worked with for years who've been responsible for determining salaries and other material benefits. They've always been quick to make sure my needs have been met along with those of other staff pastors and support teams in our church. What a blessing this has been for our whole staff. In fact, as I pen these words, our elders are once again involved in a salary review based on what it takes to make an adequate living in our community. As we've seen in this study, this process is a biblical responsibility.

# BIBLICAL BASIS

*I rejoice greatly in the Lord that at last you have renewed your concern for me. Indeed, you have been concerned, but you had no opportunity to show it. I am not saying this because I am in need, for I have learned to be content whatever the circumstances.* —Philippians 4:10–11

Paul seldom talked about his own needs, but when he had one, he admitted it. There was no subtle pride in his personality. He lived within his means, but when he lacked, he was not too proud to accept help.

As he wrote to the Philippians, thanking them for their gifts, his words reflected this humility. He was rejoicing that they had once more helped him in a time of need. He had missed their help for a period of time, but he quickly and sensitively communicated that he knew they had never stopped being concerned. Rather, he said, "You had no opportunity to show it."

We can only speculate as to why the Philippians had temporarily stopped supporting Paul materially. Perhaps they didn't know about his needs in Rome. Maybe they were so poverty stricken themselves that they couldn't help. Whatever the reason, Paul wanted them to know he understood but was excited about their renewed help.

After letting the Philippians know how happy he was about the gift they had sent, Paul hurried to tell them he was not playing on their sympathy. Paul was very concerned that his motives never be misinterpreted. On some occasions, as we saw earlier, he actually refused what was coming to him as an apostle of Christ to avoid being a stumbling block to non-Christians or to new believers (1 Corinthians 9:1–18; 1 Thessalonians 2:9).

## *Supracultural* Principle 80

### OPENNESS WITHOUT MANIPULATION

*Be open and honest about your material needs, but*
*avoid any form of dishonesty or manipulation.*

Some people, including some Christians, work at giving the impression they're always in need. Those who make their living doing religious work can also be tempted to take advantage of members of Christ's body. This should never be. Unfortunately, some believers do engage in dishonesty or manipulation, which makes it difficult for others to overcome the resulting attitudes of distrust and reluctance to help. Again Paul was a marvelous example. May God give us more Christians with such integrity.

## BIBLICAL BASIS

*I know what it is to be in need, and I know what it is to have plenty. I have learned the secret of being content in any and every situation, whether well fed or hungry, whether living in plenty or in want.*
—Philippians 4:12

Paul had an unusual capacity to adapt to various situations and circumstances and still reflect contentment (2 Corinthians 11:23–12:10). The situations he wrote about in his letter involved his material needs—being well fed or hungry, and living in plenty or in want.

## *Supra*cultural Principle 81

### OVERALL CONTENTMENT

*Learn to be content in the difficult times,*
*as well as in the prosperous times.*

It's true that God has promised to meet our needs. But this doesn't mean we'll always have everything we need to make life *comfortable*. It's one thing to be happy and content when we have food on the table, clothes on our backs, shelter over our heads, and some money in the bank. But what if all these things were missing? How content would we be? How would we adapt? Paul could say, "I have learned to be content *whatever* the circumstances" (Philippians 4:11).

## BIBLICAL BASIS

*As you Philippians know, in the early days of your acquaintance with the gospel, when I set out from Macedonia, not one church shared with me in the matter of giving and receiving, except you only; for even when I was in Thessalonica, you sent me aid again and again when I was in need. Not that I am looking for a gift, but I am looking for what may be credited to your account. —Philippians 4:15–17*

Paul was a great believer in maintaining a ministry of encouragement. As he concluded this letter to the Philippians, he commended them for their *exceptional commitment* as compared with other churches, for the *abundant gifts* they had sent him, and for their *sacrificial spirit*—their willingness to give even when their own material needs were not being met.

Paul used an analogy—"credited to your account"—to communicate how he felt about the gifts the Philippians had sent him (Philippians 4:17). These key words were also used by people in the lending institutions of Paul's day. R. P. Martin explains: "What the Philippians gave as their *gift* was like an investment which would repay rich dividends in the service of the kingdom, as accumulating interest (*karpos*) stands to the credit (*logos*) of the depositor. At the last day, such generous and unstinted service which expressed itself in practical monetary support would not go unrecognized or unrewarded."[1]

## *Supra*cultural Principle 82

### ETERNAL TREASURES

*Christian leaders who make their living in the ministry should serve Jesus Christ with the view that they're storing up treasures in heaven for those who support them financially.*

Those who support Christian leaders in the ministry are accumulating special rewards in heaven based on the fruit that results. But the lesson we learn from Paul in his letter to the Philippians is that those who are supported by others should serve the Lord with this in mind. Part of our motivation should be to accumulate eternal rewards for our supporters. Paul exemplified this principle: he was more excited about what was being credited to the Philippians' account in heaven than he was about the gift he had received and how this would enhance his own eternal reward (Philippians 4:17).

This truth has given me a new perspective. As I do my work for God, I am not only serving the Lord, but I am serving those who support me. It's exciting to know that whatever spiritual results come from my earthly ministry will be shared in eternity with those who have made my efforts possible.

## BIBLICAL BASIS

*I have received full payment and even more; I am amply supplied, now that I have received from Epaphroditus the gifts you sent. They are a fragrant offering, an acceptable sacrifice, pleasing to God. And my God will meet all your needs according to his glorious riches in Christ Jesus.*
—Philippians 4:18–19

Paul made a similar statement to the Corinthians: "God is able to make all grace abound to you, so that in all things at all times, having all that you need, you will abound in every good work" (2 Corinthians 9:8). As Christians are faithful in their giving, God will meet their needs.

When interpreting this text in Paul's letter to the Corinthians, our committee looked at how God meets the *personal* needs of *every* Christian when each is faithful. However, there's a broader meaning, both in God's promise to the Corinthians and in the restatement of that promise to the Philippians. He also promises to take care of *groups* of Christians when they are faithful as a body of believers.

## *Supra*cultural Principle 83

### CORPORATE PROMISES

*God's promise to meet needs applies to the church as well as to individual believers in that church.*

As Christians who live in the Western world, we're so used to thinking in terms of individualism that we lose sight of the corporate nature of Christianity. Consequently, we tend to personalize all promises in the Bible and fail to realize that many promises are *collective* in nature. This is true in the area of giving. When Paul wrote to the Philippians, thanking them for their generous gifts, he said, "My God will meet all your needs according to his glorious riches in Christ Jesus" (Philippians 4:19). He was confident that not only would God meet the needs of the individual members of the church in Philippi, but he would also meet their needs as a corporate body. And in meeting their needs as a corporate body, he would also be meeting personal needs.

To be more specific, when a church is faithful in giving, God may choose to bless certain individuals in the church who, in turn, can help others in the church who are giving more sacrificially. In this sense, Paul's statement to the Corinthians can apply to Christians within specific local churches as well as to churches helping other churches: "Our desire is not that others might be relieved while you are hard pressed, but that there might be equality" (2 Corinthians 8:13).

## Chapter 22
# A Personal Letter to Philemon

Philemon was a wealthy Christian businessman who lived in Colosse and who had become a believer as a result of Paul's missionary efforts (Philemon 19). Since the apostle evidently did not have a direct ministry of evangelism in Colosse, Philemon may have become a Christian on one of his business trips to Ephesus, where he probably heard Paul teach in the lecture hall of Tyrannus (Acts 19:9).

Paul identified Philemon in his personal letter as a "dear friend and fellow worker" (Philemon 2). Since they evidently had not traveled together in evangelistic work, Philemon may have supported Paul financially and, like the believers in Philippi, became a fellow worker by developing a partnership in the gospel (Philippians 1:5; 4:15–16). Philemon's economic status is obvious from several factors in this brief but enlightening letter.

First, the church in Colosse met in his home (Philemon 2). We can't reconstruct the exact size of his dwelling, but structures have been discovered in the New Testament world that could comfortably seat up to five hundred people in the garden room alone. These homes were built not to house four or five people, as in our culture today, but to provide living quarters for an extended family—including married children and servants. Philemon's home seems to fit this picture.

Second, Philemon was a man given to hospitality. Paul wrote, "Your love has given me great joy and encouragement, because you, brother, have refreshed the hearts of the saints" (verse 7). Paul was probably referring to the way Philemon opened his home to his fellow believers in Colosse and to traveling evangelists and teachers. Evidently he had, on occasion, made this provision for Paul. Whatever the facts, Paul felt free to ask Philemon for a place to stay (Philemon 22).

A third factor points to Philemon's wealth: only well-to-do people in the New Testament world had servants. A young man named Onesimus, a major subject in this letter, was one of those servants. Evidently, when Philemon became a Christian, he took Paul's instructions seriously to treat his slaves as fellow believers—as brothers and sisters in Jesus Christ (Ephesians 6:5–9; Colossians 4:1). But Onesimus was initially a rebellious and irresponsible young man and did not respond to the gospel of Christ. He took advantage of his new freedom and new relationship with his master and escaped, perhaps stealing certain items.

# BIBLICAL BASIS

*If he has done you any wrong or owes you anything, charge it to me.*
—Philemon 18

In the providence of God, Onesimus ended up in Rome and came in contact with Paul while he was in prison. The apostle led him to a personal relationship with Jesus Christ and taught him the Word of God. Onesimus responded to Paul's loving exhortations, and a deep friendship developed between this old servant of Christ and the young slave.

Onesimus became a great source of encouragement to Paul. Though the apostle wanted Onesimus to stay with him in Rome, he reminded his friend of his responsibility to his real master. Consequently, Paul wrote this letter to Philemon in order to rebuild a relationship between Onesimus and his former master: "I appeal to you for my son Onesimus, who became my son while I was in chains. Formerly he was useless to you, but now he has become useful both to you and to me" (Philemon 10–11).

Philemon's attempt to do God's will in his relationship with his slaves points to another supracultural principle.

## *Supra*cultural Principle 84

### RISKS AND VULNERABILITY

*Putting God first in our lives may open the
door for people to take advantage of us.*

If Christians are given to hospitality as God says we should be, there will always be people who will abuse our generosity. This shouldn't surprise us. Obeying Christ always involves risk. That doesn't mean we should *allow* people to take advantage of us. But some people will, no matter how hard we try to avoid it.

Being a follower of Christ at times means suffering with him— including the way people took what they could get from Jesus and then walked away. This is what happened when he fed the multitudes (John 6:1–15). The people were initially elated and followed Jesus because their needs were met (John 6:26). But when he tested their true motives, "many of his disciples turned back and no longer followed him" (John 6:66). Yet we must never allow this kind of fickleness and manipulation to keep us from loving people and using our material possessions to help others. God wants us to use discretion but always to be generous.

# BIBLICAL BASIS

*I did not want to do anything without your consent, so that any favor you do will be spontaneous and not forced. . . . If he has done you any wrong or owes you anything, charge it to me. I, Paul, am writing this with my own hand. I will pay it back—not to mention that you owe me your very self.* —Philemon 14, 18–19

Onesimus had wronged Philemon and may have owed him repayment of stolen money or goods. Consequently, Paul informed his friend that he would pay it back for Onesimus. But in the same breath, he reminded Philemon that he owed his very conversion to their previous interaction about the gospel of Christ. In fact, the apostle implied that Onesimus's debt to Philemon should be more than canceled in view of what Philemon owed Paul for his new life in Christ.

Though this may look like manipulation, it was Paul's gentle but straightforward way of being honest. Philemon did owe Paul a debt he could never repay with material possessions.

What Paul wrote also reflected the deep friendship and love that existed between him and Philemon. Perhaps his friend even recognized in Paul's words a bit of tongue-in-cheek communication. Whatever we read between the lines, Paul's message was clear. On the one hand, he sincerely offered to pay Philemon what Onesimus owed. On the other hand, he reminded

Philemon that he owed Paul—as his friend and mentor—a huge debt as well.

## *Supra*cultural Principle 85

### BALANCED COMMUNICATION

*Christian leaders should use methods of communication about giving that create both a sense of obligation and a spirit of spontaneity and freedom.*

Paul achieved this unique balance on other occasions as well. He let the believers in Corinth know that he knew how eager they were to help the poor Christians in Jerusalem. He even told them he didn't feel it was necessary to write to them about it; but just in case they didn't understand, he did write. In addition, he sent the brothers in order that his boasting about them would not prove untrue. He wanted the Corinthians to be ready with their gift so he wouldn't be embarrassed—and neither would they.

Paul used the same basic approach with his good friend Philemon, who, unlike the Corinthians, was a mature Christian. All of us, then, need a certain amount of healthy pressure to be faithful and obedient to God. True, we may feel some guilt. But when we're outside of God's will, we *should* feel guilt. If we don't, we may already have allowed our consciences to become seared regarding the Word of God and the Holy Spirit (1 Timothy 4:2).

Paul's communication model reflects balance. He illustrated with his own life that we should not manipulate people. But at the same time, he didn't hesitate to let others know they had an obligation to be generous and benevolent, even if it did create a little discomfort.

# BIBLICAL BASIS

*I do wish, brother, that I may have some benefit from you in the Lord; refresh my heart in Christ. Confident of your obedience, I write to you, knowing that you will do even more than I ask. And one thing more: Prepare a guest room for me, because I hope to be restored to you in answer to your prayers.* —Philemon 20–22

Here Paul illustrated another important principle in his communication with people about the way they should use their material possessions. He expected the best, particularly from those he knew truly loved Jesus Christ. He was confident that his friend would respond positively. In fact, he told Philemon that he knew he would do even more than was asked.

What is Paul hinting at? Some believe he was suggesting that Philemon give Onesimus his complete freedom. As we mentioned earlier, Paul did not condone slavery, but he never attacked it head on. He approached this social problem by telling masters to love their slaves as Christ loved them and by instructing slaves to serve their masters as if they were serving Christ. Legalities don't make much difference if people are practicing principles of love. Philemon and Onesimus were brothers in Christ and in this sense equals, both experiencing freedom in Christian fellowship. If I had to speculate on what took place, I would guess that Philemon did give Onesimus his freedom.

Paul's final request in verse 22 indicates again the degree of friendship that existed between these men. The apostle seldom asked favors for himself. But in this instance, he didn't hesitate to ask Philemon to prepare a guest room for him. He knew his request would not be misinterpreted. Paul felt secure in this relationship, for if he sensed he had offended Philemon with his previous comments, he certainly would have hesitated to impose on him for lodging.

## *Supra*cultural Principle 86

### SHARING FINANCIAL NEEDS

*Don't hesitate to ask for help when there's
a need, both for others and for yourself.*

In some respects Paul was acting out of character when he asked Philemon for personal help. On the other hand, he showed that Christian leaders do have a right to make their ministry needs known.

In today's world, Christians tend to two extremes. Some have no qualms about asking for help from people to whom they've never ministered and with whom they have no personal relationship. Others are so timid and reserved that they never make their needs known to anyone. Both approaches are aberrations from scriptural principles. Paul consistently looked to those he had ministered to in a special way for his financial support. Though he was cautious and sensitive, he was also specific. Let us learn to follow his example of godly balance.

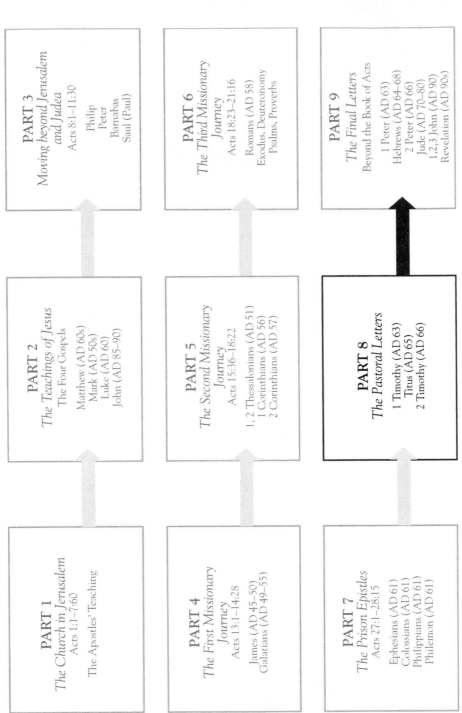

**PART 1**
*The Church in Jerusalem*
Acts 1:1–7:60

The Apostles' Teaching

**PART 2**
*The Teachings of Jesus*
The Four Gospels

Matthew (AD 60s)
Mark (AD 50s)
Luke (AD 60)
John (AD 85–90)

**PART 3**
*Moving beyond Jerusalem and Judea*
Acts 8:1–11:30

Philip
Peter
Barnabas
Saul (Paul)

**PART 4**
*The First Missionary Journey*
Acts 13:1–14:28

James (AD 45–50)
Galatians (AD 49–55)

**PART 5**
*The Second Missionary Journey*
Acts 15:36–18:22

1, 2 Thessalonians (AD 51)
1 Corinthians (AD 56)
2 Corinthians (AD 57)

**PART 6**
*The Third Missionary Journey*
Acts 18:23–21:16

Romans (AD 58)
Exodus, Deuteronomy
Psalms, Proverbs

**PART 7**
*The Prison Epistles*
Acts 27:1–28:15

Ephesians (AD 61)
Colossians (AD 61)
Philippians (AD 61)
Philemon (AD 61)

**PART 8**
*The Pastoral Letters*

1 Timothy (AD 63)
Titus (AD 65)
2 Timothy (AD 66)

**PART 9**
*The Final Letters*
Beyond the Book of Acts

1 Peter (AD 63)
Hebrews (AD 64–68)
2 Peter (AD 66)
Jude (AD 70–80)
1,2,3 John (AD 90)
Revelation (AD 90s)

A Research Paradigm (For studying the subject of material possessions as described in the biblical story.)

# PART 8
## PRINCIPLES FROM THE PASTORAL LETTERS

After his two-year imprisonment in Rome, Paul was released and evidently completed a fourth missionary journey. During this time, he wrote the Pastoral Epistles to Timothy and Titus. As you read these letters, you can see some unique changes in Paul's perspective. He was still a highly motivated man, but he now knew he might face death through martyrdom rather than old age. He was well aware of Nero's unpredictable nature. Earlier, Paul had hoped to be alive when Christ returned, but even this perspective had changed. When he wrote 2 Timothy, he expected to die rather than to be among those who heard the "trumpet call of God" (1 Thessalonians 4:16) when he was still alive.

Knowing his time might be short, he began to look more and more to the younger men who had served with him to continue the ministry they had begun together. This is one of Paul's purposes in writing the Pastoral Epistles: two letters to Timothy, and one to Titus. And as he approached this final stage in his life, still high on his list of concerns was how Christians use their material possessions.

## Chapter 23

# The First Letter to Timothy

After Paul was in prison in Rome for two years, he was released and apparently made a fourth missionary journey. He and Timothy traveled again into the province of Asia and visited Ephesus. Paul then traveled on into Macedonia, leaving Timothy behind to deal with a leadership crisis. Concerned that his young companion be able to follow through on the challenging task, Paul at some point penned a letter to him. As we'll see, the apostle was very concerned about materialism in the church in Ephesus and shared some instructions on how to avoid it.

## BIBLICAL BASIS

*The overseer must be above reproach, the husband of but one wife, temperate, self-controlled, respectable, hospitable.* —1 Timothy 3:2

All Christians should be given to hospitality (Romans 12:13; Hebrews 13:1–2; 1 Peter 4:8–9). However, in Paul's first letter to Timothy, as well as in his letter to Titus (1:6, 8), he recommends this quality especially in those who are to be appointed as spiritual leaders in the church. This was particularly important in the New Testament world because Christians had no choice but to meet in homes.

Eldership and hospitality, then, are corollary concepts. Selfishness and being a Christian leader are incompatible, both from a divine and a human perspective. Unfortunately, there were men in the early church who aspired to be spiritual leaders but wanted only the position, not the responsibility to serve others.

## *Supra*cultural Principle 87

### Being Hospitable

*Spiritual leaders should be generous Christians who are willing to use their material possessions to serve those they shepherd.*

This principle does not imply that spiritual leaders must be affluent. They must be willing, however, to share what they have—little or much—to minister to others in the church. The size of their homes is not the issue, nor is the amount of money they make or can give. What's important is the degree to which they're willing to sacrifice and share with others what is theirs.

## BIBLICAL BASIS

*The overseer must be above reproach, . . . not a lover of money. . . . Deacons, likewise, are to be men worthy of respect, . . . not pursuing dishonest gain.* —1 Timothy 3:2–3, 8

The Bible doesn't teach a Christian should be free from money, but rather, free from the *love* of money. It's a human tendency to put a great value on material possessions. When Paul wrote to Timothy and Titus (Titus 1:7), he was concerned that spiritual leaders not succumb to this temptation. The apostle Peter showed the same concern when he exhorted the elders in various churches to not be "greedy for money, but eager to serve" (1 Peter 5:2).

## Supracultural Principle 88

### BEING NONMATERIALISTIC

*Christians who occupy leadership roles
in the church should be free from
materialistic attitudes and actions.*

As the church grew and expanded throughout the New Testament world, so did the number of people who wanted to get into leadership roles in the church for the wrong reasons. Though selfish motivation is an age-old problem (as we noted with Simon the sorcerer in Samaria), more and more people wanted to cash in on this opportunity for prestige. They were prominent personalities who were "teaching things they ought not to teach—and that for the sake of dishonest gain" (Titus 1:11).

As Paul faced the closing days of his ministry, he wanted to make sure only those individuals who were seeking first God's kingdom and his righteousness were appointed to be leaders in the church.

We face the same issues today—probably even more so. With the advent of modern media (print, radio, television, video, and the Internet), Christian hucksters have come out of the woodwork. They're experts at taking advantage of caring but naive believers. And one of their points of strategy is what has come to be called prosperity theology. These teachers appeal to our God-given desire to obey God, and they mix this with our natural tendency to want to be blessed materially. Consequently, they promote a self-centered approach to giving that is nothing short of heresy.

Unfortunately, this teaching has been accepted among many of God's people—and in the process has padded the pockets of a number of so-called spiritual leaders. Tragically, in some cases it has left sincere Christians destitute. Many who succumb to this false teaching are poor people who believe that if they give the little they have, it will be multiplied.

# BIBLICAL BASIS

*Give proper recognition to those widows who are really in need.*
—1 Timothy 5:3

This directive introduces us to one of the lengthiest sections in the New Testament having to do with material possessions. Though Paul was addressing a unique cultural situation in the Roman Empire, what he wrote yields some relevant and helpful guidelines for Christians in every culture of the world.

## The Problem

When Jews became Christians, they were automatically cut off from the welfare system in Israel. Since there was no official provision in the Roman Empire for these people, caring for needy Christians became the sole responsibility of local churches. As Christianity spread and grew in numbers, more and more people emerged who had special needs.

Predictably, more and more people also began taking advantage of the generous spirit that existed among believers. In actuality, it was a two-sided problem. Not only did older people tend to look to the church to meet their needs, but family members who had older parents and relatives in need also began to look to the church rather than accepting their own responsibility to care for these people.

## *The Solution*

Paul addressed the issue because it was becoming a serious problem in Ephesus. He was concerned for those widows who were not having their needs met. On the other hand, only those who were really in need should receive consistent support.

The apostle made it clear that children and grandchildren of widows had the primary responsibility to take care of them (1 Timothy 5:4). He then spelled out how serious it was for any family member to neglect a relative in need: "If anyone does not provide for his relatives, and especially for his immediate family, he has denied the faith and is worse than an unbeliever" (1 Timothy 5:8).

Next Paul set up some guidelines regarding widows asking to be consistently supported by the church. If no family member was available to take care of them, of course the church should consider supporting them. However, Paul declared that no widow should qualify for financial support unless she met these requirements:

- She was more than sixty.
- She had been faithful to her husband.
- She was well-known for her good deeds, such as bringing up children, showing hospitality, washing the feet of the saints, helping those in trouble, and devoting herself to all kinds of good works (1 Timothy 5:9–10).

Paul wasn't proposing a system that would neglect people with true needs. He was simply addressing the issue that anytime Christians practice principles of generosity, some will try to take advantage of that generosity. In the New Testament world, those tempted to do so included young widows. But it wasn't just the young widows themselves; family members were choosing to burden the church with the responsibility of caring for these young women rather than facing the financial responsibility themselves.

## *Supra*cultural Principle 89

### CHOOSING WHOM TO HELP

*The selection of people who receive
consistent help from the church should
be based on specific scriptural guidelines.*

The church should certainly be a caring community of believers. People in need should be helped. However, just as the church in the first-century world needed guidelines, so the twenty-first–century church must use wisdom as well.

### *Biblical Guidelines for Today*

Though the cultural dynamics are different in many societies in today's world, the guidelines outlined by Paul still apply when considering financial support for needy people—particularly on a consistent basis.

First, the church should make sure there are no other available sources of support—including assistance from governmental agencies.

Second, people in need should look first to their own families for help.

The third guideline relates to the qualifications of those who want to receive consistent financial support from the church:

- The person should be a *true believer*. As we saw in Paul's letter to the Galatians, this in no way means that the church should not help unbelievers (Galatians 6:10). But consistent and long-term support should be reserved for born-again Christians.
- The applicant should be an *older believer*.
- He or she should be a *mature believer* with a good reputation.

Fortunately, the American church doesn't face these problems as often as churches in other cultures. Our more affluent society and its welfare systems help reduce the need. Yet there are still people who are truly in need.

Some people, however, will try to take advantage of the church—particularly when we function according to New Testament principles. Wherever there's a positive, Satan will try to turn it into a negative. But this in no way excuses us for neglecting our God-given responsibility to help those truly in need. This is why we must understand and apply these biblical, supracultural principles.

At Fellowship Bible Church North, we take seriously the injunctions in Scripture to be generous and to help people who need assistance. We have set up a Love Fund for this purpose, supplied monetarily from special Christmas Eve services at the end of the year. We also seek to follow the scriptural guidelines for being accountable with the monies entrusted to us.

Consequently, we have set up the following guidelines:

1. The purpose of the Love Fund is primarily to meet unusual, short-term financial needs within our church body. Examples of these needs could include, but need not be limited to, medical expenses, rent, food, and short-term living expenses.

2. We encourage all who request financial help from the church to consider the following potential sources of funds, in this order, before disbursements from the Love Fund are considered:
   a. personal assets
   b. family
   c. friends
   d. commercial credit
   e. government assistance

3. Recommendations for disbursements are normally made by small-group leaders or staff pastors who are familiar with all the circumstances pertinent to the situation.

4. Disbursements from the Love Fund normally are approved by two staff pastors and two nonstaff elders, either in person or by telephone.

In addition, we encourage people to give back to the Love Fund if and when they're able, to help someone else in need as they have been.

## BIBLICAL BASIS

*The elders who direct the affairs of the church well are worthy of double honor, especially those whose work is preaching, and teaching.* —1 Timothy 5:17

Elders who do an exceptional job leading the church "are worthy of double honor." The Greek word *tim* (translated "honor") refers to remuneration or honoraria. The word for "double" indicates generous or ample financial support. The amount given should be contingent both on the time demands and on how well a spiritual leader functions. Again, Paul's focus was on those who devote a great deal of time to preaching and teaching the Word of God, which correlates with the directive in his letter to the Galatians (Galatians 6:6).

Paul was bringing balance to his earlier statements regarding the qualifications for elders. He had warned Timothy not to appoint leaders in the church who love money (1 Timothy 3:3) or who were in any way dishonest (1 Timothy 3:8). He also had cautioned against supporting people who didn't measure up to very high standards (1 Timothy 5:3–16). To make sure the believers in Ephesus didn't overreact to these exhortations, Paul clarified that he didn't want faithful elders or pastors to be penalized financially because of his earlier statements.

## *Supra*cultural Principle 90

### ADEQUATE REMUNERATION

*Pastors and teachers who are hardworking, efficient, and productive in ministry should be rewarded financially.*

This principle indicates first and foremost that "the worker deserves his wages" (1 Timothy 5:18). But it also is a reminder that all of us need rewards and recognition. Interestingly, one of the most motivating rewards, even for Christian workers, is financial remuneration that reflects appreciation for a job well done. In this sense, the Scriptures themselves promote merit pay. As Paul said, "The hardworking farmer should be the first to receive a share of the crops" (2 Timothy 2:6).

When our elders at Fellowship Bible Church North appointed a task force to study the financial needs in our church—which also led to this biblical study—one of the group's recommendations was to review staff salaries. In order to make the study objective, we didn't share with this group any specific salary figures. We simply asked that they look carefully at academic preparation, experiential qualifications (including years of service), and job description. We also asked them to factor in what it cost to live reasonably in our community.

Based on their findings, the task force recommended salary ranges. In some instances their suggestions were much higher than the existing salary amounts. Our elders immediately began making adjustments. Needless to say, this was very encouraging—especially to our pastoral staff who, when their salaries were measured against the recommended amounts, were the most underpaid.

## BIBLICAL BASIS

*The love of money is a root of all kinds of evil. Some people, eager for money, have wandered from the faith and pierced themselves with many griefs.* —1 Timothy 6:10

Paul concluded his letter to Timothy with a series of warnings against the negative impact of materialism. Much of what he wrote echoes what Jesus taught and what James later wrote in his epistle.

Unfortunately, all of us—both Christians and non-Christians— are tempted to love material things. But we need not submit to this temptation. It's possible to maintain a proper balance. God has provided a way of escape (1 Corinthians 10:13) if we will only trust him to help us find it and then act on what we know to be his will.

The following teachings are clear cut and self-explanatory, especially in view of other scriptural exhortations and illustrations we've already considered with in this study:

> Godliness with contentment is great gain. For we brought nothing into the world, and we can take nothing out of it. But if we have food and clothing, we will be content with that. (1 Timothy 6:6–8)

> People who want to get rich fall into temptation and a trap and into many foolish and harmful desires that plunge men into ruin and destruction. (1 Timothy 6:9)

> Command those who are rich in this present world not to be arrogant nor to put their hope in wealth, which is so uncertain, but to put their hope in God, who richly provides us with everything for our enjoyment. (1 Timothy 6:17)

> Command them [the rich] to do good, to be rich in good deeds, and to be generous and willing to share. In this way they will lay up treasure for themselves as a firm foundation for the coming age, so that they may take hold of the life that is truly life. (1 Timothy 6:18–19)

## *Supra*cultural Principle 91
### A PROPER FOCUS

*Focus on godliness and contentment rather than on riches, which often bring discontentment.*

Paul wasn't saying that poor people are always content and wealthy people are always discontent. This would contradict scriptural teachings, not to mention observable reality. Scripture teaches that poverty brings with it a lot of difficulties (Proverbs 19:7; 14:20; 19:4).

Having but little of this world's goods can be a painful existence. Perhaps that's one reason there are so many exhortations in Scripture not to mistreat the poor. But many proverbs also warn about the problems that can come with wealth. In fact, there are far more exhortations of this nature than those that deal with the plight of the poor:

> A good name is more desirable than great riches; to be esteemed is better than silver or gold. (Proverbs 22:1)

> Riches do not endure forever, and a crown is not secure for all generations. (Proverbs 27:24)

> Cast but a glance at riches, and they are gone, for they will surely sprout wings and fly off to the sky like an eagle. (Proverbs 23:5)

The more we study God's Word, the more we understand that it teaches balance. Certainly this is the goal of Proverbs 30:8–9: "Give me neither poverty nor riches, but give me only my daily bread. Otherwise, I may have too much and disown you and say, 'Who is the LORD?' Or I may become poor and steal, and so dishonor the name of my God."

When we set our goals to become rich rather than to become godly, we're headed for serious trouble. Ultimately, we will not find contentment. And if our focus is on wealth, we won't be able to resist the temptations that invariably come our way; we'll eventually find ourselves in a trap, controlled by many "foolish and harmful desires that plunge men into ruin and destruction" (1 Timothy 6:9). It's in this context that Paul says, "The love of money is a root of all kinds of evil" (1 Timothy 6:10).

If, on the other hand, if we set our goals to be godly people—to seek first God's kingdom and his righteousness, everything else will come into focus. As Jesus said, "All these things will be given to you as well" (Matthew 6:33). If *God* brings wealth and prosperity, he will also enable us to handle the temptations that come with these blessings—provided we use what he gives us not to only meet our own basic needs but also to invest in his eternal kingdom.

## Chapter 24
# Paul's Final Correspondence

### The Letter to Titus

At some point on his post-prison journey, Paul again met up with Titus, a Gentile convert who had come to faith in Christ early in Paul's ministry. After reuniting, these two men boarded a ship and traveled to Crete. We're not told how long Paul and Titus ministered on this island, but it could not have been a lengthy period, because the time span between his first and second imprisonments in Rome was only about three years. But the Holy Spirit opened many hearts to the gospel in the major population centers of Crete.

At some point Paul traveled on alone, leaving Titus behind to "straighten out what was left unfinished and appoint elders in every town" (Titus 1:5). On the way to Nicopolis, he penned a follow-up letter. One of his primary concerns was that Titus appoint spiritual leaders who were godly models and who would counteract the influence of leaders whose motives were selfish and materialistic.

### BIBLICAL BASIS

*There are many rebellious people, mere talkers and deceivers, especially those of the circumcision group. They must be silenced, because*

*they are ruining whole households by teaching things they ought not to
teach—and that for the sake of dishonest gain.* —Titus 1:10–11

One of Paul's primary solutions to silence false teachers was to have
Titus appoint men who were opposite in terms of what they believed
and how they lived. Not only would a leader need to model
Christlikeness and nonmaterialistic motives, but he must also con-
front those troublesome individuals. "He must hold firmly to the
trustworthy message as it has been taught, so that he can encourage
others by sound doctrine and refute those who oppose it" (Titus 1:9).

## Supracultural Principle 92

### CHURCH DISCIPLINE

*Leaders who teach false doctrine and manipulate people
in order to pursue dishonest gain should be silenced.*

Why it is difficult to practice this principle? First, we don't have the
same revelatory insight and direct authority as the various apostolic
leaders. For example, when Peter confronted Simon the sorcerer in
Samaria about his personal-profit motives, he wasted no words in
condemning his materialistic goals: "May your money perish with
you, because you thought you could buy the gift of God with money!"
(Acts 8:20). And when Paul encountered Elymas the sorcerer on the
island of Cypress, he called him a "child of the devil and an enemy of
everything that is right" (Acts 13:10). Then with God's supernatural
power, he struck this man temporarily blind (Acts 13:11).

But there's a second reason it's difficult to practice church
discipline. Many leaders who are guilty of this kind of behavior
are outside our realm of responsibility and accountability. Even

some of these individuals who are leading local churches are difficult to control or to hold accountable, primarily because they're operating more like despots than servants of Jesus Christ and his people. They've developed around them a group of yes people who dare not question their authority.

The third reason it's difficult to practice this principle is that our legal system is so complex that even the government finds it difficult to prosecute or silence anyone. Consider, for example, the scandals surrounding televangelists.

So what can we do? Let me suggest five steps we can take to protect the church from ungodly leaders.

1. We must make sure our local churches have a system of checks and balances that make it virtually impossible for a leader to be dishonest. Furthermore, the primary leader in the church should initiate this kind of financial accountability.

2. If church leaders do not and will not make financial records available for inspection and proper audits, Christians should discontinue supporting that church with contributions or attendance. They should seek out a place of worship that practices biblical principles of accountability.

3. Believers should not support any Christian organization in which its leaders are violating the basic principles outlined in Scripture regarding material possessions. If all Christians took these measures, we would take giant steps in silencing leaders who are "ruining whole households by teaching things they ought not to teach—and that for the sake of dishonest gain" (Titus 1:11).

4. Christian leaders who have the authority to do so should not avoid confronting and exposing people who are violating the principles of God's Word. This must be done, however, in a biblical fashion, following the guidelines outlined in Scripture (see Matthew 18:15–17; Galatians 6:1; Titus 3:10–11).

5. Believers should pray that God will protect all Christian leaders from falling into Satan's trap. Furthermore, we should do all we can to support leaders who are committed to practicing the principles outlined in Scripture.

## The Second Letter to Timothy

At some point Paul was suddenly taken into custody and imprisoned again in Rome. Before he was sentenced to death, probably by Nero, he wrote his final letter to Timothy. This epistle contains the apostle's final words to the Christian world. Still believing that the Lord's return was imminent, he issued a strong warning.

## BIBLICAL BASIS

*There will be terrible times in the last days. People will be lovers of themselves, lovers of money . . . lovers of pleasure rather than lovers of God—having a form of godliness but denying its power. Have nothing to do with them.* —2 Timothy 3:1–2, 4–5

Paul made clear that Christians are to disassociate themselves from people who are self-centered, materialistic, and hedonistic. Understand, of course, that Paul was not teaching isolation from unsaved people. We can only carry out the Great Commission by being light and salt in this world. Rather, Paul was warning against participating with these people in their worldly behavior.

It's always difficult to keep our hearts and motives pure when we have close fellowship with people who are living sinful lives. So we must be on guard against fellowshiping with those who will pull us down to their level. In some instances, we should not even associate with those who have given themselves over to materialism and sensuality. If we do, we're in danger of becoming like them. This is a particular risk when developing close relationships with people who are materialistic. Many Christians have succumbed to temptation and have developed the same mind-set, in some cases without even realizing it.

## *Supracultural* Principle 93

### A PROPHETIC TREND

*Don't let the world's system cause you to love self, money, or pleasure more than God.*

When evaluating and applying Paul's exhortations in his final letter against the backdrop of our present culture, we can quickly establish two facts: First, we are closer than ever to the Second Coming of Christ. If the time was near when Paul wrote his second letter to Timothy, what can be said about two thousand years later? Second, the world in general reflects the trends outlined by Paul. This is certainly true in our American culture. Many people are "lovers of themselves, lovers of money," and "lovers of pleasure rather than lovers of God" (2 Timothy 3:2, 4). We're manifesting these characteristics more every day.

The challenge we all face as Christians is that we not allow ourselves to "love the world or anything in the world" (1 John 2:15). This is why Paul exhorted the Roman Christians to avoid allowing their lives to "conform any longer to the pattern of this world" (Romans 12:2).

There's only one solution to this problem. We must be continually "transformed by the renewing" of our minds. It is only then that we will "be able to test and approve what God's will is—his good, pleasing and perfect will" (Romans 12:2). This is foundational to everything we do—including the way we view and use our material possessions.

As the Day of Christ draws near, believers should intensify their efforts to practice biblical principles. We should give increased attention to being "strong in the Lord and in his mighty power" (Ephesians 6:10). We should take seriously Paul's exhortation to the Ephesians to "put on the full armor of God" so we can take our stand "against the devil's schemes" (Ephesians 6:11).

**PART 3**
*Moving beyond Jerusalem and Judea*
Acts 8:1–11:30

Philip
Peter
Barnabas
Saul (Paul)

**PART 2**
*The Teachings of Jesus*
The Four Gospels

Matthew (AD 60s)
Mark (AD 50s)
Luke (AD 60)
John (AD 85–90)

**PART 1**
*The Church in Jerusalem*
Acts 1:1–7:60

The Apostles' Teaching

**PART 6**
*The Third Missionary Journey*
Acts 18:23–21:16

Romans (AD 58)
Exodus, Deuteronomy
Psalms, Proverbs

**PART 5**
*The Second Missionary Journey*
Acts 15:36–18:22

1, 2 Thessalonians (AD 51)
1 Corinthians (AD 56)
2 Corinthians (AD 57)

**PART 4**
*The First Missionary Journey*
Acts 13:1–14:28

James (AD 45–50)
Galatians (AD 49–55)

**PART 9**
*The Final Letters*
Beyond the Book of Acts

1 Peter (AD 63)
Hebrews (AD 64–68)
2 Peter (AD 66)
Jude (AD 70–80)
1, 2, 3 John (AD 90)
Revelation (AD 90s)

**PART 8**
*The Pastoral Letters*

1 Timothy (AD 63)
Titus (AD 65)
2 Timothy (AD 66)

**PART 7**
*The Prison Epistles*
Acts 27:1–28:15

Ephesians (AD 61)
Colossians (AD 61)
Philippians (AD 61)
Philemon (AD 61)

A Research Paradigm (For studying the subject of material possessions as described in the biblical story.)

# PART 9
## THE FINAL LETTERS

Peter, John, Jude, and an unknown author wrote the remaining letters during the closing years of the New Testament era. Much of what these men wrote about material possessions reinforces what we've already noted in the biblical story. But they also addressed some new concerns, particularly as false apostles, prophets, and teachers exploited the true message of Jesus Christ.

Chapter 25
# The Last Letters

## Peter's First Letter

The apostle Peter wrote his first letter to encourage Christians facing persecution. These believers were primarily Jewish but also included Gentiles. He addressed his first letter, "To God's elect, strangers in the world, scattered throughout Pontus, Galatia, Cappadocia, Asia and Bithynia (1 Peter 1:1).

## BIBLICAL BASIS

*For a little while you may have to suffer grief in all kinds of trials. These [trials] have come so that your faith—of greater worth than gold, which perishes even though refined by five—may be proved genuine and may result in praise, glory, and honor when Jesus Christ is revealed. —1 Peter 1:6–7*

In the midst of this persecution, Peter encouraged these believers to focus on spiritual and eternal values, not on the things that were being taken away from them—in some instances, their earthly existence. Peter explained that one of God's primary purposes in allowing trials is to test a believer's faith (1 Peter 1:7). He then went on to outline some other lessons we can learn when we face difficult circumstances:

- We can understand more fully that our redemption is based upon the blood of Jesus Christ, not on "perishable things such as silver or gold" (1 Peter 1:18–19).
- We're able to perceive more clearly the enduring nature of God's Word and the eternal life it gives, as compared with the decaying material world—including our bodies (1 Peter 1:23–25).
- We can also appreciate—because of persecution—that our real citizenship is in heaven, not on earth (Philippians 3:20).
- We have the opportunity—as difficult as it may be—to be purified from the world's system and to stand out as Christlike examples (1 Peter 2:11–12).

Peter challenged the believers to not lose sight of their responsibility to care for each other and to share what they had (1 Peter 4:9), even though much of their world's goods were in jeopardy. This too is a lesson for all believers today.

Finally, Peter warned the spiritual shepherds to check their motives and not to succumb to the temptation to take advantage of their flocks materially (1 Peter 5:2). Unfortunately, some so-called Christian leaders today use economic crises to manipulate believers by playing on their sympathy. This is particularly tragic when they use untrue stories or inaccurate information to solicit money to pad their own pockets. I would hate to stand in their shoes when we all appear before the judgment seat of Christ.

## *Supracultural Principle 94*

### SPIRITUAL PURIFICATION

*Economic challenges can help us focus on the spiritual and eternal dimensions of life rather than on the material and temporal.*

Though it's generally God's will that Christians not suffer and that we be able to "live peaceful and quiet lives in all godliness and holiness" (1 Timothy 2:1–4), history demonstrates that periodic difficulties help us refocus our values from the things of this world to the things of heaven. When life is persistently free from difficulties and we're able to accumulate more of this world's goods, we tend toward a materialistic mind-set. If we're not careful, the more we get, the more we want. Like our pagan counterparts, we subtly begin to exchange "the truth of God for a lie" and to worship and serve "created things rather than the Creator" (Romans 1:25). When we do, we're conforming to the pattern of this world (Romans 12:2).

What does this say to us in America? Is it possible for Christians to refocus their priorities before God allows external pressure to force it to happen? As a pastor, I've observed Christians during economic ups and downs. Though many seem to become more protective of their money and even begin to withhold their first fruits when times are tough, I've also seen believers positively adjust their priorities. They become more attentive to the Word of God and make more intensive efforts to do his will.

Does this renewal last? Does it endure when our economic

situation improves? Unfortunately, many believers forget quickly—just as people have done for centuries. Our challenge is to always seek the kingdom of God first—during the good times and the bad.

## The Letter to the Hebrews

Hebrews was written by an unknown author to help Jewish Christians understand and appreciate their heritage, but also to establish their new identity in Jesus Christ. They were now a part of the church. Their focus was to be on a spiritual kingdom, not an earthly one.

At least three exhortations are included in this letter regarding how Christians are to view and use material possessions. We have looked at similar directives in previous epistles, but these add additional light and perspective.

## BIBLICAL BASIS

*Do not forget to entertain [that is, to show hospitality to] strangers, for by so doing some people have entertained angels without knowing it.*
—Hebrews 13:2

Showing hospitality is not a new concept in our study. Both Paul and Peter exhorted believers to this practice (to review, see Romans 12:13; 1 Timothy 3:2; Titus 1:8; 1 Peter 4:9). But the Hebrew Christians were encouraged to show hospitality to *strangers*—to believers they didn't know personally.

*Overcoming Legalistic Attitudes*

The need for this specific exhortation may be related to the fact that those receiving the letter, Hebrew Christians, were deeply influenced by a legalistic approach to caring for others. For example, some orthodox Jewish sects, such as the Essenes, actually "refused to eat with anyone whose carefulness in dietary, tithing, and purity rules was not proved by being a member of his own sect."[1] When these people became Christians, they often retained their legalism and refused to allow anyone to enter their homes unless they kept the same rules they did. Such people were considered strangers, and since the Jewish believers had no way of knowing how they conducted their lives, they refused to show them hospitality. This exhortation, then, would be a corrective to an overly cautious and community-centered approach to helping fellow Christians.

Not only were the believers to care for the needs of others involved in their own local churches, but they were to be willing to help all Christians, no matter where they lived. F. F. Bruce gives this helpful comment: "Christians traveling from one place to another on business would be especially appreciative of hospitality from fellow-Christians. Inns throughout the Roman Empire were places of doubtful repute, . . . and would provide very uncongenial company for Christians."[2]

### Entertaining God's Messengers

The author of Hebrews went on to say that "some people have entertained angels without knowing it" (Hebrews 13:2). This was probably a reference to Abraham's experience when he entertained three men near the great trees of Mamre. One of these men turned out to be the Lord himself, accompanied by two angelic beings (Genesis 18:1–19:1).

Though the reference to entertaining angels in Hebrews may

refer to actual angelic beings, it doesn't necessarily follow that the author is referring to "supernatural beings traveling incognito."[3] The term *angels* can also refer to messengers who are serving Jesus as apostles, prophets, evangelists, pastors, and teachers. Christians may be "angels" or "messengers" assigned by Christ to equip and build up his universal body (Ephesians 4:11–13). Among the strangers who knocked on the doors of Christian dwellings might have been true servants of God, called in a special way to carry out the Great Commission. The author of Hebrews was telling these believers that in neglecting strangers they may be missing a unique opportunity to minister to some of God's greatest servants.

# BIBLICAL BASIS

*Keep your lives free from the love of money and be content with what you have, because God has said, "Never will I leave you; never will I forsake you."* —Hebrews 13:5

Thomas Hewitt provided this worthwhile commentary on the exhortation in Hebrews: "The Christian's habits of thought and life in connection with money are a touchstone of his character. Such habits must be free from covetousness and avarice, for the love of money can be as detrimental to a man's spiritual life as sensuality. The way of victory over this evil is to *be content with such things as ye have.*"[4]

Paul's words to Timothy in his first letter also are an excellent supplement to the rather concise statement in Hebrews (1 Timothy 5:6–10, 17–18). His reassuring words to the Philippians elaborate on this as well: he affirmed that he could do everything through Christ, who gave him strength (Philippians 4:13). This adds meaning to the quoted portion from Hebrews: "God has said, 'Never will l leave you; never will I forsake you'" (Hebrews 13:5).

## BIBLICAL BASIS

*Do not forget to do good and to share with others, for with such sacrifices God is pleased.* —Hebrews 13:16

Under the old covenant, the children of Israel repeatedly offered animal sacrifices to atone for sins. In the new covenant, Jesus Christ became the ultimate and final sacrifice (Hebrews 10:11–18). And once believers receive the wonderful gift of salvation, they are to offer their bodies as living sacrifices (Romans 12:1–2)—not to atone for their sins but to offer worship, praise, thanksgiving, and appreciation to God for his mercy and grace. As we've seen before—especially in Paul's letter to the Philippians—one way believers can offer these spiritual sacrifices to God is by using their material possessions to help others (Philippians 4:18).

The author of Hebrews underscores this truth. In a fitting conclusion, he reminded the recipients that God is pleased when we share what we have with others. It is a sacrifice especially acceptable to him—one that brings joy to his heart.

## *Supra*cultural Principle 95

### SHARING WITH STRANGERS

*Take advantage of opportunities to show hospitality by sharing not only with believers in the local Christian community but also with those you don't know personally.*

It's important to understand that this scriptural principle doesn't mean believers are to have an open-hands policy for every stranger who passes by and claims to be a Christian in need. We must be discerning, even as our fellow believers had to be in New Testament days.

I remember on one occasion a family visited the church where I served as senior pastor. The father said he was a traveling evangelist and claimed he was out of money and needed help to care for his family. Though they were strangers, I invited them to our home for dinner. During the meal, he demonstrated some self-centered and judgmental attitudes. The man then asked for money, assuring me he would pay it back.

I would gladly have given him the money as a gift if I had felt assured he was for real. But by this time, I was beginning to suspect his credibility and integrity, primarily because of his self-righteous and prideful behavior. I also sensed that his wife was embarrassed by his argumentative spirit. In spite of my hesitancy, as I looked at his children I felt a responsibility to help them; so I wrote out a relatively small check and prayed that God would be with them as they traveled on.

I'm sure you can guess what happened. Though he had my address and my phone number, my wife and I never heard from them—or saw the money—again. In retrospect, I believe the man was a fraud. At least we know he wasn't the kind of angel mentioned in the book of Hebrews.

Some people will take advantage of our willingness to share our possessions with others. They know Christians are to be generous—even toward strangers—and they'll play on people's sympathy and their desire to do God's will. Yet the exhortation in Hebrews to do good and share with others still stands. Fortunately, there are some biblical guidelines for dealing with fraudulent Christians, and we'll look at these guidelines in the next sections of this chapter.

## Peter's Second Letter

The persecution Peter wrote about in his first epistle had subsided, and the church was facing a new problem: false teaching. Peter addressed this issue in his second letter.

# BIBLICAL BASIS

*In their greed these [false] teachers will exploit you with stories they have made up.* —2 Peter 2:3

The greed or covetousness Peter referred to includes three selfish and insidious motives—sex, power, and money. As always, these false motives were based on dishonesty, which combined to form a subtle means of exploiting Christians by using fabricated stories.

False teachers quickly learned they could exploit innocent and sincere believers. Mixing truth with error and good with evil, they became "experts in greed" (2 Peter 2:14). Peter had little patience with these individuals: "These men blaspheme in matters they do not understand. They are like brute beasts, creatures of instinct, born only to be caught and destroyed, and like beasts they too will perish. They will be paid back with harm for the harm they have done" (2 Peter 2:12–13).

## Jude's Letter

Jude, who was probably James's brother, another half brother of Christ, was also deeply concerned about false teachers. He pulled no punches in warning against them.

# BIBLICAL BASIS

*These men are blemishes at your love feasts, eating with you without the slightest qualm—shepherds who feed only themselves.* —Jude 12

I have read enough fund-raising letters while being privy to the facts to know that many have been written by experts in greed. Some actually contain fabricated stories designed to move people emotionally—stories that are exaggerated or cannot be verified. Though some of these contain half-truths, they're nonetheless false. I remember evaluating one such letter. It went something like this:

> *Dear Mary,*
>
> *This morning in my prayer time, God brought your name to mind. God told me, Mary, that you had a special, immediate need. He also told me, Mary, that if you sent my prayer ministry $25, he will meet this immediate need. But God also made it clear to me, Mary, that you have a long-term need and that if you sent me $100, he will meet your long-term need.*
>
> *I'm praying for you, Mary, and hope to hear from you today.*
>
> *Signed personally*
> [probably with electronic equipment]

How tragic! This person reported to me that she had attended a large meeting where this man spoke. She had signed a card and given her address but had never met or talked with this well-known pastor-evangelist. The rest of the story is predictable. The letter was computerized, with the first name filled in periodically to make it appear personal. Knowing this man and other dishonest tactics he used to raise money, it was easy for me to conclude that this was a fabricated story. Fortunately, he was eventually exposed as a fraud who was using biblical truth mixed with error to pad his own pockets. Though this example is extreme, such tactics are prevalent today, to varying degrees. As Christians we must be on guard.

Does this mean it's wrong to tell stories to motivate people to give and share their material possessions? Not at all. We need to know what the needs are, and there's no better way to communicate a need than to tell a real-life story. But the story must be true in all respects.

Fund-raising letters are not wrong. Even the apostle Paul used a letter to make his needs known when he wrote to Philemon. However, "experts" claim that people don't respond to the simple facts. So these people have learned how to get others to open their pocketbooks. If no real crisis exists, part of their strategy is to create one. Or perhaps they'll fabricate a breathtaking story of dramatic conversions to Christ.

## *Supra*cultural Principle 96

### FALSE TEACHERS

*Be on guard against false teachers who are motivated
by selfishness and greed and who mix truth with
error in order to exploit people.*

A lesson for Christians today is never to respond to such fund-raising letters or any form of appeal without knowing the reputation of those involved. Otherwise we may be responding to needs that don't exist and giving money to organizations that are not accountable for the way they spend the money. Sadly, people who respond to these appeals often neglect their responsibility to support fellow believers in their own local churches, where there is a *real* need. This is perhaps the greater tragedy—and very discouraging to pastors and other Christian leaders who abide by the principles of Scripture and never resort to dishonest tactics.

## John's Three Letters

The apostle John probably wrote his three epistles about the same time he wrote his Gospel. They were written for the churches in Asia sometime in the last third of the first century. Tensions that existed between the Jews and Christians were mostly over, and arguments over justification by faith versus works had subsided.

But the church faced a new problem. With a great number of Gentiles believing in Christ, Christians were faced with a heretical doctrine called Gnosticism, which taught that spirit is good but matter is evil. Consequently, this affected their view of Jesus Christ—how he, who was God, could inhabit a material body. John wrote to clarify that Jesus Christ was in every sense the God-man, and anyone who denied that Christ had come in the flesh could not be of God (1 John 2:22–23).

Regarding material possessions, John made a powerful statement in his first letter about the world and the things in the world. It's all-inclusive and is certainly foundational in helping

Christians formulate a biblical philosophy of how they should view and use their possessions.

## BIBLICAL BASIS

*Do not love the world or anything in the world. If anyone loves the world, the love of the Father is not in him. For everything in the world—the cravings of sinful man, the lust of his eyes and the boasting of what he has and does—comes not from the Father but from the world.* —1 John 2:15–16

The world and the things of this world were not originally evil. What God created "was very good" (Genesis 1:31). But the entrance of sin changed everything (Romans 8:20–21). People began to love what God created rather than God himself (Romans 1:25). When this happens, we're on a toboggan slide of sinful behavior motivated by the cravings of our sinful hearts, the lusts of our eyes, and the boasting of what we have and do.

Our material possessions, of course, are an intricate part of the world. And again, they are not sinful in themselves. That's why Paul made clear to Timothy that the *love* of money—not money itself—is a root of all kinds of evil (1 Timothy 6:10).

Matter itself, then, is not evil as the Gnostics taught. Thus Jesus Christ could indeed become a man and inhabit a human body without being evil. And Christians—who also live in bodies of flesh—can live lives worthy of God, so long as they present their bodies to him as living sacrifices (Romans 12:1). Furthermore, Christians can possess material things and still use them for the glory of God.

We will be tempted, of course, to love what we have. So we

must be on guard against the sinful cravings and lusts that are a part of our flesh, which has not been eradicated through conversion to Jesus Christ. This is why Paul exhorted Timothy: "Command those who are rich in this present world not to be arrogant nor to put their hope in wealth, which is so uncertain, but to put their hope in God, who richly provides us with everything for our enjoyment" (1 Timothy 6:17).

## *Supracultural* Principle 97
### A FALSE DICHOTOMY

*Guard against establishing false distinctions between what is "material" and what is "spiritual."*

It shouldn't surprise us that as believers we have difficulty harmonizing what belongs to us and what belongs to God. It's easy to *say* everything we have is the Lord's (it eases our consciences) and then proceed to keep most of it for ourselves.

### The Grace Givers

This can easily happen to people who put a strong emphasis on God's grace. For example, many of these believers resist, and even resent, any kind of approach to giving that suggests percentages or particular amounts. They're quick to point out that we're under grace in the New Testament—not under law as in the Old Testament. They don't believe the Old Testament tithe system any longer applies.

Yet often, when what these Christians actually give is recorded, measured, and evaluated, it doesn't come close to any form of regular or proportional giving. Unfortunately, some of them use grace as an excuse for their tendency to love money.

## The Defensive Givers

This false distinction is often manifested in the way some people react to messages about money. As long as their spiritual leaders concentrate on moral issues, they affirm what is being taught. But the moment they're exposed to what the Bible says about material possessions, they become defensive, uncomfortable, and sometimes critical. Frequently, these are the same people who are not regular and systematic givers. They haven't integrated material possessions into their definition of spirituality.

## The Secret Givers

Another manifestation of this false dichotomy is the way Christians react against any form of openness about how they use their material possessions. They insist this part of their life is private. Unfortunately, many people who take this approach have a guilty conscience and are coming up with scriptural excuses to cover up their lack of faithfulness. A true interpretation of what Scripture teaches regarding material possessions leads to openness rather than secrecy.

Christians who have a proper view of their material possessions and who are giving regularly, systematically, and proportionately are not defensive on the subject of money. They're as excited about what the Bible teaches about money as they are about the other great truths of Scripture. They enjoy the things that have been given to them for their benefit, but they don't love these things more than they love God. They don't allow their sinful cravings and the lust of their eyes to lead them into materialism. Neither do they let their tendency toward pride lead to arrogance. They have properly integrated the material with the spiritual and are seeking first the kingdom of God.

# BIBLICAL BASIS

*If anyone comes to you and does not bring this teaching [that Jesus Christ has come in the flesh], do not take him into your house or welcome him. Anyone who welcomes him shares in his wicked work.*
—2 John 10–11

In Hebrews, Christians are encouraged to "entertain strangers" (Hebrews 13:2). But the apostle John made very clear that this does not apply to those who deny the true nature of Jesus Christ. John was speaking directly to the form of Gnosticism that began penetrating Christian thought in the latter part of the first century. Since Gnostics taught that matter is evil and spirit is good, it follows naturally that they would deny that God, as infinite, pure spirit, could inhabit a physical body. Consequently, they denied that Jesus Christ was perfect God and perfect man.

John's warning to not let this kind of person enter our homes and to not even greet them may seem contradictory to his repeated emphasis on demonstrating love to those who don't know the Lord Jesus Christ as personal Savior. We must understand, however, that John was directing these concerns toward false teachers who were leading Christians astray and using these opportunities to take advantage of them financially. In that sense, they were like the "mere talkers and deceivers" Paul described in his letter to

Titus. They were "ruining whole households by teaching things they ought not to teach—and that for the sake of dishonest gain." Thus, Paul wrote, they must be silenced (Titus 1:10–11).

We also must understand that John was not addressing the issue of private hospitality per se. He was writing to participants in a house church. These Christians were not to officially welcome false teachers and allow them to address the church body. To do so would be to expose believers to what John earlier identified as a "deceiver" and an "anti-Christ" (2 John 7).

Inviting someone into our homes to discuss the Scriptures is a different matter. For example, Jehovah's Witnesses deny that Jesus Christ is God. However, their door-to-door visitation may open a door of opportunity to discuss with them what the Bible really teaches—that the "Word" John described in the opening chapter of his gospel was not *a* god. Rather, the "Word *was* God" (John 1:1), and "the Word became flesh and made his dwelling among us. We have seen his glory, the glory of the One and Only, who came from the Father, full of grace and truth" (John 1:14).[5] Even in such situations, however, Christians must be careful not to be deceived by these false teachers.

## *Supracultural Principle 98*
### WITHHOLDING FINANCIAL SUPPORT

*Don't give financial support to religious teachers and leaders who claim to be Christians but deny that the Lord Jesus Christ came as God in the flesh.*

Applied more specifically to the twenty-first–century world, this principle means that Christians should not be in fellowship with leaders who don't teach the truth regarding Jesus Christ. For example, we shouldn't associate with a church where the leaders don't teach the deity of Christ. And we certainly should not give money to support such an organization.

This, of course, gives us another guideline for our giving. Not only must people and organizations be above reproach in the kind of lifestyle they promote in order to be worthy of financial support, but they must also be sound in doctrine.

## BIBLICAL BASIS

*Dear friend, you are faithful in what you are doing for the brothers, even though they are strangers to you. . . . We ought therefore to show hospitality to such men so that we may work together for the truth.*
—3 John 5, 8

In John's third letter, the Holy Spirit again brings the balance of Scripture. After warning against false teachers in his second letter and forbidding believers to show hospitality to false teachers, in this third letter John commended Gaius for practicing hospitality toward *true* Christian workers.

He also publicly exposed another church leader named Diotrephes who violated this principle. Diotrephes actually refused to welcome the apostle John. He even excommunicated Christians from the church who attempted to practice the principle of hospitality (3 John 9–10). Clearly, his motives and actions were based on selfishness. John wrote, he "loves to be first" (3 John 9).

## *Supra*cultural Principle 99

### SELFISH LEADERS

*Christian leaders who receive financial support from the church they serve must not refuse to share financial help with other Christian leaders in need.*

Unfortunately, there are Diotrepheses in churches today—pastors who are self-oriented and refuse to support other Christian leaders and organizations simply because they want more for themselves. True, there must be balance here. It's not right for a church to increase its missionary budget and neglect to care for the financial needs of its own ministers. Often such a mentality on the part of a church board or missionary committee becomes a stumbling block to pastors who are struggling financially.

The other side of this issue, however, is that sometimes pastors develop a self-oriented approach to church finances and stand in the way of helping others. This goes against the heart of the Christian message and is a form of hypocrisy. May God give us more spiritual leaders like Gaius and fewer like Diotrephes.

## The Book of Revelation

This final document in the New Testament is unique in that it's the only piece of New Testament literature devoted exclusively to prophecy. Little is said about material possessions except in the short letter written to the church in Laodicea. But what *is* said is an appropriate conclusion to what the New Testament teaches about how a Christian should view and use material possessions.

# BIBLICAL BASIS

*You say, "I am rich; I have acquired wealth and do not need a thing."*
*But you do not realize that you are wretched, pitiful, poor, blind and*
*naked. I counsel you to buy from me gold refined in the fire, so you*
*can become rich; and white clothes to wear, so you can cover your*
*shameful nakedness; and salve to put on your eyes, so you can see.*
—Revelation 3:17–18

The church in Laodicea is the last of the seven churches mentioned in Revelation. Though I don't believe dogmatically that the seven churches forecast the development of the church throughout history, I can't deny the fact that there appears to be a chronological unfolding of one basic truth in these seven letters. The imminence of Christ's return seems to grow more prominent over the course of the exhortations the Lord himself gave to the churches (Revelation 2:5, 16, 25; 3:3, 11, 20). Christ's final message to the church in Laodicea appears related to the grand culmination of history with his return: "Here I am! I stand at the door and knock" (Revelation 3:20).

The state of this church reflects a materialistic mind-set that has become conformed to the world's system. Jesus made clear that it is possible to be lulled into complacency and a carnal state by cultural affluence. Again and again throughout this study, we've encountered warnings against this faltering. What is most dangerous, this can happen to Christians without their really being aware of what's taking place.

Jesus pointed out that the Christians in Laodicea needed three things: gold, clothing, and eye salve. Gold refined by the fire was an illustration used in connection with *faith* (1 Peter 1:7). White garments symbolize *righteousness* (Revelation 19:8). Salve for the eyes indicates *restored vision*—the ability to see clearly how materialistic they had become. In essence, Jesus was saying there's hope for churches who have become Laodicean. They can be restored and renewed.

## *Supra*cultural Principle 100

### SELF-DECEPTION AND RATIONALIZATION

*As Christians living in an affluent society, we must be*
*on guard against self-deception and rationalization.*

John penned the very words Christ spoke to him when he was in exile on the island of Patmos (Revelation 1:9–19). Jesus was saying to Christians of all time that it's easy to be content with worldly wealth and to feel we have everything we need. But in reality, we can have an abundance of material possessions and yet be "wretched, pitiful, poor, blind and naked" (Revelation 3:17).

This message seems vital for Christians living in twenty-first–century American society. Never have we had more materially; yet never have we given so little to the Lord's work. Statistics demonstrate that something is desperately wrong at the heart of American Christianity. We listen to the teaching of God's Word. We sing songs of praise. We claim to love God. But when it comes to giving, too many of us have "a form of godliness" but are "denying its power" (2 Timothy 3:5). We are violating the Word of God by not giving from our first fruits systematically, regularly, and proportionately. If Jews under the Old Testament law gave an average of 23 percent of their annual income to do God's work, how much should we who live under grace offer up in order to be proportionate givers?

## Chapter 26
# Overarching Biblical Truths

Looking back over the entire biblical story, two overarching principles emerge that describe how Christians should use their material resources.

### *Supra*cultural Principle 101

#### THE LOCAL CHURCH

*By divine design, local churches are the primary
context for Christians to use their material possessions
to further the work of God's kingdom.*

Every true believer is a part of the universal church (1 Corinthians 12:13; Ephesians 4:11–16). However, approximately 95 percent of all references to the *ekklesia* in the New Testament are references to local, visible, and organized expressions of the universal church.[1] Luke's historical record in the book of Acts is an account of the founding of local churches. Moving out from Jerusalem, assemblies of believers were established throughout the Roman world. We cannot, therefore, bypass the local church when discussing how Christians should use their material resources.

This is especially relevant as we practice accountability. In fact, spiritual leaders in the church should take the initiative and responsibility to make sure this happens—just as Paul did. He was an outstanding model in wanting to be above reproach in receiving and distributing monies and other material goods: "We want to avoid any criticism of the way we administer this liberal gift. For we are taking pains to do what is right, not only in the eyes of the Lord but also in the eyes of men" (2 Corinthians 8:20–21).

Yet there is no feasible way for Christians to be held accountable when they're not participating members of a local body of believers. God designed churches to be this kind of accountability system in all areas of our Christian lives—including the way we give. Christians who purposely avoid being accountable to other believers and to their spiritual leaders are just as guilty of being unsubmissive to the will of God as are Christian leaders who refuse to make themselves accountable to other members of the body of Christ.

## Parachurch Ministries

*Does the Bible teach that Christians should give only to their local churches in order to practice the principle of accountability?*

The answer to that question is a decided no. God allows freedom in form when it comes to doing his work in the world. Consequently, a number of ministries exist that are involved in carrying out the Great Commission. Many of these parachurch organizations are also performing a number of functions God designed for local churches.

It's not wrong for these ministries to exist. Neither is it inappropriate for Christians to support them. In fact, many of these organizations are able to reach biblical goals in our society that are virtually impossible for local churches to achieve. The tasks are too enormous and the opportunities too numerous for even groups of local churches (denominations) to do all that needs to be done.

It's important, however, to evaluate our giving patterns to organizations outside our own local churches by considering other important guidelines God gives us in Scripture. The following questions are important in helping all of us to decide whether to support a particular ministry and how much we should give.

*To what extent are we supporting those ministering to us?*

This is a foundational guideline in determining whether to support a parachurch ministry or an individual involved with another Christian organization. The Scriptures make it clear that we have a responsibility to first and foremost take care of and encourage in material ways those who have ministered to us in spiritual ways (Romans 15:27). God intends for this to happen primarily within the local church.

*What percentage of our income should we give to our local church before we consider supporting other Christian ministries?*

A good rule of thumb is for Christians to give at least 10 percent of their income to their local churches before they support additional ministries. God's plan in the Old Testament required the Israelites to give 10 percent of their resources to support their spiritual leaders. If we use this as an example, local church leaders will never be neglected by the very people to whom they minister. If all Christians were committed to giving at least a tithe to their local church, and then to give proportionally beyond a tithe to other ministries, financial problems in local churches or parachurch ministries would be few.

*What system of accountability does the parachurch organization under consideration practice?*

It's difficult to hold Christian leaders accountable outside of local church structures unless they themselves determine to be accountable to the Christian public through a careful and comprehensive system of reports and by setting up a responsible board of directors. Even then, it's possible for these leaders to waste money, misuse funds, or misappropriate gifts given for specific needs. We've all seen this illustrated in recent years.

A Christian should never give to any organization that does not make concerted efforts to be accountable to its donors and to the Christian public at large. Fund-raising appeals and real-life stories are legitimate ways for ministries to raise funds. But such appeals must be truthful in all respects. The major problem Christians face is how to determine if information is factual and if funds are being used appropriately. One thing is sure. If no regular financial reports are made available, the organization is not acting responsibly toward the public it supposedly serves.

In recent years, Christian leaders involved in parachurch ministries have been concerned about their responsibility to practice accountability. They've formed the Evangelical Council for Financial Accountability. Though there are other ways to maintain and communicate accountability to the Christian public, any organization that is a member of this council is attempting to demonstrate that it is credible and worthy of financial support.

*What kind of reputation does the parachurch ministry have, both in the Christian community and in the world at large?*

Christians should access a broad base of information before they support organizations outside their local churches. One important factor to consider is the established reputation of an organization and its leaders. They should be above reproach both in the Christian community and in the secular world. Furthermore, this reputation should have been established and maintained for a period of time. If the organization is new, it's doubly important to consider the already established reputation of its founders and leaders. In other words, respectable Christians who launch a new parachurch ministry usually can be trusted to maintain a proper accountability system.

Christians can also feel comfortable supporting individual missionaries and Christian workers who, like the apostle Paul, have established a good personal reputation. These individuals, however, should be involved with Christian organizations that also have established reputable credentials in carrying out the Great Commission. The organizations should be sound doctrinally and should be well-known for holding their employees accountable for the way they use their time and resources in furthering the work of God's kingdom.

## Supracultural Principle 102
### THE PERFECT WILL OF GOD

*Being generous is an integral part of living in the good, acceptable, and perfect will of God.*

The most comprehensive supracultural principle that describes how Christians should use their material resources is implicit in

Paul's powerful exhortation to the Romans:

> I urge you, brothers, in view of God's mercy, to offer your
> bodies as living sacrifices, holy and pleasing to God—this is
> your spiritual act of worship. Do not conform any longer to
> the pattern of this world, but be transformed by the renew-
> ing of your mind. Then you will be able to test and approve
> what God's will is—his good, pleasing and perfect will.
> (Romans 12:1–2)

Paul, of course, had in mind many facets of our Christian lives
when he penned these powerful words. But one stands out on the
pages of Scripture—our priorities regarding material possessions.
When we offer our material gifts to God, we're also engaging in a
"spiritual act of worship" that reflects the degree to which we are
living in God's "good, pleasing and perfect will."

Paul affirmed this when he wrote to the Philippians and
thanked them for the money they sent to sustain him in prison.
He considered those material gifts an extension of the way they
had given themselves to God. Compare Paul's statement to the
Romans with what he wrote to the Philippians:

> Therefore, I urge you, brothers, in view of God's mercy, to
> *offer your bodies* as *living sacrifices*, holy and pleasing to
> God—this is *your spiritual act of worship*. (Romans 12:1)

> I have received full payment and even more; I am amply sup-
> plied, now that I have received from Epaphroditus the *gifts*
> *you sent*. They are a *fragrant offering*, an *acceptable sacrifice*,
> *pleasing to God*. (Philippians 4:18)

Note the following specific comparisons:

*Romans 12:1*                                   *Philippians 4:18*

Offer your bodies......................................The gifts you sent

Living sacrifices...............................An acceptable sacrifice

Pleasing to God............................................Pleasing to God

Your spiritual act of worship....................A fragrant offering

Writing to the Corinthians, Paul again underscored this correlation. Referring to the Christians in Macedonia (probably the
Philippians or the Thessalonians), he wrote, "They gave as much
as they were able, and even beyond their ability. . . . *They gave
themselves first to the Lord* and then to us *in keeping with God's will*"
(2 Corinthians 8:3, 5).

Clearly, Christians who are not giving their first fruits to God
are not living within his perfect will. We may be obedient in
many other areas of our lives, but if we're not generous with our
material possessions, we're out of harmony with what God has
designed for us. Once we're saved by grace through faith, as Paul
wrote, "We are God's workmanship, created in Christ Jesus to do
good works, which God prepared in advance for us to do"
(Ephesians 2:10).

Unfortunately, statistics demonstrate that the majority of
believers in our culture are not walking in harmony with those
good works designed for us by God—namely, the way we handle
material possessions. Consequently, when we stand before the
judgment seat of Christ, many of us won't experience God's
commendation, "Well done, good and faithful servant!"

(Matthew 25:21) regarding this important dimension of giving ourselves as a living sacrifice—unless we make changes in our lives while we still have that wonderful opportunity.

Let us remember the principle in Paul's second letter to the Corinthians: God accepts and honors believers' gifts once they begin giving regularly and systematically, even though they may not yet be able to give as proportionally as they will once their economic lives are in order (2 Corinthians 8:10–12).

God wants all of us to begin now to organize our financial affairs so we can put God first in the use of our material possessions. He will honor you based on your willingness rather than on the amount you have to give at this point in your life. And once you begin, you may be amazed how quickly God enables you to give proportionately and generously. Will you take the first step today?

# CONCLUSION
## THE PRINCIPLES COMPILED

## Chapter 27
# 102 *Supracultural* Principles for Becoming *Rich in Every Way*

This final chapter is designed to allow you not only to review all of the supracultural principles outlined in this study but also to once again observe how they emerge from God's unfolding revelation in Scripture. In addition, these principles can be used as criteria for evaluating how you and your church measure up to God's will regarding generosity.

## Chapter 2

1. THE POWER OF LOVE AND UNITY: Using our material possessions in harmony with the will of God will create love and unity among believers, which in turn will motivate and encourage non-Christians to believe in Jesus Christ.

2. MODELING GENEROSITY: Spiritual leaders should model the way all Christians are to use material possessions.

3. SPECIAL NEEDS AND SPECIAL SACRIFICES: Be willing to make sacrifices to meet special material needs within the body of Christ.

4. BECOMING ENCOURAGERS: Share your material possessions to encourage others in the body of Christ.

5. SHOWING APPRECIATION: Show appreciation to Christians who are faithful in sharing their material possessions.

6. PERSONAL AND CORPORATE MODELS: Christians need to be able to observe other believers who are faithful in sharing their material possessions.

7. PURE MOTIVES: Our material gifts should always be given to honor God, not ourselves.

8. ADEQUATE FORMS: Every church should have an efficient system for helping to meet the true material needs of others in the body of Christ.

9. DELEGATING TASKS: Spiritual leaders must at times delegate administrative responsibilities to other mature believers who can help them in meeting material needs.

# Chapter 3

10. BLINDING SELF-SUFFICIENCY: Having a lot of material possessions may make it difficult to recognize and acknowledge our need for God's grace in salvation.

11. MAKING RESTITUTION: Material gifts are acceptable and pleasing to God only when we've done our part to be in harmony with brothers and sisters in Christ.

12. LOVING OUR ENEMIES: We should minister not only to those who love us but also to those who resent or even try to harm us.

# Chapter 4

13. **GLORIFYING GOD:** Evaluate your motives to see whether you're giving to glorify God or to glorify yourself.

14. **PRAYER AND PETITION:** Pray and thank God for daily sustenance.

15. **CREATIVE GIVING:** Whatever excess material possessions God enables us to accumulate should be used in creative ways to further his kingdom.

16. **TRUE PERSPECTIVE:** We can detect our true perspective on material possessions by evaluating the consistent thoughts and attitudes of our hearts.

17. **MATERIAL BONDAGE:** It is possible for a Christian to be in bondage to material possessions.

18. **PUTTING GOD FIRST:** If we put God first in all things, he will meet our needs.

19. **TRUSTING GOD:** Don't worry about the future or how your material needs will be met.

# Chapter 5

20. **SPECIAL BLESSINGS:** God will reward us when we help meet the material needs of others who serve God.

21. **FAMILY RESPONSIBILITY:** Those who are able should care for their parents' material needs.

22. SACRIFICIAL GIVING: God will reward us in his eternal kingdom based on the degree of sacrifice in our giving.

23. INVALID OFFERINGS: We invalidate our gifts to God when we deliberately withhold our love from him and from one another.

## Chapter 6

24. ECONOMIC AWARENESS: We should develop an awareness of the economic structures and practices in every culture in which we're attempting to communicate God's truth so we can use these economic experiences to teach people spiritual truths.

## Chapter 7

25. SELFISH MOTIVES: There will always be people who will try to use the Christian message to benefit themselves.

26. GOD'S PATIENCE: God is sometimes more patient with uninformed people who are materialistic than with people who have more direct exposure to the truth.

## Chapter 8

27. A GOSPEL FOR ALL: Though it's often difficult for wealthy people to respond to the gospel, God wants us to reach out to rich and poor alike.

28. SELF-FUNDING MISSIONARIES: God desires to use people who can give great segments of their time to ministry while still providing for their families.

# Chapter 9

29. TIME AND TALENT: God wants to use Christians who may not have an abundance of material possessions but who unselfishly use what they do have, including their skills, to do his work.

# Chapter 10

30. SINCERE SEEKERS: God's heart responds to non-Christians who are sincerely seeking to know and please him and who express their sincerity by being generous with their material possessions.

# Chapter 11

31. A COMMUNITY EFFORT: All Christians, according to their ability, should share their material possessions to carry on God's work in the world.

# Chapter 12

32. EQUALITY IN CHRIST: Christians who have few material possessions should not feel inferior to those who have more.

33. NO ROOM FOR PRIDE: Christians who have a lot of material possessions should demonstrate humility, realizing that their only true treasures are those they've stored up in heaven.

34. CARING FOR THE POOR: People who are in need—and the Christians who help meet those needs—have a special place in God's heart.

35. AVOIDING FAVORITISM: Never show favoritism toward people who are wealthy or prejudice against people who have few material possessions.

36. A TEST OF FAITH: The way we view and use our material possessions is one of the most significant ways our saving faith is tested for validity.

37. A BIBLICAL PRIORITY: Do all economic and financial planning with an intense desire to be in God's will in every respect.

38. GOD'S DISPLEASURE: Non-Christians who put faith in their material possessions and who abuse and misuse other people in order to accumulate wealth must be warned that God will judge them severely.

39. BEING ON GUARD: Accumulating wealth brings temptations for both Christians and non-Christians.

# Chapter 13

40. SUPPORTING SPIRITUAL LEADERS: Local church leaders whose primary ministry is to teach the Word of God should be given priority consideration in receiving financial support.

41. HELPING ALL PEOPLE: Plan ahead so you can be prepared to minister economically, first and foremost to fellow Christians who are in need but without neglecting non-Christians.

# Chapter 14

42. DEMONSTRATING PURE MOTIVES: Christian leaders should look to fellow believers for financial support, not to the unbelievers they're attempting to reach with the gospel.

43. AN EXEMPLARY WORK ETHIC: Work hard to provide for your economic needs so you're not criticized by unbelievers for being lazy and irresponsible.

44. CHURCH DISCIPLINE: Separate yourself from other believers who are persistently irresponsible, not providing for their own economic needs.

45. WITHHOLDING ECONOMIC ASSISTANCE: Christians who can but won't work for a living should not be given economic assistance.

# Chapter 15

46. BEING ABOVE REPROACH: Though God has commanded that spiritual leaders be cared for financially by those to whom they minister, at times it is wise to give up that right.

47. SYSTEMATIC AND PROPORTIONAL GIVING: Set aside a percentage of your income on just as regular a basis as you are paid so you can give systematically to God's work.

48. LEADERSHIP ACCOUNTABILITY: Those who handle and distribute money given to God's work should be above reproach and should be held accountable.

## Chapter 16

49. CORPORATE MODELS: Every local body of believers needs real-life examples of other churches that are positive models of giving.

50. PERSONAL ACCOUNTABILITY: All Christians need accountability when making financial commitments to God's work.

51. EXCELLING IN GENEROSITY: Be generous in sharing your material possessions.

52. GRACE GIVING: God wants us to share our material possessions not in response to a command but rather out of love, reflecting sincere appreciation for his gift of salvation.

53. RESPONDING IMMEDIATELY: God accepts and honors our gifts once we begin giving regularly and systematically, even if we're not yet able to give as proportionately as we will once our economic lives are in order.

54. BIBLICAL EQUALITY: God is not pleased when Christians with abundance refuse to help others in need.

55 TEAM EFFORT: No one Christian leader should handle the financial needs of the Christian community alone.

## Chapter 17

56. FAITH-PROMISE GIVING: Take a step of faith and trust God to enable you to give based on your future earnings.

57. JOYFUL GIVING: Organize and plan your giving so you can give generously, not grudgingly.

58. GENEROUS BLESSINGS: If we give generously, we will receive generous blessings; if we're not generous in our giving, we won't receive generous blessings.

59. A CHEERFUL GIVER: Each of us is responsible to give to God on the basis of our heart's decision.

60. GOD'S PROVISION: When we're faithful in our giving, God will meet our material needs.

61. CONTINUED GENEROSITY: When we're generous, God will enable us to continue being generous.

62. PRAISE AND THANKSGIVING: Generous Christians cause others to praise and worship God.

63. RESPECT AND LOVE: People respect and love Christians who are unselfish and generous.

# Chapter 18

64. RESPECTFUL CITIZENS: Be a responsible and honest citizen by paying all governmental taxes and revenues.

65. PAYING DEBTS: Whether money, goods, or services, always pay what you owe.

66. OUR OBLIGATION: All Christians have an obligation to support God's work in material ways.

# Chapter 19

67. PROTECTING THE POOR: Never take economic advantage of poor people.

68. HELPING OTHERS: If we obey God's Word, we'll be able not only to meet our own economic needs but also to help others.

69. DEMONSTRATING GRACE: Be gracious to people who borrowed money with good intentions but encountered crises beyond their control that make it difficult to repay their loan on time.

70. BORROWING WISELY: Before borrowing money for any purpose, seek wisdom from others who can help you evaluate all aspects of the decision.

71. GUARANTEEING LOANS: Before guaranteeing another person's loan based on your own assets, make sure you'd be able to repay the loan without defaulting on other financial obligations, including your indebtedness to the Lord.

72. DECEITFUL BORROWING: We are outside of God's will when we knowingly borrow money we can't pay back according to a predetermined agreement.

73. LEAVING GOD OUT: We are outside of God's will when we cannot give him the first fruits of our income because we've obligated ourselves to pay off debts.

# Chapter 20

74. HONESTY AND GENEROSITY: Work hard to make an honest living, not only to take care of your own needs but also to help others.

75. WORKING FOR THE LORD: Work hard to serve your employer (whether Christian or non-Christian) as if you were actually serving the Lord Jesus Christ.

76. EQUITABLE TREATMENT: Treat employees fairly in every respect, including fair and equitable financial remuneration.

## Chapter 21

77. CAUSE FOR REJOICING: Faithfully supporting God's servants in material ways brings joy to the hearts of those who receive our gifts.

78. JOYFUL PRAYING: When you faithfully support God's servants in material ways, you make their prayers a joyful experience.

79. HONORING FAITHFUL SERVANTS: Honor Christians who make special sacrifices to help meet the material needs of God's servants.

80. OPENNESS WITHOUT MANIPULATION: Be open and honest about your material needs, but avoid any form of dishonesty or manipulation.

81. OVERALL CONTENTMENT: Learn to be content in the difficult times, as well as in the prosperous times.

82. ETERNAL TREASURES: Christian leaders who make their living in the ministry should serve Jesus Christ with the view that they're storing up treasures in heaven for those who support them financially.

83. CORPORATE PROMISES: God's promise to meet needs applies to the church as well as to individual believers in that church.

## Chapter 22

84. RISKS AND VULNERABILITY: Putting God first in our lives may open the door for people to take advantage of us.

85. BALANCED COMMUNICATION: Christian leaders should use methods of communication about giving that create both a sense of obligation and a spirit of spontaneity and freedom.

86. SHARING FINANCIAL NEEDS: Don't hesitate to ask for help when there's a need, both for others and for yourself.

# Chapter 23

87. BEING HOSPITABLE: Spiritual leaders should be generous Christians who are willing to use their material possessions to serve those they shepherd.

88. BEING NONMATERIALISTIC: Christians who occupy leadership roles in the church should be free from materialistic attitudes and actions.

89. CHOOSING WHOM TO HELP: The selection of people who receive consistent help from the church should be based on specific scriptural guidelines.

90. ADEQUATE REMUNERATION: Pastors and teachers who are hardworking, efficient, and productive in ministry should be rewarded financially.

91. A PROPER FOCUS: Focus on godliness and contentment rather than on riches, which often bring discontentment.

# Chapter 24

92. CHURCH DISCIPLINE: Leaders who teach false doctrine and manipulate people in order to pursue dishonest gain should be silenced.

93. A PROPHETIC TREND: Don't let the world's system cause you to love self, money, or pleasure more than God.

# Chapter 25

94. SPIRITUAL PURIFICATION: Economic challenges can help us focus on the spiritual and eternal dimensions of life rather than on the material and temporal.

95. SHARING WITH STRANGERS: Take advantage of opportunities to show hospitality by sharing not only with believers in the local Christian community but also with those you don't know personally.

96. FALSE TEACHERS: Be on guard against false teachers who are motivated by selfishness and greed and who mix truth with error in order to exploit people.

97. A FALSE DICHOTOMY: Guard against establishing false distinctions between what is "material" and what is "spiritual."

98. WITHHOLDING FINANCIAL SUPPORT: Don't give financial support to religious teachers and leaders who claim to be Christians but deny that the Lord Jesus Christ came as God in the flesh.

99. SELFISH LEADERS: Christian leaders who receive financial support from the church they serve must not refuse to share financial help with other Christian leaders in need.

100. SELF-DECEPTION AND RATIONALIZATION: As Christians living in an affluent society, we must be on guard against self-deception and rationalization.

# Chapter 26

**101. THE LOCAL CHURCH:** By divine design, local churches are the primary context for Christians to use their material possessions to further the work of God's kingdom.

**102. THE PERFECT WILL OF GOD:** Being generous is an integral part of living in the good, acceptable, and perfect will of God.

Appendix

# Guidelines for Developing
# *Supra*cultural Principles

**Guideline 1: To formulate biblical principles, we must look at the
totality of Scripture on a particular subject.** Applied to the subject
of this book, our group did an in-depth study of material possessions
as detailed in the Scriptures. We looked particularly at both functions (activities) and directives (exhortations, instructions, etc.).
The functions appear most frequently in the book of Acts—logical,
since Luke recorded the acts (or activities) of Christians during the
time the church came into existence in Jerusalem and as it
expanded throughout the Roman world.

Directives, or exhortations, appear most frequently in the
Epistles—the letters written to local churches or to men like
Timothy and Titus who were helping establish these churches.

Functions and directives are like two sides of a coin. Luke's
account in Acts is primarily a description of the functions of
Christians as they used their material possessions. The Epistles
include directives to these local churches as well as to the leaders
of local churches to instruct them *how* to use material possessions.
That's why we see functions primarily in the narratives of
Scripture and directives primarily in the didactic sections.

**Guideline 2: As we study a particular subject in Scripture, we must follow God's unfolding revelation.** To delineate accurate supracultural principles relative to any aspect of God's will, we must study God's Word as it was revealed. To do this in relationship to the way New Testament Christians used their material possessions, we began our study in the book of Acts. At the same time, we consulted sections in the Epistles as they were written chronologically in harmony with events in Acts (see page 7).

**Guideline 3: We must be sure to interpret Scripture accurately.** As we study scriptural revelation chronologically, we must always look at the larger context of Scripture. Fortunately, many helpful tools are available to help us in this process—interlinear translations, Greek and English concordances, a variety of Bible translations, word studies, commentaries, journals, and historical studies.

Our research team devoted itself to this process week after week. After each interactive session, I wrote summaries of our observations, which we used in subsequent sessions to review and maintain continuity in the process.

Studying scriptural events and injunctions out of context can lead us to draw false conclusions about any subject in Scripture. For example, one false teaching that has become prevalent is prosperity theology—the teaching that God will multiply Christians' earthly possessions if they tithe regularly. Certain Bible teachers have taken scriptural statements out of context to make the passages say things the authors did not intend. Some fail to recognize (or admit) that this so-called doctrine of Scripture tends to produce results only in capitalistic and affluent societies where it's possible to better oneself financially through a free-enterprise system.

**Guideline 4: We must make general observations that summarize our more specific discoveries.** After we looked carefully at every reference to material possessions as scriptural passages unfolded chronologically, our team began making more general observations. After looking at the trees, so to speak, we looked at the forest. In other words, when making observations on the biblical story, we need to see the specifics in relationship to the whole.

**Guideline 5: We must look carefully at verifiable and consistent repetition.** In order to determine supracultural principles from Scripture relative to the way we should use our material possessions, it's important to observe the extent to which New Testament activities and teachings are repeated, verified, expanded, and reinforced throughout the whole counsel of God as recorded in both the Old and New Testaments. This process is very important in order to avoid taking Scripture out of context to support our own personal agendas. Looking carefully at God's truth as it is unfolded throughout Scripture will help us understand *God's* agenda.

**Guideline 6: We must make sure what we call a principle is truly supracultural.** A properly stated principle from Scripture does not include *the way* that biblical truth is applied in any given cultural situation. Principles relate to activities (functions) and directives (teachings), not to forms, patterns, and methodologies. Though it's impossible to engage in functions (the application of principles) without some kind of methodology and structure, it is possible to state a principle that describes a function without prescribing a form that principle should take when it is applied.

This is what makes a biblical principle truly supracultural. If it is, indeed, a correctly worded biblical truth, it can be applied anywhere in the world, no matter what the cultural conditions. Furthermore, it is applicable at any moment in history—in the first century as well as in the twenty-first century, anytime in-between, and in the future.

In terms of material possessions, being able to apply biblical principles does not depend on the existence of certain economic structures. Furthermore, it is not dependent on one's economic status in society, either as an individual Christian or as a group of Christians. In fact, being able to apply these principles does not depend upon *any* cultural factors. Though it may be more difficult to apply them because of certain cultural restrictions and pressures, their supracultural nature makes it possible for the principles to work in some form or fashion wherever believers may be.

# Notes

### Introduction: A Quest for God's Agenda

1. For Guidelines for Discovering and Formulating Supracultural Principles, see Appendix.

### Chapter 1: The Mystery Revealed

1. In subsequent Scripture quotations, all italics have been added for the sake of emphasis and will not be noted.

2. Three times a year, faithful Jews participated in three special events in the holy city—three great festivals when pilgrims came from all over the world: the Feasts of Passover, Pentecost, and Tabernacles (Deuteronomy 16:1–16). Jesus ascended back to heaven during the Feast of Pentecost. More precisely, scholars tell us that this special festival began on the same day Jesus rose from the grave and culminated fifty days later on the Day of Pentecost. This was the moment the Holy Spirit descended on the 120 believers gathered in the Upper Room (Acts 2:1–4). Many would have arrived earlier to participate in the passover meal—the paschal supper Jesus had with His disciples in an Upper Room. If so, these faithful Jews were there at the time of the crucifixion which took place the next day. Furthermore,

since there were thousands of people still "staying in Jerusalem" (Acts 2:5) when the Day of Pentecost came, these travelers had stayed on in Jerusalem for at least a fifty-day period.

3. Joachim Jeremias, *Jerusalem in the Time of Jesus*, trans. F. H. and C. H. Kay (London: SCM, 1969), 83.

4. The first tithe in Israel involved a tenth of all yearly produce and a tenth of all the flocks and cattle. This tithe was to be used to support the Levites and priests (Leviticus 27:3–34). The second tithe was known as the festival tithe, which was 1/10th of the 9/10ths that was left. This tithe was to be set apart and taken to Jerusalem. If it was impossible to make the trip with the produce and animals, a tenth of their possessions could be sold. The money could be used to make the trip and then to purchase food or animals for offering in Jerusalem (Deuteronomy 12:5–7; 14:22–27).

## Chapter 2: An Unparalleled Work of Faith

1. The apostle Paul used the same grammatical technique (the personal pronoun) when he wrote to the believers in Corinth and used his personal experience to illustrate the need for that church to grow together and reflect the life of Jesus Christ: "When I was a child, I talked like a child, I thought like a child, I reasoned like a child. When I became a man, I put childish ways behind me" (1 Corinthians 13:11).

2. Gene A. Getz, *Elders and Leaders: God's Plan for Leading the Church* (Chicago: Moody Press, 2003), 281–83.

## Chapter 3: The Sermon on the Mount (Matthew 5)

1. William Hendriksen, *New Testament Commentary: Exposition of the Gospel According to Matthew* (Grand Rapids: Baker, 1973), 310.

### Chapter 4: The Sermon on the Mount (Matthew 6)

1. W. E. Vine, *The Expanded Vine's Expository Dictionary of New Testament Words* (Minneapolis: Bethany House Publishers, 1984), 536–37.

### Chapter 5: More Teachings from Jesus (Matthew)

1. Jeremias, *Jerusalem*, 92.

2. Ibid., 97. For a scholarly and thorough treatment of the economic status of many people in Jerusalem, see the following chapters in Jeremias's book: "Industries," 3–30; "Commerce," 31–57; "The Rich," 87–99.

3. R. A. Cole, *The Gospel According to Mark: An Introduction and Commentary*, 2nd ed., vol. 2 of *The Tyndale New Testament Commentaries* (1989; repr., Grand Rapids: Eerdmans, 1997), 271.

4. Hendrikson, *New Testament Commentary*, 831.

### Chapter 7: The Gospel in Samaria

1. Merrill C. Tenney, *New Testament Survey* (Grand Rapids: Eerdmans, 1961), 242.

### Chapter 11: Beyond Judea and Samaria

1. Harold Hochner, "Chronology of the Apostolic Age" (PhD diss., Dallas Theological Seminary, 1965), 46.

2. Ibid., 48.

3. Kenneth Gapp, "The Universal Famine Under Claudius," *The Harvard Theological Review* 28 (October 1935): 261–62.

### Chapter 15: The First Letter to the Corinthians

1. Jewish authorities differ in their opinions regarding the third tithe. Josephus indicated that it was offered every third year and was in addition to the first and second tithe. Others believe

that every third year the second tithe (the festival tithe) was given to the poor and needy in their local communities instead of taking it to Jerusalem.

### Chapter 16: Second Corinthians 8

1. Lyle Eggleston, "The Church That Learned to Give," *Moody Monthly*, July–August 1988, 32.

### Chapter 18: The Letter to the Romans

1. Douglas J. Moo, *The Epistle to the Romans*, *The New International Commentary on the New Testament* (Grand Rapids: Eerdmans, 1996), 812.

2. Frederic Louis Godet, *Commentary on Romans* (Grand Rapids: Kregel, 1977), 484.

### Chapter 19: Borrowing, Loaning, and Debt

1. A. E. Willingale, *"Debt, Debtor"* in *The New Bible Dictionary*, 3rd ed., rev. ed. D. R. W. Wood, consulting eds. I. H. Marshall et al (Downers Grove, Ill.: InterVarsity Press, 1996), 268.

2. Carl Bernhard Moll, *The Psalms*, Vol. 5 of *Commentary on the Holy Scriptures*, (New York: Charles Scribner's Sons, 1884), 256. Moll has given a helpful commentary on this verse: "The wicked, through God's curse resting upon him, is reduced to poverty, so that he is compelled to borrow, and cannot pay; whereas the righteous hath even abundance not only for his own wants, but for the wants of others." In essence, Moll is stating that what David wrote in Psalm 37:21 is a *proverb* that was derived from the *promise* in Deuteronomy: "For the Lord your God will bless you as he has promised, and you will lend to many nations

but will borrow from none" (Deuteronomy 15:6).

3. C. F. Keil and F. Delitzsch, *The Pentateuch*, vol. 1, *Commentary on the Old Testament*, trans. James Martin (1973; repr., Grand Rapids: Eerdmans, 1980), 370.

4. Ibid., 369.

5. Wilhelm J. Schroeder, "Deuteronomy" in *Commentary on the Holy Scriptures*, vol. 3, John Peter Lange (New York: Charles Scribner's Sons, 1900), 136. The clear reference to the land-rest or release, which was for the year, and the force of the Hebrew word rendered *exact*, more correctly *urge* or *press*, and the whole spirit of the Mosaic law, which was not to destroy obligations of this kind but to guard the poor and the unfortunate against undue severity or oppression, are all in favor of the interpretation which regards the release as for the year. This interpretation is now almost universally accepted.

6. Otto Zöckler, "The Proverbs of Solomon" in *Commentary on the Holy Scriptures*, vol. 10, John Peter Lange, 192.

7. Larry Burkett, *Answers to Your Family's Financial Questions* (Pomona, Calif.: Focus on the Family, 1987), 113.

8. Ibid.

9. Ibid.

## Part 7: Principles from the Prison Epistles

1. Some believe Paul may have written these letters while in prison in Caesarea. However, the most probable view is that he was in Rome. Merrill Tenney commented: "Probably the traditional view that they were written from Rome is correct, for the allusions to Caesar's household (Philippians 4:22) and to the Praetorian Guard (1:13) would apply better to Rome than to Caesarea. He

seemed to be in a center of travel, where his friends came and went with ease, which would be much more characteristic of Rome than of Caesarea" (Tenney, *New Testament Survey*, 314).

## Chapter 20: The Twin Epistles: Ephesians and Colossians

1. For a careful study of the way the word *church* (*ekklesia*) is used in the New Testament, see Gene A. Getz, *The Measure of a Church* (Ventura, Calif.: Regal, 2001), 245–64.

## Chapter 21: Philippians: An Intimate Epistle

1. Ralph P. Martin, *The Epistle of Paul to the Philippians: An Introduction and Commentary*, vol. 11, *The Tyndale New Testament Commentaries* (Grand Rapids: Eerdmans, 1959), 181.

## Chapter 25: The Last Letters

1. George Wesley Buchanan, *To the Hebrews: Translation, Comment and Conclusions*, 2nd ed. in *The Anchor Bible* (Garden City, N.Y.: Doubleday, 1972), 230.

2. F. F. Bruce, *Commentary on the Epistle to the Hebrews* (Grand Rapids: Eerdmans, 1964), 370.

3. Ibid., 371.

4. Thomas Hewitt, *The Epistle to the Hebrews: An Introduction and Commentary*, vol. 15, *The Tyndale New Testament Commentaries* (Grand Rapids: Eerdmans, 1960), 206–207.

5. The Greek grammatical construction leaves no doubt that this is the only possible rendering of the text in John 1:1. See Walter Martin, *The Kingdom of the Cults*, rev. ed., Hank Hanegraff (Bloomington, Minn.: Bethany House Publishers, 1997), 138.

## Chapter 26: Overarching Biblical Truths

1. Getz, *The Measure of a Church*, 245.